C000163655

8 ∂

JACK'S WAR

JACK'S WAR

Lower-deck recollections
from World War II

G. G. Connell

WILLIAM KIMBER · LONDON

First published in 1985 by
WILLIAM KIMBER & CO. LIMITED
100 Jermyn Street, London, SW1Y 6EE

© G.G. Connell, 1985
ISBN 0-7183-0565-5

Typeset by Rapid Set and Design Ltd., London WC1
Printed in Great Britain by
The Garden City Press Limited
Letchworth, Hertfordshire, SG6 1JS

Contents

List of Illustrations

Text Illustrations

Acknowledgements

My thanks are due to all those who have contributed to the contents of this collection of World War Two lower-deck experience. I am especially indebted to Eric Smith, Donald Goodbrand, William Hope and Sidney France who gave me unrestricted access to their autobiographical manuscripts and wartime documents. All contributors to the book are listed in the Sources appendix.

I have again enjoyed much encouragement and the generous loan of books of reference from Geoffrey Green (Naval and Marine bookseller). The Naval Historic Section of the Ministry of Defence (Navy) and the Public Records Office gave their excellent expert advice and assistance.

G.G.C.

Foreword

Most books covering World War Two naval history concentrate on the operations of a particular ship, formations or fleets, a specific naval action or the role of a commander. Because of my own experience as a rating I felt that hitherto the opinions, recollections and influence of men in the lower-deck have not been adequately recorded.

The general high morale and achievements of the men manning the fleets are all the more remarkable because of the physical discomforts and the out-moded discipline to which they were subjected. They were led by highly professional and dedicated officers who were often unaware of the acute strains imposed upon the regular engagements ratings in the months leading up to the war and the first year of hostilities by the massive dilution of ships' companies with reservists, civilian volunteers and conscripted Hostility Only new entries. These men brought with them new problems to the restricted shipborne life.

In the older battleships, constructed in World War One, the layout of the secondary armament broadside messes had hardly changed in 150 years. Except for more headroom, sailors of Nelson's ships, who were often cooped up for years in the lower-decks of ships of the line, would have recognised much that was familiar. Crowded in the limited space between gun mountings and casements of the broadside batteries, mess fittings were identical, bare scrubbed wooden tables suspended from deck-heads, flanked by mess stools and headed at the inboard end by an oak bread cask that doubled as a seat for the senior hand of the mess of twelve or fourteen men. There were only a limited number of slinging billets for hammocks above the table or near vicinity, and men were forced to sleep on and below the table with other places for hammock bedding on each mess stool.

New construction of capital ships in the late 1930's and then during the war did introduce some improvements, better supplies of fresh water, showers and larger bathrooms, general messing and in a few ships, bunks instead of hammock billets; however, this modification was not universally popular.

When the Americans entered the war the superior living conditions in their ships, including the cafeteria system of messing, had an accelerating influence on the design and provision of lower-deck accommodation in the ships of the Royal Navy.

This book sets out to record some of the surviving recollections and experiences of life on the lower-deck during World War Two from Regular Engagement Service ratings, recalled pensioners, the various classes of reservists and the volunteer and conscripted hostility only civilian entries, and their views on some of the great naval actions and campaigns they witnessed.

G.G.C.

CHAPTER ONE

Prelude Years and 1939

Ships of the Reserve Fleet which had been brought forward for urgent refits, update and commissioning into the active fleet during the 1938 run up to the Munich crisis had not all, by mid 1939, reverted to their original reserve care and maintenance status. An enhanced fleet continued in being, which required a large number of recalled pensioners and Royal Fleet Reservists retained for active duty. The Royal Naval Reserve and Royal Naval Volunteer Reserve portion of the reserve organisation had virtually all been released back to their merchant and fishing fleet and civilian shore-side occupations.

The active strength of the Royal Navy distributed between the Home and Overseas commands consisted of 15 battleships and battle-cruisers, 8 aircraft carriers, 38 Fleet plus 23 trade route and convoy cruisers, 3 anti-aircraft cruisers, 114 Fleet destroyers, 101 escort destroyers, sloops and corvettes and 38 submarines. There were also a large number of support and auxiliary vessels.

The Royal Navy Active Service strength on 1st January 1939, officers and men, was 118,932, and 12,390 officers and men of the Royal Marines. The reserves stood at 73,240 officers and ratings.

A short and somewhat frenzied semi-mobilisation of the fleet in 1938 and the resultant impact of reserve men on the regular lower-deck navy had a profound effect. The regulars were at that time coming to terms with the first intakes of special service engagement ratings and national service conscript adult entries. These young men of nineteen to twenty years of age had started to have an noticeable influence.

One of the first problems the navy faced was that of married new entries. At that time Naval Regulations did not permit members of the lower-deck, the majority of whom had joined the Royal Navy at thirteen years of age via the boys' service, to draw marriage allowance before they were twenty-five and in fact actively discouraged marriage before this age. Their Lordships of the Admiralty were thus acutely embarrassed to find that many of the adult new entrants were married and were petitioning members of parliament and writing to the press demanding the allowance that was denied to their regular long service shipmates. They very soon had obtained results and a concession in the form that the marriage allowance was to be available for ratings from the age of twenty-one subject to the proviso that the claimant had to make a minimum prescribed allotment to the wife from his daily pay.

Their Lordships had not given up however; they still frowned on marriage before the age of twenty-five and as they forecast that the 1938 emergency or even a war, would only last a short period and therefore the need for adult new entrants or conscripts would cease to be necessary to man the fleet, the relevant articles in King's Regulations and Admiralty Instructions were not cancelled, merely suspended indefinitely. In fact when the KR and AI's were reissued in the fifth year of the war, 1944, the article confining the allowance to men over twenty-five years of age re-appeared but was again suspended temporarily.

The pay for an able seaman in 1939 was 3s. 0d. per day (15p new pence) unless the rating had joined the navy prior to 5th October 1925, and then his pay was 4s. 0d. (20p new pence). This difference was reflected in pay rates of all senior ratings as well and furthermore affected the amount of marriage allowance that could be qualified for, on a pro rata basis. The newcomers to the Navy did not succeed in getting these somewhat squalid pay differences amended, so they remained unaltered until the end of the war. Men carrying out the same job, enduring the same discomforts and dangers could be receiving different rates of pay, something that did not occur in the officer pay scales, except for the chaplains, who were also subject to the 1925 differentials.

It was a sad fact that from the 1797 mutiny on, it required a mutiny or the threat of one to obtain an increase in pay or significant improvements. As World War Two progressed there seemed to be every possibility that the history of unrest over naval pay would be repeated; so much so that in 1944 a retired naval officer wrote a book, *Service Pay*. In this booklet the author traced the history of naval pay disasters and offered comprehensive proposals to avoid a new outbreak of lower-deck discontent and a breakdown of morale.

The remarkable ability of the Admiralty to ignore anomalies and to create new ones and unnecessary distinctions continued. For example, an insistence after mobilisation that the various classes of reservists should wear special badges to distinguish them from their continuous service counterparts, in some instances to have further pay differentials, retained some of the irritants that contributed to the 1931 Invergordon mutiny. Another factor was that although no man had been flogged in the navy since the late 1860's and that the authority of any commanding officer to order a man to be flogged had been suspended in 1879, everyone knew that up to 25 lashes remained as punishment No 2 in the current King's Regulations and Admiralty Instructions and in fact until the 1950's. The Army abandoned flogging altogether in 1881 and this one area of retention, the 'Cat', in temporary suspension as a form of naval punishment for nearly 150 years, can perhaps illustrate the Admiralty's reactionary attitude to pay, conditions of service and what senior officers considered to be suitable accommodation standards for the lower-deck ashore and afloat immediately prior to 1939. These attitudes modified only slowly as the service became massively diluted by officers and ratings from all walks of life and occupations, as they became sucked into World War Two.

It was therefore unreal, even incongruous, that in the middle of a titanic struggle at sea, in 1943, a small recruitment book should be written by a serving naval officer, entitled *Naval Life and Customs*. The foreword, written by Admiral Sir William James GCB MP, bore no relation to the realities experienced by the overwhelming numbers of men in the fleet. The Admiral eulogised on the luxuries enjoyed by the wartime sailor. He wrote of closed-in messes with pantries, hot water in plenty in bathrooms, spacious cooking plants presided over by skilled cooks, chapels, book stalls, laundries, plates, knives, forks. None of these ocean liner facilities existed except in an austere version and then only in a very small number of recently completed major war vessels, battleships, cruisers and aircraft carriers. For the remainder of the fleet these facilities were totally unknown.

In spite of these problems the Royal Navy was in a high state of readiness, efficiency and morale, its continuous service officers and ratings extremely professional and enjoying, in general, a high regard and respect for each other. It was nevertheless a situation containing a number of paradoxes: for instance, many members of the Royal Naval Volunteer Reserve on being mobilised, a few in 1938, and then the entire reserve in 1939, were at first taken aback to find officers referred to as 'Naval Pigs' and then to discover that this stemmed from the very considerable social chasm that existed at that time between the officer class and ratings, the attitude of 'Us and Them' as well as the vastly different living conditions and standards both ashore and afloat.

Long commissions of at least two years were the norm for ships serving in overseas stations of the Empire: Mediterranean, China, West Indies and others. Some officers, the most senior, had their wives with them on the overseas stations but there were no opportunities for ratings to be accompanied except in the rare event where a rating had obtained permission to marry a local girl. It was most unusual for a married rating to go ashore frequently during an overseas commission; most spent their off duty time dhobying, snobbing, tailoring, or haircutting and providing a variety of services for shipmates and officers to augment marriage allowances, sending every possible penny home to enable their families to survive.

Notwithstanding the well-known problems of bad pay and conditions, strict discipline and long overseas commissions, the Royal Navy was regarded with pride by the public at large. Its role as the policeman of the world's sea-lanes and oceans appeared inviolate and there had been no serious challenge to the blockade of Spanish ports during the Civil War, maintained by units of the Home Fleet during the years 1936 to 1939. In the uneasy months of 1938 and 1939 when war seeme 1 unavoidable, the lower-deck of the navy was first choice for thousands of young men who were faced with the possibility of being conscripted or who wished to volunteer to join the armed services.

One of the new breed of adult pre-war volunteer new entry was Thomas 'Lofty' Alfred Bywater, who was sent to Portsmouth base and depot for training,

> Portsmouth depot was to me 'Home'. I lapped it up and loved ships and the sea so much that for three months I didn't write home and was taken before the Divisional Officer for a 'quiet chat!' and then resumed writing home. The messing in Portsmouth Barracks was adequate; how new entries behaved was another matter. It was a regular chore for the cook of the mess to fetch tea in a fanny for stand-easy. Before he got back to his mess the tea was often gone, waylaid by others with cups dipping into the fanny.
>
> One character stands out, CPO Cook, our instructor and chief of the parade. He was a fatherly figure, giving us pep talks and seeing that we settled in and got our hair cut etc.

The ships of the fleet in 1938/39 were the platforms for the navy's principal weapon of offence, the gun, and to a lesser extent the torpedo. The dominant specialist department within the fleet was naturally the gunnery establishment and a lower-deck ruled by seamen who had qualified in its skills. Chief and Petty Officers who were the professional graduates of the Alma Mater of Royal Navy gunners, HMS *Excellent*, were the font and focus of drill, order, discipline and ceremonial. All other branches of the seamen's profession had their roots and dependence on the stiff-backed, loud-voiced graduates of Whale Island. The gunnery instructors and gunners' mates had nonetheless a certain panache and a rough and ready sense of humour, which tempered the rigours of gundrill, rifle and parade training.

Lofty Bywater revelled in the barrack square training where shouting, gaitered, whistle-blowing gunners' mates taught him and his new entry class, 'Fisher Class', how to march in step, in formation and rifle drill with other classes wheeling, counter-marching and drilling in the same loose gravelled dusty parade ground. He even recalls his enjoyment of living in the great barrack rooms that doubled as mess-decks, the many kit musters, inspections and cleaning chores. The barracks, HMS *Victory*, had few comforts and welfare only in the form of a barn of a beer canteen but the establishment was uncrowded; there was no lack of slinging billets for hammocks and plenty of kit lockers. General messing had recently been introduced after a long trial at Devonport barracks, HMS *Drake*, where it had been the brain child of a warrant cook, Mr Jago. The scheme forever to be known as 'Jago's' removed the responsibility of catering and the preparation of meals from the members of individual lower-deck messes where the ship's galley acted only as a cooking agency. This was the canteen messing system which prevailed in most ships of the fleet until the end of World War Two.

Jago's placed all responsibility for menu choice and the preparation and cooking to a central galley; messes would only retain a commitment under the direction of the galley staff for the preparation of sufficient potatoes for their mess. The general mess system had been introduced in naval shore establishments and to the new major war vessels.

Absence of the gross overcrowding which in the later years of the war turned these and other barrack rooms into congested hell-holes which bred pulmonary tubercolosis, the plain but substantial meals, the physical exercise and the seamanship instruction, which included much boat work under oars and sail, gave Thomas Bywater a tolerance and enthusiasm for the navy which was to sustain him right to the conclusion of an apparently interminable war. He accepted with stoic realism his punishment of leave stoppage and extra rifle drill during the dog watches as a penance for his failure to write home and eventually after three months he was rated as an ordinary seaman entitled to a daily pay rate of 2s. 0d., paid fortnightly.

Thomas remembers being introduced early to a routine to help ends meet: 'Being not overpaid in these days and only fortnightly we were often short in the blank week, so we pawned our number one suits for 5s. 0d. and then got it back on pay day for 5s. 6d in time for Sunday Divisions.'

The Jewish tailors who clustered in the three main naval ports had a remarkable reputation not only for tailoring made to measure uniforms for all ranks, of good quality, cheap and within 24 hours if necessary, but several enjoyed a good deal of respect and affection from the lower-deck for the extended credit and assistance given to men and their families.

Bywater and 'Fisher class' in 1938 started their sea training when they joined a small World War One destroyer, *Skate*, 900 tons. Her normal war complement was 90 officers and men; now she was armed only with one 4″ gun and ran with a very much reduced ship's company as a tender to the seamanship training school.

> The very first ship we were drafted to as 'Greenhorns' was for one week in the *Skate*, a really old ship, a harbour only ship. As the word 'Skate' in naval terms is someone not very nice, so was this ship; it was over-crowded. Three wash basins only for washing and bathing, dhobying a galvanised bucket. For us, that is the Fisher class on one week's sea-time experience we were introduced to the smell of shale oil and the ribald comments of the regulars and older sailors about how green we were and looked. We only went a few miles out from Spithead and then back to harbour in late afternoon. Unfortunately I caught scabies and we all had to go back to barracks into the quarantine sick-bay for a fortnight, I also lost a pair of boots. So much for the *Skate*.

Following recovery from their uncomfortable affliction, the class was drafted to a 800 ton minesweeper, built in 1919 and now used as a navigational training tender for junior officers and senior ratings, The *Alresford* was coal burning which brought a new dimension into the lives of the embryo sailors. Coaling ship, an evolution that sucked in everyone without exception in the minesweeper was a filthy, exhausting task that strained the primitive facilities for washing. The trainee ordinary seamen messed in a very confined area within the forepeak and for the first time discovered that in turn they had to be cook of the mess, responsible for turning raw issued victuals, augmented by purchases from the ship's canteen, into meals for their messmates. This they attempted with varying successes and disasters under the guidance of the leading seaman in charge of the class and who was also their mess caterer.

> . . . we had to coal ship and to do this the ship entered Portsmouth harbour and berthed on a coal lighter. We were sent down into the hold to fill coal bags which were then hoisted inboard. After it was finished we were washed down by a hose usually wielded by the Buffer who was always very particular in how he dressed. Our First Lieutenant 'Jimmy the One' was a live wire and one day took the hose off the Buffer and sprayed everyone including the Buffer who was not at all pleased.

This first lieutenant of the *Alresford* was the first of the many eccentrics they would encounter and who would have almost unlimited power over their well being; this ebullient character made his mark at the 2100 rounds – 'he used to line us all up at rounds, 9pm, and dose us all with castor oil!'

This form of idiosyncrasy was prevalent in the fleet at home and abroad, inflicted on a relatively passive lower-deck but became rapidly eradicated with the demands and pressures of war and the arrival of large numbers of reservists and volunteers who were rather less tolerant of the peculiarities of officers and senior ratings.

Some men wishing to join the fleet came to it as Royal Marines. The corps was also enjoying a rush of volunteers. Chris Buist came from a Scottish mining family with no naval or army background. Buist presented himself at the main Glasgow recruiting office where he was quickly accepted after a satisfactory medical. His pay was to be 14s. 0d. per week and he had to agree to open a Post Office account into which he had to place 5s. 0d. per week. He found soon after arrival in Plymouth that recruits were under pressure to save, on each Friday pay parade the Post Office set up a desk manned by a clerk on the barrack square, eager to accept payments into the recruits accounts. The purpose of this saving drive was to ensure that the recruits always had the necessary funds to pay their fares home for leave, for these were the days before the issue of free travel warrants for servicemen.

Recruits were required to buy their own cleaning materials for equipment and arms as well as uniform replacements, so the 9s. 0d. left to them allowed very little for spending when released from barracks. While the majority of recruits came from areas of high unemployment there were some whose families were relatively well off. One named Gear had a father who owned a chain of bicycle shops and kept his son well supplied with pocket money. Gear junior could not stand the discipline of cleaning and polishing his uniform, boots and equipment and he got around his distaste by paying Chris Buist and others 5s. 0d. per week to keep his kit and weapons up to scratch. However the ability of Gear and a few other 'barons' to pay fellow recruits to do their cleaning chores did not save them from the rigours of infantry and weapon training under the direction of unrelenting, tough sergeant instructors. Parade and ceremonial training were carried out in Stonehouse barracks and the introduction to infantrymen's skills on a wet bleak Dartmoor. Following the initial training in Plymouth where the recruits lived in long barrack rooms furnished with iron bedsteads fitted with the traditional army biscuit mattresses the embryo marines were transferred to Eastney barracks at Southsea, Portsmouth, where they were introduced to the hammocks which would have to be used by detachments serving afloat in a warship. The recruits also commenced drill on a variety of guns they would be expected to man at sea. It was here at Eastney in a very cold winter the ex-recruits, now trained marines, waited to be drafted. Chris did not have long to wait; he was sent as a replacement to the detachment serving in the cruiser *York* which sailed almost immediately for Bermuda. It was early 1939.

In contrast, and representative of the main source of seamen in the Royal Navy, Eric Smith joined as a boy seaman in the winter of 1936/1937 and was sent to the boys' training establishment at Shotley, HMS *Ganges*. By 1938 and his first draft to sea he had survived many months of a tough and spartan existence where corporal punishment was used in generous portions to stimulate progress in acquiring seamanlike agility and skills.

> What can one say about *Ganges* in the 1930's? It seemed to be staffed by some of the most sadistic and bloody-minded chief and petty officers in the Royal Navy although there were a few good ones amongst them.

So wrote Eric Smith of his boy training period and it did not surprise him to learn of a Home Secretary who proposed to use the daily training routine of the *Ganges* boys as a model for instituting a system of short sharp sentences for young offenders appearing before the courts, without, however, the boys' daily 0500 hours call followed by boat pulling or mast climbing from 0530 hours. This early start was considered too hard for young criminals.

Before leaving *Ganges* for sea training, all boys had to pass a swimming test. For those who could not swim, learning to do so was a grotesque ordeal,

The method of teaching a non-swimmer to swim was primitive in the extreme. This was for the PTI to order a boy to jump in at the deep end and then drag him out with a large boathook when he was on the point of drowning. Not a very sensible method in my opinion. All non-swimmers had to attend backward swimmers' classes on two evenings a week until such time as they could pass the Test. In my case I passed out just two weeks before going to sea. The instruction received from the PTI's was negligible, so mostly us boys finished up teaching each other. No way was I going to be left behind at Shotley while the rest of my class went off to sea.

Some of the lads found it hard and bewildering to be shouted at all the time. It served to align the physical training instructors, in the minds of the boys, with the 'Gate and Gaiter' branch of the gunners' mates, probably at that time the most hated branch in the Navy.

[One of the instructors] always carried a length of rubber hose around with him which he used frequently and with relish on any unfortunate boy whom he considered was not paying sufficient attention to his instructions . . . the rubber hose, or 'Stonarcky' as it was called, was noticeably used more frequently in the afternoon training period after he had had his 'Tot' and an interrupted sleep.

Our seamanship petty officer on the other hand was a different type of man . . . Any boy not paying attention to 'Tubby' was rewarded with a slap from his hoary hand on the nape of the neck which stung for a while but was not done viciously, he was popular with us boys. Tubby Foulsham enlivened the rigours of winter seamanship training on the river with laughter and tales of overseas commissions and faraway places.

This petty officer was one of a few exceptions at Shotley; many boys left the establishment for their sea training nursing an undying hatred for many of their instructor tormentors.

The Anson Class of boy seamen, including Eric Smith, in the latter

half of 1938 were sent to do their three months sea-training in the
battleship *Ramillies*:

> On board the 'Rolling Rammy', we soon found that we had left one hard
> ship for another. When clearing the mess-deck prior to the boys falling
> in, [the man in charge] would bawl, scream and lash out with his
> 'stonarcky' in all directions, and woe betide any unfortunate lad who got
> in his way.

The boys were allocated a couple of messes crowded between the
casement of the secondary 6″ armament. They found no change in
the routine of instruction classes and a demanding and long daily
timetable. The boys were still called at 0500, 0530 hammocks had to
be lashed up and stowed in the nettings and ship's cocoa drunk
(Kye). Soon after 0530 the boys, wearing duck suits and bare-footed,
were scrubbing or holystoning the acres of *Ramillies*' quarter-deck
while the remainder of the ship's company were being called.

> Boys were not allowed to wear boots or shoes during the scrub-deck
> period and few, if any, could afford sea-boots. As the ship's company sea-
> men were not called until half an hour after the boys, it fell to us to com-
> mence hosing down the decks with the help of a few men 'under punish-
> ment' who were also called at 0530 as part of their punishment; we still
> had to wear our canvas suits with trousers rolled up to our knees. . . We
> boys were given a holystone each, about the size of a house brick weigh-
> ing about 1½lbs, and starting from the stern we holystoned forward until
> reaching the after superstructure on the quarter-deck. In bitterly cold
> winds and half an hour of this work we were left cold and with painfully
> sore knees.
>   The autumn cruise of *Ramillies* took in wild places like Lamlash, Stor-
> naway and many ports in the north of Scotland, it was a wonder that no
> one went down with frostbite. We were by now getting hardened to the
> life and our sea training was only to last three months, by which time all
> but the most solid of the boys would have passed their examination for
> able-seaman ready for the time that they would reach the age of 19 years
> and then become eligible for rating up.

Some hard lessons had been learnt in *Ganges* and a few had been con-
solidated for the boy ratings in their sea training experience. They
had discovered that the establishment was unsympathetic or reluctant to offer protection to individuals or a group from bullying or

physical violence of some instructors. While at *Ganges* an attempt to complain to their divisional officer about ceaseless bullying by an instructor which had culminated with the wounding of a shy inoffensive classmate by a bayonet, failed. They found that their case would not be listened to. Now in *Ramillies*, their divisional officer condoned or turned a blind eye to rampaging, intemperate language and the indiscriminate use of the 'Stonacky'.

'The months in Shotley and *Ramillies* were hard,' wrote Eric Smith years later,

> and for the most part not particularly happy, but during the time our characters became moulded, taught us discipline and self-discipline, to be neat, tidy and clean, to work together and in general gave us the qualities needed to serve in the fleet of that time. We certainly all became fitter, taller and heavier.

During the last few weeks of 1937 several classes of the *Ganges* boys in *Ramillies*, the Anson class included, progressed towards term completion and the boys became aware that their mess-deck notice board had began to advertise ships that required or offered billets for boy seamen. The central notice of interest was an announcement that there were vacancies, for boys who had passed and qualified for the able seaman rate, in three cruisers preparing to commission for overseas stations. At that time there was little effort to help boys in the choice of ship, except only less than useful guidance from long serving shellbacks of the lower deck who gave advice to the boy seamen which contained a high degree of cynicism.

The notice offering overseas commissions, listed the Kent class cruiser *Kent* armed by four twin 8″ turrets and destined for the China station, a light cruiser *Arethusa* with three twin 6″ turrets and committed to join the Mediterranean fleet and the third a Leander class cruiser launched as recently as 1935 with a principal armament of eight 6″ guns in four turrets and eight torpedo tubes; *Ajax* was to relieve a cruiser in the America and West Indies squadron based on Bermuda.

The young and eager boys ready to escape from the physical disciplines of the boy training environment and very keen to volunteer for release into the active fleet ships had only the mess deck lawyers to offer them guidance. Eric Smith and his friend Harry listened to a three badge able seaman who had served on every overseas station:

There's 'undreds of ships on the China and Mediterranean stations, but there's only one ship from each of the port divisions (Chatham, Portsmouth and Plymouth) on the West Indies station. You've got a life-time to get the China or the Med; but you may not get a chance again to get to America and the West Indies, so if you really want to go I'd volunteer for the *Ajax*, personally I never volunteer for anything!

So on this cynic's recommendation Harry and Eric put their names down for the *Ajax*. Soon afterwards they were sent off for 28 days' seasonal and foreign leave prior to joining the cruiser at Chatham.

In March 1938 after an intensive few weeks in Portsmouth storing and embarking ammunition, painting ship and carrying out harbour and local sea trials, *Ajax* (Captain C.H.L. Woodhouse) sailed first to Chatham to collect her Royal Marine detachment and some specialist senior naval rates then crossed the Atlantic bound for the America and West Indies squadron base, HMS *Malabar* in Bermuda.

The cruiser was manned entirely by long service regular engagement officers and ratings; it would not experience any dilution of the ship's company by reservist and hostility only officers and ratings until several months after the start of World War Two and after the West Indies squadron had been the victor of the first major naval action of the war.

This modern cruiser contained only a few of the amenities listed by Admiral James in his foreword to *Naval Life and Customs* in 1943. She was nevertheless considered a fine smart ship and regarded with pride by her ship's company. Her messdecks were crowded and poorly ventilated, there were insufficient hammock slinging billets, kit lockers or overhead racks for ditty and cap boxes. The ship's company bathrooms for seamen, stokers and Royal Marines were small tiled compartments fitted with a few galvanised tip up basins served by a single hot and a cold tap in each bathroom space, there were a few showers but no full length baths for the ratings. The cruiser had no laundry; dhobying had to be carried out in buckets but there were several drying spaces.

There was a central galley and the ship was equipped for the general messing (Jago's) system and a bakery had been installed. A NAAFI-staffed canteen shop supplied confectionery, toiletries, stationery, fresh fruit when available and a range of sundries. A recreation space existed, sparsely furnished with cushioned lockers and benches. It had been equipped by the Royal Naval Cinema service to show films and there was also a soft drink (gopher) bar.

The sub-tropical islands, set in an azure sea and bathed in glorious sunshine, fascinated the 'first timers' in the cruiser and the boy ratings in particular, but the restraints imposed by the Royal Navy on its youngest ratings were near intolerable. Regulations for boys' shore leave, even in these exotic island settings where the risk of desertion was unlikely and almost impossible, allowed leave only on Saturday and Sunday afternoons, from 1300 to 1800 hours. Exceptionally as the ship was on an overseas station, leave could also be granted on Wednesday afternoons, otherwise except for recreation in the form of sports or organised outings the young sailors remained in the ship. There was also another limitation which inhibited even these restricted excursions ashore. Boys' pay was only 8s. 9d. per week from which was deducted a 5s. 0d. allotment to the boys' parents and a further 1s. 0d. removed for slops etc (purchases of uniform replacements, soap and tobacco). The remaining 2s. 9d. was normally only paid monthly. This left very little for entertainment ashore when a bottle of beer in Bermuda in 1938 cost 2s. 6d.

Frustration of these dimensions had little time to fester, *Ajax* for her first two weeks on station had to erase signs and stains from her long dockyard refit and the long Atlantic passage to Bermuda and to prepare for the Commander-in-Chief's annual inspection of the squadron ships and at the same time train for a regatta that concluded the round of inspections. Led by Captain Woodhouse and his departmental officers the ship's company toiled holystoning decks, washing paintwork, polishing brightwork day following day until the cruiser, its armament and boats gleamed in the Bermudan sunshine. In the dogwatches and on make and mend afternoons, men sweated at the whalers' and cutters' oars preparing for the regatta. The ship received its reward by achieving the C-in-C's commendation for being the smartest squadron ship, and then walked away with most regatta events defeating its squadron rivals, the cruisers *Exeter* and *Orion*. Eric and his friend Harry were members of *Ajax*'s triumphant boys' cutter crew that trounced the other boys' crews.

Very shortly after the regatta Orion was relieved on the station by a second Leander class cruiser, the Royal New Zealand Navy ship *Achilles*; then followed a long series of squadron exercises at sea which, although important and necessary, became monotonous to officers and men of the squadron.

It is not the objective of this book to follow the well chronicled events of the 1938 American and West Indies squadron and the climax of the South American division's commission, the sea battle of December 1939, but to follow the vicissitudes and experiences of Eric Smith, in *Ajax*, and his progress from a boy rating to ordinary seaman and able seaman. His was a typical career of a regular service rating of the 1930's which had many parallels in all ships of the fleet serving for long commissions on overseas stations.

Ajax at sea, carrying out a practice shoot in company with *Exeter*, had to break off from the exercise and proceed at high speed to Kingston, Jamaica in answer to an appeal for assistance from the Governor to help suppress violent riots in the capital and island. On passage the Royal Marine detachment checked arms and equipment and prepared for landing as armed infantrymen to deal with a civil riot; at the same time a platoon of seamen was detailed off to land in support of the Royal Marines, armed only with wooden steel-tipped entrenching tool handles. On arrival there was a brief lull in the disturbances so for two days the rather apprehensive seaman platoon exercised drills for riot control in a large warehouse owned by Fyffes Banana Co. Two members of this less than confident seaman platoon were two boy seamen friends, Eric Smith and Harry Nobbs, both ex-Ansons.

To everyone's immense relief when violence again erupted in the streets of Kingston the Royal Marines and the seamen's platoon led by a lieutenant carrying the platoon's only fire-arm, a revolver, succeeded in calming and then dispersing the mob of threatening rioters without bloodshed or any serious injuries.

On the day that *Ajax* arrived at Kingston Harry Nobbs had his eighteenth birthday and became rated up to ordinary seaman; three days later Eric Smith achieved the same age and was also rated up. Both friends were moved from the boys' mess into the same new mess, part of the Topman division. Now that they were eighteen years of age they were entitled to shore leave whenever their watch was piped for leave except that until they became able seamen or twenty-one years of age, whichever was the earlier, they could not have all-night leave and had to return to the ship by 2300 hours.

The two friends, once tensions ashore in Kingston had subsided and leave became possible for *Ajax*'s ship's company, wished to celebrate their advancement to ordinary seamen and their approach to official adulthood; money to do this was a problem. Pay had increased to 14s. 0d. per week, less allotments, but pay day was two weeks away; the only way to obtain the necessary funds was to approach one of the cruiser's 'loan sharks' or 'rubber barons'. Every ship on foreign service had one or more hard-headed stoker or sea-man who joined ship at the start of a long commission with a cash float and the intention of setting up as a money lender; they were men who rarely went ashore.

It was to one of these 'rubber barons', a three-badge able seaman torpedoman in the adjoining mess that the two friends turned. The rate was 3s. 0d. in the pound interest, repayable on the monthly pay day.

The lending of money with interest was a punishable offence which attracted severe penalties. If the lender was of petty officer rank the punishment included immediate disrating of reduction to the ranks in the case of a Royal Marine. For all ratings the additional penalties consisted of the loss of good conduct badges, reduction to 2nd class for conduct for up to six months, 2nd class for leave and stoppage of leave up to three months, loss of pay, stoppage of grog ration up to 30 days and 7 days of extra work and drill not exceeding two hours per day.

In spite of these stern penalties the rubber barons flourished and protected by their clients were only rarely discovered or brought to account. Most at the end of a commission paid off with substantial amounts of capital. For Eric and Harry their new status as adults was a heady experience and so with borrowed funds, augmented by the sale for 15s. 0d. of an Edward VIII threepenny piece, the two friends hurried off ashore for a belated celebration of their promotions knowing that for the first time they could remain ashore until 2300 hours. They were joined by several messmates who were all ready for a special party following the previous day of exacting cere-monials. The ship's Royal Marines and two platoons of seamen had spent long hours in hot sunshine acting as escorts from Government House to where *Ajax* lay berthed. The coffin being ceremoniously escorted contained the body of the Governor who had called for assistance from the Royal Navy to quell the island disturbances. It had been a trying day marching in slow time with arms reversed through the sundrenched streets of Kingston and then forming a guard of honour on the cruiser's quarter-deck as *Ajax* proceeded to a position off the port where the late governor's body was committed to the deep.

The run ashore after the exertions and tension of riot duties and a state funeral overwhelmed Eric and Harry, free to taste for the first time the dubious delights of adult experience in pubs, clubs and brothels of downtown Kingston. The results were predictable; long before the hour when underage ordinary seamen had to repair back to their ship the two young seamen, seduced by many rum-based drinks, had lost all sense of time or place. Much of the run ashore was later a complete blank; the friends had become separated and Eric came to in the dingy back room of a nondescript bar with only 1s. 6d. in his pocket.

Now seven hours and ten minutes adrift, Eric Smith was greeted by the regulating petty officer (The Crusher) and, with his feet hardly touching the deck, appeared at the rush with his cap off before the officer of the day. The remorseless routine for defaulters then took over and Eric appeared next at commander's defaulters table to try and explain why on his first run ashore as a 'man' he failed to return to the ship at the expiration of his leave period. Eric eventually joined other defaulters to receive the captain's justice. Captain Woodhouse did not take kindly to leave-breakers and so the young miscreant had to forfeit one day's pay for each three hours or part adrift, the captain adding a stern homily on the evils of drink and the crime of libertymen not returning to their ship on time.

Soon after this event *Ajax* returned to Bermuda, Eric Smith was ashore again with messmate George Lewis where they joined a crowd of libertymen from the squadron ships at a Tombola session at the fleet club. Brickwoods Sunshine Ale provided a good stimulus for a convivial evening and in the case of Eric and George, success with tombola winnings. They won several lines and houses, then to cap the evening won the final big house. While the officials poured the winnings into the friends' caps they were assailed by ribald and earthy comments, 'fiddle', 'golden bollocks' being the milder cries from older men who played regularly, when they discovered that Eric had never played before. The two winners collected all the Topmen messmates present and staked them for the remainder of the evening; the hosts were repaid by being borne back to the cruiser on time with the makings of a monumental hangover that commanded their attention for the whole of the next day. A review of funds left, at breakfast, revealed that the fortunate tombola winners still had £4 apiece which was a useful sum with which to start a cruise of the Caribbean islands followed by South American ports with intervals when the squadron ships would rendezvous for exercises.

The junior members of the lower-deck community were greatly influenced by a quartet of senior and older able seamen. They were all three-badgemen, indicating that all had twelve years or more adult service. This group spent every hour of their spare time and off duty hours doing dhobying, snobbing, tailoring and haircutting for senior ratings and many of the officers. Each of their three badges was worth an additional 3d per day pay extra to the able seaman's daily rate of pay which after six years' service as continuous service ratings was either 4s. 6d or 3s 8d per diem depending whether they were designated as 1919 rates of pay or 1925 (post 5th October 1925).

These characters refrained from going ashore until they had accumulated substantial finances; they then selected the port which would satisfy their lusty desires of the flesh. The intervals of shore leave depended on how long it took them to work out ever increasing penalties for leave breaking and to allow for their finances to be restored after losing good conduct badges and many days of stoppage of pay. Their practice was to seek out the most comfortable bordello and move in for days of drinking and whoring until their money ran out or *Ajax*'s day of departure arrived and their ship was under sailing orders, whichever event came earlier. The quartet had one unbreakable golden rule; they never failed to return to the ship before she sailed. Their escapades from time to time did, however, drag in their messmates as leave-breakers. Barbados was their next chosen port.

At Barbados *Ajax* unexpectedly stayed on for a few extra days and word filtered back to the ship that the four hard men were running short of money; a whip-round of the mess-decks produced a 'fix' to be delivered by their mess leading seaman to the Maple Leaf club where the quartet was holed up.

The 'Hookey' asked Eric Smith and Harry Nobbs to accompany him to this popular meeting place for men of visiting men of war. Eric recalls:

> The lower half of the premises was merely a bar with a few grubby tables and chairs scattered around, the upstairs part was well decorated and furnished and had a small stage for a band. There was also a long cool balcony which overlooked the main street. On arriving upstairs the first thing the three of us did was to burst out laughing, for there were the four absentees sitting at a table playing cards dressed only in girls' panties whilst overhead had been rigged two clothes lines stretched between beams from which hung four sets of white drill suits and underwear which the hostesses had washed and ironed for them. Hookey promptly handed over the money that had been collected whereupon the proprietress was paid the credit she had extended to the four, then drinks were called for all round. A little later on more of the *Ajax*'s ship's company

began to drift in and the band started up; the evening soon got lively. As there were a lot of our mess-mates there we decided to have a 'Yorkshire', the pooling of funds, according to the rank of the rating, with one elected man detailed to buy the beer until money ran out. Soon it was flowing freely. The Master at Arms came in with the Regulating Petty Officer to whom the four stripeys promised they would return to the ship before sailing time. 2300 hours arrived all too quickly, so Nobby and I decided that we may as well be hung for sheep as lambs and decided to stay ashore for the night. I don't know how we got there but we awoke the following morning in an oversized chicken house which had done nothing for our spotless white suits. Needless to say when we returned to the ship we were lined up before the Officer of the Day destined for the Commander's then the Captain's report.

This second lapse earned Smith another three days' stoppage of pay, plus 14 days' stoppage of leave and an extra seven days' number 11 punishment which consisted of turning out of his hammock half an hour before the hands and commencing work half an hour early, then three quarters of an hour work during the dinner break followed by working or rifle drill in the dog watches. Smith also received a less than friendly welcome from his Captain at the defaulter's table.

Ajax steamed south from the West Indies to Argentina, calling at Buenos Aires, capital and port in the estuary of the River Plate. In this sophisticated Latin-American city with a large Anglo-Argentinian colony the white-clad sailors enjoyed a whole range of Rabelaisian adventures. Smith and his friends distinguished themselves by escaping from a determined effort to kidnap and mug the seamen in the red light district.

The cruiser then turned north and visited the Brazilian ports of Santos and Rio de Janeiro before again turning south and calling at Montevideo in Uruguay where within a year the South America division of the America and West Indies squadron would achieve an immortal place in naval history. From Montevideo after a few days' exercise with her sister cruisers, *Ajax* made her way for a first visit to Port Stanley, Falkland Islands. Members of the ships made use of the limited resources of Port Stanley, three pubs and a few homes turned into temporary cafes to serve the visiting ship's company with familiar English cuisine of the egg and chip variety. Farmers from the outback and settlements invited groups of sailors to join them as guests, to see and explore the natural resources of the islands and to take part in shooting parties.

Eric Smith was now a stern sheetman of one of the cruiser's cutters; his boat was ordered to a jetty in a lonely creek outside Port Stanley and there they waited for a shooting party in gathering darkness and deteriorating weather. After about an hour all the party had returned except for three and when this information had been passed to the ship by aldis light the cutter was ordered to return with a boat full of assorted wild fowl that had been bagged with a miscellaneous assortment of weapons including a WW1 Lee-Enfield ·303 rifle. With visibility almost nil a very disgruntled cutter's crew were ordered to return to the jetty, where they waited for half an hour in now inky blackness until the sound of discordant singing and shouts came downwind, then a bobbing light which turned out to be a storm lantern carried by the host farmer returning his drunk and unpopular guests. The trio arrived on the jetty, two inebriates supporting a paralytic, all wearing necklaces of slaughtered wildfowl including several seagulls. The farmer who had entertained the sailors all day was clearly furious with his guests and the reason became clear when he informed the boat's crew that in addition to the fact that they had been indiscriminate in the protected birds shot, they had also shot dead his neighbour's prize bull. *Ajax* sailed from the remote Falklands with her ship's company not very popular with the kelpers.

Following a few days exercising with the squadron in an area between Falklands and the Argentinian mainland *Ajax* passed into the Magellan strait, short-circuiting Cape Horn, and engaged in survey work for several days. *Exeter* was in company when the two cruisers arrived at the Chilean port of the bleak and inhospitable land of Tierra del Fuego, Punta Arenas the southernmost city of the world where the free and easy men of the Royal Navy to their complete surprise received a very unfriendly reception from the poverty-stricken population of this desolate region. Many libertymen found themselves having difficulty avoiding premeditated fracas; one of the most easy-going and gentle characters of *Ajax*'s lower deck was in fact stabbed with near fatal consequences; only because Able Seaman Len 'Scupper' Trawley, a member of the ship's boxing team, was a very fit man, was he able to recover after a stay in the ship's sickbay. *Exeter* rejoined *Ajax* a day or so before Christmas at a place called Puerto Montt, a port that served a vast sheep rearing area of Chile. The port approaches were very shallow and the cruisers had to anchor some distance from the shore which meant long and sometimes hazardous trips in the ship's boats for the few libertymen.

While at Port Stanley, the Topmen seamen of *Ajax* and *Exeter* had, because the squadron's peacetime itinerary was known in advance,

arranged to have, with their respective commanding officers' permission, a joint 'Sods Opera' get-together in *Ajax*'s Topmen's mess-
deck on Christmas Day afternoon 1938. When the day arrived Eric
Smith narrowly avoided drowning; he was in the forenoon duty
boat's crew detailed to secure the cutter for the relief crew. The boat
was being thrown about in a short nasty seaway which plagued the
open anchorage. Smith encumbered by bulky oilskins slipped off a
near horizontal jacob's ladder and for some very long minutes with
his strength ebbing remained hanging by his hands with most of his
body submerged in a pounding seaway. Some engine-room artific-
ers, taking in lungfuls of air in shelter of the forecastle break, took
some time to realise that a seaman was about to slip under and in the
nick of time clambered out along the boom and hauled out a wet and
exhausted Smith. A stiff tot from the RPO, a hot wash down, a
change into dry clothing and Eric Smith was ready with his messmates to enjoy Christmas dinner in the decorated mess spaces.

The captain and commander, supported by the heads of departments, divisional officers, escorted by junior officers in fancy dress
and some junior ratings dressed in borrowed officers' uniform, led by
the Master at Arms toured the messes while the special meal was in
progress, to offer the season's greetings. The captain faced up to the
ordeal of being offered rum sippers at each mess stop and the occasional gulpers from illicit sources that required a seasonal turning of
a blind eye. The traditional tour of the decorated messes passed off in
high good humour with everyone knowing exactly the extent to
which normal discipline could be breached.

Immediately after the midday Christmas dinner debris had been
cleared away the Topmen's mess tables were lashed to the deckhead
and mess stools ranged alongside the bulkheads and ship side.
Everyone had received an official bottle of beer for Christmas and
since the invitation made weeks before in Port Stanley the leading
hand of the Topmen's mess had master-minded a steady import of
illicit booze from ashore, rum issues had illegally been hoarded and
there was also a homebrew of hooch with a devastating potency. The
visitors from *Exeter* arrived after a rough boat passage to be greeted
by their hosts with speeches both formal and ribald couched in East
London and Hampshire accents which were answered by the soft
burr of the West Country ratings who manned the Plymouth-based
cruiser. The guests brought concealed about their persons contribu-
tions of alcoholic refreshment to the gathering. A good vigorous and
Rabelaisian 'Sods Opera' was soon in full swing with everyone, hosts

and guests, doing and presenting their party pieces; some torpedo-
men and watchkeepers from adjoining messes mucking in as well.
The illicit booze supplies began to flow freely and without restraint
so in due course word reached aft that it was obvious that drink had
been smuggled inboard and in massive quantities.

The party was quickly wound up and after the guests had been
returned to *Exeter*'s cutter a certain nausea set in, which put a
damper on what had been a good shindig. As the result of enquiries
instigated by the commander, one leading seaman was disrated to
able seaman and a second lost his good conduct badges.

Exeter and *Ajax* parted company, and *Ajax* then paid a call at
Coronel where during World War One a German squadron commanded by Admiral Graf Von Spee destroyed a British cruiser
squadron. A modern pocket battleship bearing the name of the victorious admiral was within a year to be brought to battle by the ships
of the British South America Division of the America and East Indies
squadron who were currently showing the flag round the whole of the
South American continent.

During the first week of January 1939 *Exeter* and *Ajax* were again in
company to visit the port and city of Concepcion in Chile. Citizens of
this very Spanish city gave the British ships a rapturous welcome
that tended to overwhelm delighted libertymen whenever they stepped ashore. It was here that the disrated leading seaman of the Topmen's mess who had organised the Christmas party showed that he
still retained his genius as an organiser of parties. He became
friendly with the proprietor of one of the city's largest hotels and with
his assistance laid on a dinner and dance for his Topmen messmates.
It was a splendid event attended by beautiful female partners, and
cost the Topmen only an astonishing 5s 0d each, which included
taxis to take the under-age libertymen back to their ship by 2300
hours. After several days of wonderful entertainment offered to officers and ratings by the Chilean population of all social classes with
children's parties and sporting encounters laid on by the ships' companies everyone was reluctant to leave when the cruisers sailed
north, bound for Valparaiso.

On passage Eric Smith, Nobby Nobbs and the other ex-Shotley
ordinary seamen were rated up to able seamen with pay increased to
3s 0d per day; what appealed to the new AB's most was that they
could now enjoy all night leave ashore when it was piped. They
looked forward to this with delighted anticipation as the cruisers
approached Chile's largest port.

The welcome given by the city was a replica of the hospitality offered by the citizens of Concepcion. *Ajax*'s newly rated able seamen funded by loans from the ship's 'loan barons' were first ashore to savour their first night leave with compliant female company. For the next few days the ship's company enjoyed the heady delights offered by Valparaiso to visiting seamen until the night of 26th January 1939 when disaster struck this portion of the earthquake prone area of South America. The berthed cruisers experienced without warning an alarming underwater convulsion so violent that many sleeping sailors were hurled from their hammocks. Eric Smith was duty watch and part of the emergency party who slung their hammocks aft where the whip of the cruiser was most severe. Thoroughly alarmed and for a few minutes disorientated after falling out of their hammocks, the emergency party, having mustered to face whatever peril menaced their ship, learned from one of the duty signalmen that a bad earthquake had struck Concepcion, and the situation in that city had assumed the status of a major disaster. The British Ambassador's offer of the visiting cruisers' assistance was accepted by the Chilean Government and an immediate recall of libertymen on night leave brought men hurrying back to their ships.

The cruisers steamed south at maximum speed with their ships' companies preparing to land rescue teams and parties to assist the civilian authorities restore essential services. The British Fleet with its world-wide policing role was trained and equipped to render assistance in natural disasters and earthquakes in particular. Stores were earmarked and maintained at the Empire naval bases, while all major war vessels operating away from base were equipped to act independently and react immediately. In *Ajax* and *Exeter* as they steamed under full power, seamen platoons and Royal Marine detachments prepared to land with pickaxes and shovels to rescue victims of the earthquake and to back up if necessary the local police and fire services. Stokers stood by to land as demolition parties, tents and blankets, medical stores were made ready.

A scene of horror awaited the arrival of the cruisers; the white clean city of large buildings had been completed devastated and its surviving population wandered bewildered among the ruins. Officers and men of the squadron ships were soon ashore rounding up the dazed survivors and persuading them to collect in the main plaza where cooks from the cruisers set up feeding posts. Tents were quickly erected to provide shelter for women and children. The seamen platoons formed digging parties to release the few living and to recover some of the thousands of dead. As the day wore on the intense heat created a near unbearable stench from rotting bodies; a torpedo party supported by stokers demolished unsafe structures and Eric Smith with some of the *Ajax*'s Topmen found themselves searching the ruins of the collapsed hotel for the proprietor who a few days earlier had been their generous host. He had to be presumed dead as his body was never recovered. Makeshift field hospitals with the help of the cruiser's doctors and sickbay attendants had been created from tents carried in the ships but the more seriously injured were carried to the ships until every officer's cabin, flats and messdecks were crowded with the refugees, very many occupying the hammocks of the sailors who had toiled without a break in the devastated city.

When the cruisers returned to Valparaiso and began to disembark their homeless refugees and the desperately injured, the population seemed stunned by the magnitude of this latest earthquake catastrophe. It took many hours to complete the landing of the refugees and critically injured. When it was done Captain Woodhouse had lower-deck cleared and there he thanked and congratulated his men for their tireless effort; then he told them that before anyone could proceed ashore the ship would have to be de-contaminated from truck to the water-line, when it was finished he was going to give each watch 48 hours' leave. For two long days the entire ship inside and out was coated with a disinfectant paste, in sailors' parlance 'crab fat', then it was scraped off and followed by a complete washdown which restored the ship to its usual pristine condition.

With funds topped up after a visit to the ship's 'loan sharks' the first watch for 48 hours' leave hurried ashore to find that money was hardly necessary for the Chileans were determined to show their appreciation to the men they regarded as heroes; no bar or restaurant would accept payment, the uniformed officers and sailors were overwhelmed by invitations from strangers offering hospitality and the freedom of their homes.

In late February the cruisers left Valparaiso bearing ships' companies dazed by the gratitude shown by the Chilean people; the ships after a few days exercising day and night encounters followed by strenuous periods of general drill to shake off the residual effects of over-indulgence in shoreside delights, separated to visit singly other South American countries bounded by the Pacific ocean. *Ajax* over the next two months visited Peru and Equador but because pay was committed to repay debts owed to the 'loan barons', runs ashore by

Eric Smith and his messmates were low key affairs and it wasn't until
his ship docked in Balboa at the Pacific entrance to the Panama
Canal that he and his friends again tasted trouble ashore.

Most libertymen found their way to Panama City which had the
appearance of a small American western township made familiar to
all fans of cowboy movies, bars had slatted swing bat wing doors and
the roads, wooden sidewalks, the town was full of American servicemen watched over by baton swinging military police and US navy
shore patrols. These patrols had no compunction about entering the
bars, clubbing drunken US libertymen and hurling them out into the
street. They avoided interfering with the men from *Ajax* but with a
certain inevitability Eric Smith and others chummed up with members of the American garrison who had an unlimited stock of Bour-
bon whisky which they shared with their British friends. Smith, for
the third time since being rated up from boy seaman, failed to return
to his ship at the expiration of all night leave and so with others
appeared before his captain on a repeated offence charge. The leave
breakers received the usual scales of stoppage of pay and leave but
for Smith an extra in the form of 14 days No 11 punishment, extra
work and punishment rifle drill.

'Jack' is a pretty resilient chap, and by the time *Ajax* had passed
into the Caribbean sea and proceeded to Jamaica to join the Royal
Canadian Squadron for exercises the latest round of punishments
was over, and the Topmen were ready to sample again the rum and
gin palaces of Kingston.

Exeter and *Ajax* returned to the squadron's base in Bermuda; *Achilles* had returned to New Zealand to give leave and for a refit. A period
of several weeks followed exercising with visiting ships of the Royal
Canadian Navy and units of the Home Fleet, then a round of flag
officer inspections, the annual regatta and inter-ship sports. Money
was short after the long cruise round the South American continent
so there were few distractions to prevent a return to physical fitness.

On 2nd June 1939 *Ajax* left Bermuda to visit Dutch and French
West Indies, the cruiser called at Aruba, Curaçoa and Martinique
where many outings were laid on for the visiting British sailors. At
Martinique there happened to be an excellent exchange rate that
made champagne about the cheapest drink on the island. *Ajax*'s
Anglican chaplain, the sailors' 'sin bosun', who preached a robust
form of christianity had a great appetite for good food and a special
taste for champagne. He stood a number of the younger able seamen
a meal ashore where he provided quantities of his favourite tipple

which he downed in generous draughts. Later while waiting with his guests on the jetty for the ship's liberty boat to arrive he threw his cigarette butt into the water, *then stepped on it!* He was hauled out with a boat hook and for the rest of the commission Eric Smith and his friends wondered how he explained to the wardroom's satisfaction why he went for a swim while waiting for the liberty boat.

The next port of call was Para in the estuary of the Amazon, then a small town surrounded by dense jungle and very isolated. The cruiser was to stay for several days and it was here after making a short run ashore on reconnaissance that the quartet of 'Stripeys' decided it was a place where they could indulge their next period of unofficial leave. They had not long finally completed fully a package of penalties for the last escapade; all three good conduct badges had been restored but they were aware that next time they would have to pay dearly for another prolonged stay ashore. They were undeterred; in the town centre they located a suitable bordello, settled in, removed their Good Conduct badges from their uniforms, placed the badges in an envelope addressed to the Commander with a note: 'Dear Sir, Here are our G.C. badges in advance – we'll be off later!'

The captain and the commander were not amused; when the four friends returned to the ship shortly before she was due to sail they were placed under open arrest until they were due to appear before the captain. When they did, Captain Woodhouse awarded them punishment by warrant which reduced each member of the quartet to 2nd class for leave and conduct. They would only receive sufficient pay to buy necessities such as soap, toothpowder etc: and only a run ashore once over the next three months, on an afternoon and under the supervision of a petty officer. Their GC badges would not be restored for a very long time. The consequential penalties for this latest escapade of the incorrigible foursome were to have disastrous repercussions upon the well-being of Eric Smith.

Ajax visited Bahia Blanca, then Rio de Janeiro where many of the cruiser's Lotharios suffered disappointment when they discovered that the girls they had enjoyed during the ship's 1938 visit had either married or acquired dangerously protective local boyfriends. The cruiser remained in Rio for two weeks and was due to depart on 31st August with a lower-deck largely oblivious of the war crisis at home and in Europe. British newspapers were a rarity in the mess-decks, and if the wardroom was aware of the deteriorating political situation and its implications, this was not the era for keeping the common sailor informed.

Suddenly and without warning the ship's company libertymen were recalled from shore leave and a whole range of robust and temporary sexual encounters. *Ajax* sailed 24 hours before her planned date of departure, on 30th August; once clear of the approaches to Rio de Janeiro she turned south at high speed while Captain C.H.L. Woodhouse cleared lower-deck of all men not on watch and informed his ship's company that he had received a 'Warning' telegram from Admiralty that included orders to join Commodore Henry Harwood in *Exeter* which was already on patrol off the coast of Argentina. He also gave a brief outline on the situation in Europe and that there existed a real possibility that their country would soon be at war with Germany. Captain Woodhouse 'spoke sombrely having himself served in the battle of Falklands in 1914'.

His audience could hardly comprehend that after eighteen months of circumventing the South American continent the seemingly endless seamen's vista of girls, rum, bum and baccy was at an end. Eric Smith and his mess-mates found that mess-deck conversation topics now took a more sombre drift, the men who had fought in World War One came into their own and their words were listened to with respect.

Ajax was still on passage south on 3rd September when Captain Woodhouse ordered lower-deck to be again cleared at noon. Standing on his quarter-deck he announced to a hushed assembled ship's company that war had been declared and read the Prime Minister's statement that had been broadcast over the United Kingdom radio. Captain Woodhouse then read out the formal words of the Articles of War followed immediately by the news that a German merchant ship had been reported in the area and it was his intention to capture or sink the vessel. Before his audience could catch its collective breath he ordered his cruiser to action stations.

Within an hour of the announcement of hostilities the speeding *Ajax* sighted a luckless German freighter, the *Karl Fritzen*, 6,594 tons, trying to return home empty of cargo. The master wasted no time ordering the abandonment and the scuttling of his ship. The crew was picked up by the cruiser which without firing a round had achieved her first sinking. Shortly afterwards and still in an area between Rio Grande de Sul and the estuary of the River Plate a second ship, SS *Olinda*, 4,576 tons was sighted. Again the German ship was empty and trying to make a run for her home port, Bremerhaven. This time it required a 6-inch shell across her bow to force the master to heave to but to Captain Woodhouse's intense annoyance the master failed to obey his order to standby and receive a boarding party from *Ajax*. The German lowered his boats at speed, clearly abandoning ship after opening the freighter's sea cocks.

The merchantman took a long time to sink so once the master and his crew had clambered inboard the cruiser and joined as prisoners of war the officers and crew from *Karl Fritzen*, Woodhouse gave orders for 'B' turret to hasten the demise of the *Olinda* which had eluded his intention to secure as a prize of war.

Eric Smith tasted his first experience of a live action. As a young able seaman he had no gunnery qualifications but his action station was within the control cabinet of 'B' turret located between the right and left 6″ inch guns, a station he shared with the turret local control sight layer and sight trainer. He relished his view of the twelve rounds fired by his turret into the *Olinda*.

From this date onwards the squadron, reinforced by the county class cruiser *Cumberland* as *Achilles* had not returned from New Zealand, commenced long patrols of the icy and stormy seas of the South Atlantic.

The lower-deck was given very little information and men only guessed at vague rumours that the long patrols quartering the South Atlantic were to intercept German raiders seeking Allied shipping, armed merchant cruisers and, most alarming of all, pocket battleships. Into October, then November, the search continued; on 5th October, the Admiralty formed eight powerful hunter groups to hunt the pocket battleship *Deutschland* in the North Atlantic and her sister ship *Admiral Graf Spee* in the southern ocean. The South Atlantic squadron of the America and East Indies station became Force G with an area of search, the south-east coast of South America.

The men of *Ajax* knew little of this organisation created to bring the enemy ocean raiders to action, but they became accustomed to the tedium of long days and nights sweeping the icy wastes closed up at a two watch defence stations system with action stations at the most dangerous period of the 24 hours, dawn and at dusk. The messdecks became sealed compartments with scuttles and dead-lights firmly screwed down for weeks on end. The living areas below decks, due to running condensation were damp and noisome places that could only be ventilated and sweetened on the infrequent visits to neutral ports for refuelling. Commodore Harwood exploited the Hague Convention rules to the permitted limits, which allowed for belligerent warships to fuel once in three months in the port of a neutral country. The Commodore's squadron was operating of the coasts

off three neutrals, Brazil, Uruguay and Argentina some 1,000 miles
from its Falkland island base. It was during these rare runs ashore
that libertymen learned of reports that German capital ships were at
large sinking and capturing neutral as well as Allied merchant ships.

It was to Port Stanley that the battered ships had to return for
repair and rest. This bleak South Atlantic outpost beset by dreadful
weather conditions and possessing few recreational facilities did
become almost a desirable haven for the men from the patrolling
cruisers. When *Exeter* had to remain at Port Stanley for repairs during the later part of October, Henry Harwood transferred his Broad
Pennant to *Ajax*. With the embarkation of the commodore and his
staff the ship became better informed on the general situation. Sinkings of merchant ships were moving from the west coast of Africa into
the mid- South Atlantic, radio SOS calls from some of the victims
had included positive identification of the pocket battleship *Admiral
Graf Spee*; originating from the commodore's signal staff this intelligence became common knowledge to a very apprehensive ship's
company who were well aware that the combined gunpower of the
cruiser squadron was outmatched by *Graf Spee*'s six 11-inch plus
eight 5.9-inch gun arsenal.

In the first weeks of December *Ajax* with *Cumberland* in company
intercepted one of the pocket battleship's supply vessels, *Ussukuma*,
which blew up when the cruisers opened fire in an abortive effort to
prevent the crew from abandoning and scuttling their ship.

This flurry of action took place, while Eric Smith was in dire trouble and facing disciplinary action, which allowed no mitigation even
though, as seemed possible, the ship would be in action at short
notice. The cause of Eric Smith's appearance before his captain on a
serious breach of discipline was one of an incorrigible quartet of
leave-breakers. The group, after the ship's Para visit, were still on
maximum periods of stoppage of leave, pay and privileges; they had
all been downgraded to second class for leave and pay – also, the har-
dest to bear, stoppage of their grog ration.

Ajax in late November put into Port Stanley to refuel and to give a
few hours' recreational leave to each watch. When it came for Eric
Smith's turn for shore leave to stretch his legs and have a drink in one
of Stanley's few pubs, one of the quartet persuaded Eric to bring him
a bottle of rum. Recklessly Eric accepted the proffered 4s. 0d.; he
remembered his promise and bought a bottle of rum which he stuffed
into his jumper and belt, and then returned to his ship in the liberty

boat. What next occurred is described in Smith's own words:

As we came alongside the accommodation ladder we shuffled around preparing to climb onboard. Chief and Petty Officers always left the boat first saluting the officer of the day and then proceeded forward to their messes. Next up the ladder went the leading rates followed by the common or garden Jack-me-hearty who after saluting the quarterdeck was frisked by the duty regulating petty officer before going forward to the regulating office to retrieve their station card. I was 'rubbed down' and no contraband being discovered started my way forward. The OOD Lieutenant Desmond Dreyer (later to become Admiral Sir Desmond Dryer) my own divisional officer, ordered the RPO to search me again. I stood against 'Y' turret situated on the quarterdeck and again nothing was found. The OOD then ordered the duty petty officer to search me more thoroughly. He whispered enquiring whether I had anything or not with me. The Duty RPO on that evening was a decent enough chap, a petty officer and a leading torpedo operator, and as I did not wish to get him into trouble, I told him where the rum was hidden. This was of course confiscated and I was stood aside to await the Master At Arms to formulate charges and appear formally before the OOD, and so be placed in the commander's report the following morning.

The usual processes of naval law followed; two days later Eric appeared before his captain, he had committed one of the more serious crimes set out in Article 540, Table 1 item (g) 'Smuggling liquor on board or into a boat' – King's Rules and Admiralty Instructions 1939. The punishment Number 4 was detention with a maximum of three months and could have additional penalties, No 5 Dismissal from the Service, No 6 Disrating, No 7, Loss of Good Conduct Badges, No 8 Reduction to Second Class for Conduct, and there were three more associated penal awards at the commanding officer's disposal. Captain Woodhouse was merciful, the warrant submitted to the commodore for approval recommended seven days' cells.

The commodore had just held a conference of his captains to outline his plan to trap the *Graf Spee*. *Achilles* was on patrol off the estuary of the River Plate, *Ajax* was to sail immediately to join the New Zealand cruiser, *Exeter* was to sail on the 9th to join the squadron off the Plate and *Cumberland* to remain at sea close to Port Stanley in case the pocket battleship had plans to attack the islands on 8th December, the anniversary of the Battle of the Falklands in 1914.

Eric Smith continues his narrative of events seen at his level:

I had to appear before the whole ship's company not actually on duty at

1600 hours on the day that the warrant was read, I was then marched away to clean into a canvas suit to start 7 days cell punishment and the poor old three badge AB lost his 4/- and still had his thirst. The cells were situated right forward and one deck below, so any prisoners contained therein got the full blast of the buffeting, pitch and roll of the ship during heavy weather. In 1939, cell punishment was strictly carried out and was performed in a duck or canvas suit, without belt, shoelaces or anything else considered lethal by which means an occupant might conceivably commit suicide. Shaving was barred. No blanket was allowed unless temperature dropped below 32 degrees and the cell offender was allowed half an hour's exercise in the dog watches only. For the first three days a prisoner was allowed 3 hard ship's biscuits and two mugs of fresh water per day. On the 4th to 7th days I was allowed a bowl of soup and, potatoes at mid-day and on any subsequent days I could have had a full ship's company meal at mid-day (less a sweet dish). My bed consisted of a 6ft block of wood with a wooden pillow at one end. As can be imagined it was most uncomfortable particularly in the freezing weather we were experiencing at that time. I was visited by the padre each morning and the doctor. After the third day having complained bitterly about my lack of sleep due to the cold, I was granted one blanket. It was more than welcome. The task or work that I had to perform consisted of picking 2 lb of oakum per day. Oakum is about three 12 inch lengths of thick tarry hemp which had to be unlaid, stranded and then picked until the whole lot resembled a large ball of fluff. This may not sound much but believe me it was a whole day's hard work, although towards the end of my sentence I got quite expert. The commander inspected the finished product during evening rounds and if it was not to his satisfaction I had to do it all over again. The finished product was used for caulking the wooden decks or filling canvas punch bags.

On the fourth day of my sentence I had a really frightening experience. It was the first duty of the Master At Arms on the sounding of action stations to release all prisoners in cells. At about 2000 hours of this evening the call to Action Stations sounded over the ship's tannoy system, feet were heard scurrying over my head and outside my cell door as the crew hurried to their appointed stations, I was expecting the Royal Marine sentry or the Master At Arms to unlock my cell at any moment. Nothing happened and a few minutes later the main armament opened up firing broadsides. The cell plating began to vibrate with their thunder. Thinking that we had run into the German raider I banged on the cell door feeling that I was trapped like a rat. All to no avail, I began to get really worried. The gun salvos increased in intensity and I pummelled the door again. This time the cell door spy-hole was pushed aside and an eye appeared only to vanish immediately. Nearly a year before I had almost drowned and now I was in danger of being entombed within a 6ft by 4ft steel cell and a watery grave should the ship suffer direct hits and go down. After about ¾ of an hour the firing ceased followed by the 'carry-on' being sounded

A wave of relief passed over me when I heard the boots of the 'Boot-neck' sentry stop outside the cell door; his key turned in the lock and he looked in to see how I was. When I asked him what was going on he merely replied, 'Oh, we've only been doing a night encounter exercise with the *Exeter*.' For the next few minutes he heard all about what sailors thought about stupid 'Sea Oxen' and what I thought about him in particular. He slammed the door on me and I was left alone with my thoughts.

All things come to an end: on completion of my seventh day of sentence I was escorted to the bathroom for a shower and shave prior to being released to rejoin my mess. For some reason I had been released late and had not been victualled for supper. This was rubbed in by my messmates singing the old naval refrain, 'F-K you Jack, I'm all right,' but [the three badge AB] who was now a Petty Officer's messman came up trumps; he took me into his pantry where he lashed me up to a good meal plus a can of Barclays beer that he had somehow acquired from the midshipmen's gun-room. I savoured my release with a few turns round the upperdeck before turning into my hammock for the best night's sleep in a week.

A few days later the squadron on station off the estuary of the river Plate sighted the *Graf Spee* at dawn on 12th December 1939. It was here that Commodore Harwood's squadron fought the brilliant action that ended when the powerful raider *Graf Spee* retired into Montevideo later to scuttle herself, defeated by three lightly armed cruisers who for many months had rehearsed the tactics which on the day gained an historic naval victory. The price paid by the men of the squadron was high; *Exeter* suffered 61 dead and 23 wounded, *Ajax* 7 dead and 5 wounded and *Achilles* 4 dead. The enemy in the pocket battleship lost 36 dead and 60 wounded.

Recollections of the battle were later recorded in Eric Smith's memoirs:

The first time one goes into action for real, one wonders, 'Will I be up to it? Will I be afraid? Will I let my shipmates down?' A thousand and one questions flashed through my mind, this particular dawn before coming back to reality and getting on with the job I had been trained to do.

On the morning of 13th December we went to the usual dawn action stations at about 0500 and were then stood down to 'cruising stations' about half an hour later. I left my action station in 'B' turret and because I had the morning watch (0400 to 0800) made my way up to the 4" anti-aircraft director above and abaft the bridge.

The ship's company, now off watch and released from dawn action stations, went below to wash and breakfast before taking over the fore-noon watch at 0800. Hardly had we settled down in our cruising stations than a signal was received from *Exeter*; 'Have sighted an enemy warship, believed to be a pocket battleship'. At the same moment our own mast-head lookout reported smoke on the horizon and following his directions with a pair of binoculars my officer of quarters, a lieutenant Royal Marines, also reported smoke. Soon I too could see the outlines of a large warship. At first I had a feeling of numbness, this was the real thing, then as action stations sounded for the second time that morning, I scrambled down the side of the HA director, shot down two ladders leading from the bridge and crashed into Commodore Harwood clad in his pyjamas as he left his sea cabin. Shouting a quick 'Sorry Sir' I dashed to 'B' turret just as *Exeter* opened fire. Training and practice of the past years came to the fore and all stations were manned quickly and efficiently. I was of course one of the first into the turret and climbing into the cabinet I opened the sighting ports as *Exeter* crossed my line of vision with her guns blazing. The time was about 0614. Next into the cabinet was Les Dennis, the turret layer, soon followed by the trainer clad only in a towel; he had been on his way for a shower when action stations was sounded. He entered 'dripping' at all officers who wanted to play war games twice in one day. It was a few seconds before I breathlessly convinced him that this was the 'real McCoy'.

By this time all stations were closed up and we were racing for the enemy and we got the order to open fire. I will not dwell on the action here other than to explain that it was the job of us in the turret cabinet to keep the points of our instruments in line with those of the 6 inch control director from where the salvos were actually fired by the director layer but I did have the opportunity to occasionally glance out of the sighting ports to see the fall of shot from the enemy's 11 inch guns, some perilously close at times. Poor *Exeter* – she bore the brunt of the enemy's fire and I had a glimpse of her blazing furiously and listing, but still firing her after guns from time to time. After 20 to 30 minutes of furious action she had to retire to fight, the fires sweeping her upper deck and to deal with the damage she had suffered but not before inflicting serious damage on the enemy whom we now knew to be the *Graf Spee*. Many deeds of heroism were performed in *Exeter* that day and many good men were killed. By now however, with the help of *Ajax*'s spotter plane, an ancient Seafox, directing our fall of shot, we had got the German's measure and our salvos were doing increasing damage to her from one side while *Achilles* tackled her from the other. *Exeter* had meanwhile suffered further damage and was ordered to disengage and make for the Falklands. *Ajax* and *Achilles* now closed the enemy working to a pre-arranged plan and continued to fire rapid salvos.

Then we, ourselves, received a direct hit on 'X' turret, the one manned by the Royal Marines, killing some of the crew and putting the turret out of action. 'Y' turret had also been damaged. It was now about 0715 and *Graf Spee* was firing everything she had at us, 11 inch and 5.9 inch guns and also fired torpedoes at us at about 0730 which our Seafox reported and we were able to turn away, so that they missed us completely. At 0800 it was reported that we had only 20% ammunition left, 'X' turret was still out of action and the ammunition hoist in 'B' turret was jammed. With *Achilles* we continued to harry the *Graf Spee* until she broke off the action and made off in the direction of the River Plate. We continued to shadow her throughout the day intending to fight a night action with her if necessary. Meantime the guns crew were, stood down in the vicinity of their action stations and at 1100 hours the cook's staff together with other supernumeraries brought round corned beef sandwiches and tea which was very welcome, very few of us had had anything to eat since the previous evening.

The finale of the action is well known, but Eric Smith records a postscript on what happened to the cruisers when the ships learned that the *Graf Spee* had scuttled herself and her captain had later committed suicide:

The two British ships now joined by *Cumberland* steamed round in circles at the month of the Plate, cheering and hoorahing as much from relief I suppose as from anything else. The following day certain off-duty men were allowed ashore (into Montevideo). In one of the bars they met up with some *Graf Spee* men who invited them over for a drink and they ended up the best of friends. So much for the futility of war. No further leave was given to our ship's company, after this because of the unfortunate behaviour of some of the *Cumberland's* men who had been serving for the previous years on the perhaps more rumbustious China Station. . . .
So now in company with *Cumberland* we proceeded to the Falklands; *Achilles* had sailed for New Zealand where she was given a tumultuous welcome. We entered Port Stanley to find *Exeter* already there; her wounded being well looked after in the local hospital. Our own worst wounded personnel were also landed for treatment, our seven killed having been buried at sea. I had been through my first sea battle and found that I had not been as scared as I thought I might have been. . . .
The day after the battle I was one of the party detailed to help clear up the mess aft caused by a direct hit on 'X' turret. It was not a pleasant job as there were bits of torn flesh from those killed floating around in the filthy water; the sight of violent death is never pleasant but here again the sight of similar violent death in the Chilean earthquake earlier that year had perhaps immunised me to a certain extent, I was not as upset as I had expected to be. We spent Christmas in the Falklands together with those of our friends from the Topmen's mess in *Exeter* who had survived, but it was a sad occasion, so many having been killed.

Exeter limped home returning to Plymouth after three years away; *Ajax* arrived at Chatham soon afterwards in February 1940. Both ships' companies were honoured in London's Guildhall on 16th February.

The cruisers paid off and went into dockyard hands while the ship's company, including Eric Smith and his messmates, departed on 'foreign service' leave.

The experience of *Ajax* on the America and West Indies Station and then as part of the South Atlantic Command was an example of the pre-war service of men in regular continuous service engagements drafted to any of the twenty-five to thirty cruisers deployed to overseas stations and commands for commissions lasting for two to three years. Now it remains to sketch in some of the background of the reserves which were mobilised partially in 1938 and then totally in 1939.

The reserves available for mobilisation on 1st January 1939 numbered approximately 73,000 officers and men. They included retired officers of the Royal Navy in the Emergency List, retired Pensioner Ratings under 55 years of age, the Royal Fleet Reserve (men on obligatory five years on the reserve after completing seven years' active service), the Royal Naval Reserve (officers and ratings in the Merchant Navy) and finally officers and men of the Royal Naval Volunteer Reserve.

This last, and the smallest, reserve numbered 800 officers and 5,300 ratings. The establishment of 800 RNVR officers would by the end of the war in Europe in 1945 grow into tens of thousands of officers holding temporary, war-service only, RNVR commissions in spite of the fact that the majority came from Hostility Only Conscript origins. The Admiralty shrank from granting these thousands of officers temporary Royal Navy commissions, but very many acquired considerable naval expertise and commands of major war vessels. It seemed that they were granted the Volunteer Reserve status so that they could be retained in a subordinate role in the command structure.

The 5,300 Royal Naval Volunteer Reserve ratings, in contrast to the officers of the Reserve, by the second and third years of the war had vanished into the huge complement of the fleet. By 1945 the numbers in the fleet had reached 860,000. A hint of what motivated these volunteer civilian sailors should be recorded briefly.

The Reserve in early 1938 was at full strength but many in it were fearful that the betrayal which had turned their World War One predecessors into soldiers fighting ashore would be repeated. Then, men who had trained in their own time and expense to be efficient seamen capable of taking their place alongside the professionals found themselves formed into platoons and battalions of the Royal Naval Division. The RND was sent to fight in the Low Countries where many finished up interned in Holland and there were heavy casualties. The survivors went on to be decimated in Gallipoli and later in the mud and trenches on the Western Front in France. The irony was that as these trained seamen were dying in the trenches the navy was suffering an acute shortage of seamen.

Fears of the 1938/39 successors of the 1914 RNVR were stirred by every inspecting admiral who praised and congratulated the RNVR divisions for their bearing on parade and skill in arms drill; their unease reached a peak during the September 1938 semi-mobilisation when only RNVR signalmen and telegraphists were called up and drafted to merchant ships earmarked for conversion into armed merchant cruisers, into minesweepers and trawlers awaiting minesweeping equipment. But no RNVR seamen were called up to join ships of the fleet.

The civilian trained volunteer signalmen and telegraphists found that they had joined hundreds of reservists of the RFR and RNR categories and recalled pensioners who were packing into Chatham barracks. Every train that arrived at Chatham Town station brought more reservists responding to the mobilisation telegrams.

The barrack rooms became saturated with men, there were hundreds without messes or hammock billets and it was soon obvious that there were more men available than there were ships to be manned. A quasi-comic situation soon developed as men were forced to camp out on the parade ground, a few worried RNVRs among them and built dozens of small laagers constructed from their hammocks and swollen yellow waterproofed kit bags, a protection from the cold east wind. Inside the laagers hoary recalled pensioners, some with little kit other than a crown and anchor board, stripped incautious reservists of whatever cash they had in the pocket of their uniform belts.

Fortunately the emergency was over in 36 hours and the reserves were stood down and sent home, but the fact that there seemed to be no organisation or plans to draft many hundreds of men into ships, carried on the threat of the formation of another RND to fight ashore as soldiers. Those who had been witness to the confusion at Chatham passed on their fears to shipmates in the RNVR London headquarters ship *President* berthed at Blackfriars, London. These fears could

have been put to rest, but the RNVR commanding and senior officers followed the example set by their opposite numbers in the regular
service and ignored the need to provide information to the lower-
deck, an incongruous and strange situation in a volunteer reserve
where officer and ratings often worked in the same civilian occupation. The facts were that the Admiralty had by September 1938
decided that RNVR seamen were to be trained to be anti-aircraft
gunners and to serve in units which would be drafted to sea-going
ships of war. The *President* and other H/Q ships of other RNVR divisions were soon to be equipped to train these units.

Officers and men of the regular service universally considered the
men of the RNVR as being strange and more than slightly mad to
give up their civilian holidays to serve for two weeks in the spartan
crowded messdecks of the King's Ships. In the capital ships,
battleships, battle-cruisers and cruisers it was unusual for the RNVR
officer or rating to be allowed to do very much more than watch what
was going on. The professionals, especially the senior ratings,
regarded 'Rocky' sailors with suspicion and considered that they
were incapable of acquiring seamanlike skills; they would not con-
cede that anyone who had not started in a boys' training establishment or ship would ever be safe or trusted in a HM ship. Yet, the
RNVR rating was fascinated and absorbed by mess-deck life, its
order, conventions and rituals, excited also by an almost hilarious
panic when trying to comprehend the many 'pipes' that controlled
the routine and order to shipboard life. Without tannoy speaker sys-
tems, commands and routine orders were relayed through the capital ships by relays of bosun's mates and call boys. Unable to recog-
nise the individual trills and warbles, the rising and falling notes
made on the seamen's call or pipe, the shouted order that followed
often rendered unintelligible by the variety of dialect, left the RNVR
only hoping for the best and with no alternative but to join every
body of men seen rushing up ladders, between deck spaces, on to the
upper deck, by day or night, urged on by shouting petty officers and
leading seamen, rarely knowing what was going on until reaching a
muster station.

Sometimes, as a privilege – a break from scrubbing and holystoning decks, washing paintwork, the 'Rocky' sailor was allowed to
polish bright work and to handle a tin of Blue Bell polish. The cauti-
ous petty officer, captain of the top, would chose brass or steel fittings
that were safe from the critical eye of the commander. It was essential for the RNVR to retain a sense of humour, without it he was lost

Mess-deck, RN Barracks
Portsmouth, HMS *Victory*.

kate, seamanship training
ip at Portsmouth, 1939.

at St Lucia, America and
t Indies station 1939.

(*Left*) *Ajax*. Eric Smith and Len Pittman, 1939. (*Right*) 'Mast', HMS *Ganges*.

'Kit Inspection', HMS *Ganges*.

but there were occasions when the amateurs came into their own and surprised even the most cynical critics in the ranks of the regular chief and petty officers. In the ship's boats, whalers and cutters, the RNVR ratings often were able to demonstrate to startled instructors in the fleet that they were expert in handling the boats under oars and sail. Manning boats secured to the lower booms in which they were carrying out sea training, with the boats plunging into cold spray-plumed seas of Invergordon or Scapa Flow held few terrors for the civilians dressed as sailors.

In early weeks of 1939 the RNVR divisions received the armament equipment for anti-aircraft gunnery training and at last the volunteer reserve ratings were informed of their secure role in the fleet in the event of a future war mobilisation. In the *President*, which had returned from a rapid refit in Sheerness to her moorings at Black-friars, training was underway to form four anti-aircraft units comprising two officers and 50 ratings who would man four 4″ guns capable of high and low angle fire and the control team of director and data transmitting station crews.

By August four London RNVR division seaman gunnery units were trained and ready for sea training and live ammunition firing trials with towed air and sea targets. The first unit joined for two weeks' training in the Ceres class cruiser *Coventry* at Portsmouth on 20th August 1939. The cruiser, first commissioned in 1918 originally armed with five 6 inch calibre centre line guns and eight torpedo tubes, was converted to an anti-aircraft role with ten 4 inch high angle and low angle guns (HA/LA), a eight barrelled 2 pounder multiple pom pom mounting and several .5 inch multiple mountings. On 25th August the London division RNVR's second and third units joined two other converted cruisers, *Cairo* at Portsmouth and *Calcutta* at Hull. The fourth unit joined *Curlew* refitting in Chatham, several weeks later.

The unit for *Coventry* joined the cruiser by the ship's cutters as she lay at anchor at Spithead. The RNVR lieutenant in command of this first RNVR anti-aircraft unit accompanied by his sub-lieutenant led his men on to the quarter-deck of the cruiser where the ship's gunnery officer Lieutenant (G) E.W. Briggs RN, flanked by his two gunnery instructors Chief Petty Officers R. Bracking and C. Goldring, greeted this new phenomenon, a complete gunnery unit manned entirely by civilian volunteer officers and ratings. Captain R.F.J. Onslow DSC MVO RN, with his executive commander in attendance, stood aft on his quarterdeck and shared the curiosity of his ship's company who from forward vantage points, as curious spectators, watched what they regarded as the impossible.

The cruiser was commissioned and manned by regular long ser-vice officers and men but a number had been sent ashore for courses so that the RNVRs could experience occupying their own messes, fending for themselves in the canteen system. The GI's in the man-ner of their profession busied themselves allocating the reservists to their guns for the next two weeks and their places in the ship's watch and quarter bill. While this was going on during dog watches the cruiser weighed anchor and sailed for Plymouth and the gun firing practice areas. A few hours after anchoring in Plymouth Sound Cap-tain Onslow received a recall to Portsmouth and on passage he ordered the RNVR unit to muster on the quarter-deck where he informed the reservists that they had been mobilised by Royal Proc-lamation. They were to be given 36 hours' leave on arrival at Portsmouth to settle their civilian affairs and had to return to the *Coventry* by noon on 25th August.

Following a few frantic hours at home to sever civilian ties the RNVR sailors returned to their ship to find that more than half her peace-time ship's company had been drafted to other ships and to courses, their places were being filled by a motley trickle of recalled pensioners and reservists from the RFR and RNR. Suddenly the RNVR anti-aircraft unit who had not as yet fired any live ammuni-tion became the only trained gunnery nucleus, with the exception of the Royal Marine detachment who manned the two guns located on the quarterdeck. Hours of feverish activity followed, with every new arrival from barracks turned to for work immediately, embarking ammunition, naval stores, armament stores and victuals up to full war book standards. The ship was under sailing orders.

By midnight on the 25th the cruiser was stored and starting at 0530 hours the next day the chief and petty officers commenced their task of organising what was after all now a scratch ship's company so that the ship could sail that day with other ships ordered to reinforce the Mediterranean fleet. *Coventry* sailed at 1035 from South Slip jetty with exhausted and hard-pressed regular senior ratings chasing, persuading, bullying the motley collection of the remnants of the original highly trained ship's company and the new arrivals, recalled pensioners and the mobilised reservists, including the RNVR unit. The ship left harbour without displaying any signs of the convulsive changes that had occurred since the cruiser three days earlier entered harbour with a highly trained long service crew lining her upper deck and handling the berthing wires. *Coventry* sailed with her decks this time lined by immaculate ranks of men who were still stunned by having joined a few hours earlier to work unceasingly storing ship and had no time to find their way round this old first world war cruiser converted to an anti-aircraft role. Berthing wires and fenders had been stowed and as the ship proceeded down harbour the Royal Marine bugler and piping party saluted senior ships and the Commander-in-Chief then acknowledged the courtesies from junior ships. This facade of ceremonial disguised the fact that *Coventry* was not a worked-up ship and was only able to proceed to sea through the exertions of the Chief Bosun's Mate, Chief Petty Officer D. Davenport, the captains of the tops, petty officers whom Captain Onslow had succeeded in retaining, the two chief gunnery instructors, Bracking and Goldring, and other senior ratings in below deck departments, the engine-room and boiler-rooms.

Coventry arrived at Alexandria on 2nd September having called at Gibraltar and Malta. Every hour of the passage including the brief refuelling stops at the two naval bases had been occupied with training in every aspect of the cruiser's fighting function. The senior non-commissioned officers drove themselves and the junior mixed bag of ratings remorsely. Gun drill with day and night live firings using targets, air and surface, produced from Gibraltar and then Malta-dominated priorities, followed by an endless repetition of the whole range of seamanship skills and for the civilian sailors the special importance of learning to live in claustrophobic conditions below decks where to avoid constant bodily contact was an impossibility. Where to carry out bodily functions had to be endured sitting like roosting hens in primitive heads.

In brilliant sunshine the Mediterranean fleet lay in Alexandria harbour in arrogant majesty, battleships, an aircraft carrier, cruisers, destroyer flotillas and support craft all manned by the regular peacetime manpower. It was an incredible sight for the RNVRs in *Coventry*, as their ship berthed with two anchors and stern to a detached mole, then spread awnings.

The first day of a war that would eventually engulf millions who were to be destroyed started for the Mediterranean fleet ships as a day of perfection, brilliant sky and a smooth azure sea beyond the harbour breakwaters and its men secure in the belief of the Empire and a pride in the might of the fleet. Five weeks followed of Monday to Friday fleet exercising; it was a deceptive period when the fleet manoeuvred on day and night exercises against a probable enemy. Meanwhile in home waters the main fleet was face to face with the realities of war: ships were being sunk by aircraft, submarine torpedo and aircraft bomb with *Coventry*'s London RNVR shipmate units in the three other AA cruisers, *Calcutta*, *Cairo* and *Curlew* working up to battle efficiency in the bleak waters of Scapa Flow then going into action in defence of East coast convoys in terrible weather conditions with ships ill-equipped to provide shelter against the elements and individuals without protective clothing.

In the Mediterranean there were perils of a less lethal kind for the men of the fleet and to a lesser extent the civilian sailors in *Coventry*. The fleet, after exercising in seductive sea conditions, returned to Alexandria where all hands could bathe over their ship sides in water that was crystal clear, free from pollution; they were halcyon days where on make and mend days feluccas laden with ice-filled petrol cans and buried beer bottles sailed out of harbour crowded with sailors bound for golden western desert beaches populated with welcoming Lebanese and Greek females.

There were limitless temptations ashore in the Egyptian port, every form of vice and corruption to tempt the weak and unwary. Amongst the recalled pensioners and fleet reservists there were a few men of grotesque evil who because of their previous service and status as trained seamen had a malevolent influence and command over the boy seamen and to some extent the civilian sailors in *Coventry* who were still comparatively innocent; the boy seamen were in terrible danger of corruption. The cruiser was fortunate that not only had its captain succeeded in retaining an exceptional group of senior chiefs and petty officers but the RNVR had its own men of special strength of character led by a veteran Leading Seaman Alfred Drouet who had joined prior to the First World War and had served with the Royal Naval Division in Gallipoli and then the trenches in France. From the tragic fraction of survivors he was one of a handful who rejoined the RNVR when the Reserve was reformed in 1921. He now was receiving his reward for perseverance, a seagoing ship of war, fighting his King's enemies. The ex-civilian postman's steadying influence, supported by his two RNVR colleagues Leading Seaman Douglas MacDougall and Derek Gardiner, kept many of the AA unit and their shipmates on the rails of moderate behaviour and free from acts of gross and degrading stupidity ashore. The young RNVRs were reluctant to shock their father figure, Leading Seaman Alfred Drouet.

Coventry was ordered from the Mediterranean where conflict with the Germans was still a remote possibility and the ship returned to home waters and the reality of war. For a few weeks the cruiser acting as flagship of four anti-aircraft cruisers operated out of the Humber protecting east coast convoys. The cruisers *Coventry, Calcutta, Cairo* and *Curlew* made many refuelling and storing calls into Grimsby. Grimsby pubs in the winter of 1939/40 vibrated with a rumbustious earthy life energy, frequent fights, blood spilt, noses broken, fists and bottles hurled but somehow the incidents were devoid of the mindless viciousness that would be the experience of later years.

Beer-stimulated rivalries, mainly rough-humoured, were constant between the local fishermen, the navy and sometimes the regulars, versus amateur volunteers manning the white ensign ships. There was also the inevitable sexual excitement and competition for the favours of independent, beautiful often reckless, promiscuous women of the port. Two pubs, the Lincoln Arms and on the opposite corner the Sheffield Arms, known to thousands of sailors as the 'Rats Nest' were the centre of Grimsby's rough and very physical beer-based nights ashore.

Beyond blackout double curtained doorways of the Rats Nest a long bar counter illuminated by shaded blue lights was packed and throbbing with men and women; more than half the men in naval uniform and Grimsby men fast being recruited and volunteering for trawlers turned into minesweepers, drank and caroused as if there would be no tomorrows after the next departure to sea.

The cruisers and other ships on East Coast convoy protection duties often called in to Immingham and then libertymen for Grimsby embarked in a single deck tram that ran at 20 minute intervals across open fenland. The trams maintained a service ferrying dockworkers and ships' crews and since the start of hostilities ran at night blacked out except for a single dim blue light in the interior; at speed the trams had a devastating effect on returning libertymen filled with Grimsby ale. Interiors fusty dark and dank, suffocating with tobacco smoke, dipped and swayed, a ghastly motion often given an extra out of rhythm wrench by gales rampaging off the North Sea trying to throw the tram off its rails. Singing and roistering libertymen were silenced by the motion long before reaching the terminus at Immingham. Many a braggart shouting of his conquests among Grimsby women was turned into a helpless vomiting wretch.

Men drank to dull the effect of that return tram journey to be followed by wet, rough often perilous boat journeys in open cutters back to their ships and the dreadful conditions. No special foul or cold weather clothing had been issued to the majority of the fleet so men wore a strange and mostly unsuitable mixture of clothing, private gear to supplement the inadequate issue gear and worn under issue oilskins in a vain attempt to keep out raw and freezing easterly winds. Battened down messdecks, dimly lit, overcrowded and damp with constant running condensation from steaming clothing, made living spaces cold, clammy and comfortless. Once hammocks were slung it became impossible to move around between decks unless bent double; there were few places where a man could stand upright. The constant bad weather of the winter of 1939 turned the messdecks of the East Coast convoy escorts into dreadful spaces of swirling water, spilt gash buckets and vomit; for men whose sleeping billet was on the deck below their mess tables shipboard life acquired an added torment.

The last four months of 1939 and the first of what was going to seem to be an endless war, saw the settling down of the reservists with the regulars coming to terms with the first wave of hostility only entrants. Promotion had for many years been a slow process for men of the Royal Navy, most leading seamen were hoary old three badge-men and they regarded the bewildered new drafts as 'virgins or pink tits'. Some of the recalled pensioners for a while regaled and bored the regulars and the new men with highly embroidered accounts of actions at sea during World War One, their brand of line shooting soon began to tail off with the common sharing of appalling sea conditions in this first winter of the new world war, the ferocity of enemy air attacks and the menace of the massive German laid east coast minefield.

Very many of these old hands with an acquired wealth of sea wisdom borne from long foreign commissions acted as 'Sea Daddies' to the civilian sailors. One veteran is still remembered with affection by a civilian sailor who profited from his advice. Bill Sands, an RNVR able seaman, had been called up with other reservists to man ships of the Reserve Fleet, which was reviewed by King George VI in Weymouth Bay in early August. Sands was resentful and considered that he and others had been pressganged as they had not been allowed to return to their civilian jobs or given leave to wind up their business and domestic responsibilities; they had been retained in what they had believed to be a temporary draft to the 7,550 ton cruiser *Emerald* which sailed to Scapa Flow to commence working up to war efficiency before the Royal Proclamation mobilising the reserves. From Scapa Flow the *Emerald* proceeded to long patrols of the Denmark Strait and the North Sea, Bill Sands recalls his most significant war conversation:

> An old three badgeman able seaman (recalled pensioner) took pity on a gut miserable uncooperative RNVR rating and spelt it out for me. It was quite simply the need to prove oneself worthy of the ship's special duty jobs and to discover the benefits of not having to work part of ship. I took his advice to heart and never looked back. I did most special duty jobs at different times and in several ships, found them interesting and the privileges worth the effort to master them . . . I found a better war on the lower deck, I am still alive; many friends who took commissions died in action.

By 31st December 1939, 222 British, Allied and neutral ships had been sunk: by enemy U-boats (114), mines (79), warship raiders (15), aircraft (10) and unknown causes (4). Of this number 116 ships had been sunk in home waters with another 47 in the Western Approaches. In spite of the agony and effort of the mobilised fleet commanded by long service professional commanders, only nine U-boats had been detected and sunk, with just one enemy commerce raider cornered and forced to scuttle after the River Plate action.

The fleet losses had been grievous and included the aircraft carrier *Courageous* with 514 officers and men killed and drowned; then the battleship *Royal Oak* with greater losses, 833 deaths. The chill of war had began to grip the very vitals of men serving in the fleet, there was the constant gnaw of anxiety for the homeland which seemed to be at the mercy of a powerful and overwhelming enemy airforce which had not as yet revealed its might. One glimmer of hope raised spirits in the 1939 Christmas when details of the South Atlantic squadron's victory became known.

CHAPTER TWO

1940

The New Year saw no let up in the unusually prolonged gales of great ferocity that tormented the North Atlantic, Western Approaches and the North Sea. The exceptionally severe weather continued into February and March, while the ships of the Home Fleet struggled to contain the depredations of the U-boats and enemy aircraft which continued to increase; only nine U-boats paid the price for the sinking of a further 108 merchant ships, a total of 343,610 tons.

Ships of the fleet were remaining at sea for unprecedented periods: in February the average for every ship of the fleet was 23 days spent maintaining patrols bridging the gaps between Scotland and the Faroes, the Faroes to Iceland and the Denmark strait between Iceland and Greenland. The patrols searched for blockade runners trying to break back to Germany and for armed merchant and warship raiders attempting to break out into the North Atlantic to decimate Allied shipping. Other ships of the Home Fleet guarded convoys to and from Norway. Here they achieved impressive results from their endless vigilance, 1,337 ships were escorted to and from Norway in these two months with the loss of only two, both stragglers.

Elsewhere in the North Atlantic, Western Approaches and the short sea routes, in particular along the east coast, in hellish weather conditions with mounting frustration, ships strove to give protection to the supply convoys with less success, the enemy continued to sink ships with few losses to himself. A new class of small escort vessel had been introduced, the corvette. The small ship's performance at sea was extremely lively and exhausting to the crew, the violent movement rendered the early types of asdic submarine hunting equipment ineffective.

It was inevitable that in addition to lives being lost due to enemy air and U-boat action, the elements took their toll. The very new hostility only seamen conscripts with only six weeks' shore training before joining their first ships were especially vulnerable victims of the sea. Frequently as reliefs, they joined a battered escort ship in harbour for a few hours just to refuel and store. The new member of the crew, without time to find his bearings or way round an unfamiliar shipboard world, would find himself at sea in a tumult of cold and greyness of the war's first winter. Without sea sense or legs, often helpless with sea sickness, he was at the mercy of every lurch, pitch and roll of the ship, and prey to waves sweeping across the low freeboard of destroyers, corvettes and minesweepers.

Petty Officer George Frederick 'Bob' Burns DSM was a seaman captain of a top in the World War One V & W destroyer *Wild Swan*. He had joined the navy as a boy seaman in 1932 and recently as a leading seaman had weathered his apprenticeship of war experience in the sloop *Fleetwood* on east coast protection duties. He describes a typical loss of two hostility only ordinary seamen who had in their short time in *Wild Swan* impressed their personalities on their shipmates and on this regular service petty officer:

After returning from a gruelling convoy we had barely time to oil and store at Liverpool when we sailed again at short notice into the teeth of a gale force 10 north westerly, ordered to a sighted U-boat position in the Irish Sea, eighty miles northwards. I was on the 12 pdr gun deck amidships mustering the watch and detailing off lookouts and other duties when an urgent message was brought to me from the bridge. It was that the wardroom hatch cover was not properly secured and was shipping water. At that moment the first lieutenant 'Dutchie Holland' appeared and on his orders I gave him the two nearest seamen, both HO's (Hostility Only). Not very long afterwards with the sea running so high that one felt like a submariner, a very shocked first lieutenant reappeared crawling and dragging himself along the iron deck. He managed to inform me that he and the two seamen had been swept onto the quarter-deck guardrails and that their combined weight had snapped all three wire rails; they were washed overboard. Lieutenant Holland told me that he had in despair and instinctively shot up an arm and by sheer good fortune had grasped one of the guardrails. Still holding on he was miraculously washed back inboard winded and bruised but able while flat on the deck to grasp a stanchion and to hold on while he recovered his breath and strength before crawling forward.

The two HOs had disappeared. *Wild Swan*'s commanding officer with his ship fighting to survive as he drove towards the reported U-boat position could not turn to search for the men overboard; if he had risked a turn and broaching to it would have been of little avail, for his men heavily clad in woollen gear, oilskins and seaboots would have only lived for a few moments. Bob Burns can still recall the two hostility only ordinary seamen:

Ordinary Seaman Gordon Russell was in civvy street a Glasgow furrier,
a charming talented lad with a flair for charcoal drawings . . . Ordinary
Seaman Norman Shinwell was a printer from the *Daily Herald* offices in
Manchester, a dour down to earth Lancastrian eager to learn and in his
own words 'To be a good matelot'. He left a wife and two children.

Wild Swan was one of the forty plus 'stock' of the versatile and effective V & W class destroyers, 1,500 tons and capable of 33 knots with
a main armament of 4 x 4.7 inch guns and two triple torpedo tube
mountings. The destroyers had an original design complement for
115. *Wild Swan*, like her sister ships, now had numbers increased to
134 to man and service new and additional equipment; asdics, anti-
aircraft weapons etc. By 1942 the ship's company would grow to 170;
the upper seamen's messdeck had 60 to 65 men living, eating and
sleeping in a space designed for only 43. Plans had been approved to
install electric heating, lagging and the lining of mess spaces but
operational demands would not allow for these elementary improvements to primitive and congested accommodation until the ships
entered port for repairs or major refits.

The conditions in these destroyers are vividly recorded by 'Bob'
Burns:

Without doubt, throughout my experience, conditions in the old V &
W's were almost intolerable. Invariably fresh provisions were exhausted
after three days at sea, the interminable diet of tinned food, no fresh
bread, no vegetables caused more distress to the troops than any U-boat
or aircraft attack. In addition the living conditions for the complement
were primitive beyond measure, never enough billets for hammocks to
be slung for more than half the troops, a place on the deck sufficed for
most. In the cold inhospitable Atlantic with salt water often awash in living places, no facilities to dry wet clothes resulted in complete misery.
For HO's pitched after minimal shore training into these conditions
must have been heart-breaking. Many suffered permanent sea sickness
and their vomiting did not always take place on the upper-deck. Vile
smells from inadequate lavatory facilities permeated everywhere.

I recall one HO from Sheffield about thirty years of age, a painter by
trade, immediately promoted by the first lieutenant to ship's painter on
joining us at Liverpool's Gladstone Dock. He weighed around twelve
stone on joining and within eight weeks through violent sickness looked
like a skeleton. My pleadings with No 1 resulted in him being put ashore
for medical exemption from small ships. With typical Admiralty cockups
the poor man was drafted to a Flower class corvette, later to lose his life.

This first pitiless winter of the war took its toll of seamen not only on the high seas, but also from ships at uneasy rest in harbour. The cruiser *Cairo* with an RNVR anti-aircraft unit of guns crews and a control team embarked as part of the ship's war complement lay at anchor overnight in the Humber with orders to sail at first light to resume convoy protection duties. Large ice floes passed down the ship's side, it was a night of inky blackness with intermittent and heavy snow showers. After hours of ferrying men and stores to and from Immingham jetty with the coxswain and his crew exhausted by the hazardous conditions and straining to spot faint blue leading lights on the jetty and cruiser, the duty cutter returned to *Cairo* after its last trip and prepared to be hoisted inboard for the night.

Leading Seaman Philip Dorer RNVR nursed the cutter through ice floes to the lowered boats falls, lower-deck had been cleared and a silent ship's company stood ready to man the falls in the dark and hoist the boat and its crew clear of the menacing estuary flow. This was done quickly, and the watch below dismissed while the duty watch cleared away and reeled up the falls; Dorer and his bowman secured the fore and aft davit-head bottle screw slips in readiness to turn the cutter inboard. Philip Dorer ordered his crew out of the boat who felt their way over ice-coated davits and jumping ladders to the port waist deck; he followed but a seabooted foot slipped on the ice, outstretched hands failed to make contact with safety lines and Dorer fell between the cutter and the *Cairo*'s shipside into the black ice-floed outgoing tide, vanishing forever. Philip Dorer was the first casualty of the London units of RNVR gunners mobilised and serving in four anti-aircraft cruisers.

The grim progress of a war at sea continued with the fleet spending endless day and nights, in atrocious winter conditions, seeking an elusive enemy. This continued up to April when the uneasy neutrality of Norway ended with the invasion of this unfortunate country by Germany. The enemy's small ex-navy succeeded with few losses in landing a large invasion army and it was only with the first and second battles fought in the narrow confines of the Narvik fiords on the 10th, then 13th April, that Home Fleet destroyers supported by the battleship *Warspite* achieved a substantial naval victory. Eight enemy destroyers, one U-boat and seven merchant ships were sunk in fierce actions fought in the waters of Ofotfiord, Beisfiord and Rombaksfiord. The Home Fleet lost two destroyers sunk and had one badly damaged. This was to be only a temporary success in a disastrous campaign for the Allies that started on 8th April and concluded on 15th June after the Allies had withdrawn from Norway. It was a horrible and abortive battle for the British army whose main forces were battalions of ill-equipped territorials opposing highly professional German troops trained for fighting in mountainous terrain and Arctic conditions. Ships of the Home Fleet, cruisers, destroyers and sloops who had escorted the troopship convoys remained to fight a supportive battle against an enemy air force that had near complete freedom of the skies above narrow fiords which restricted freedom to take avoiding action by the ships from the screaming full power dives of Stuka Ju87 bombers.

Air attacks on supply shipping and the defending warships went on through the full 24 hours of Arctic daylight. The strain reached unendurable limits, men cracked under the endless torture of no rest or sleep and continuous attacks, a few had to be restrained below decks in straitjackets from there to continue to torment their shipmates with their cries until either they collapsed into a coma or when it was possible, they were transferred to a hospital ship or vessels returning to the United Kingdom.

Men died horribly from shell, bomb and torpedo but somehow it seemed that death came more uselessly and with a greater poignancy when it came not from enemy action but from terrible and avoidable accidents. *Curlew*, the fourth anti-aircraft cruiser to be manned by a unit of London civilian RNVR sailors, was on passage to Norway escorting two aircraft carriers with fight aircraft desperately needed by the ships and troops fighting in the fiords and mountains. The force was approaching the Lofoten islands and *Curlew* had stood down from dawn action stations, reverting to defence stations and then inflicted grievous self-inflicted casualties on some of her ship's company. The defence stations crew of the eight barrelled 2 pdr pom pom commenced the routine 'Quarters clean guns', the captain of the mounting had led the four members of his crew round to the front of the mounting to sponge out the eight gun barrels. They started on the first barrel when with an awful whomping staccato bark, the hallmark of this weapon, nicknamed in the service, The Chicago Piano, a torrent of contact fused shells obliterated the gun's crew into shapeless flesh, shattered bone and blood soaked rags. Only one of the five survived and he with eyelids and hair scorched and wounds in his legs lay on the deck midst the debris of his shipmates. One shell had ricocheted through a flash shield and mortally wounded a young HO ordinary seaman of A gun on the deck below. It was later discovered that a corroded firing switch circuit in the pom-pom director had been the cause of the accident.

Long stunned seconds passed as the full horror and shock of the incident sank into the men nearest and at hand, the situation required and got the action needed, tough, abrasive brutal shouted orders from the gunnery instructor, Petty Officer Ruggles, which broke the paralysis setting in upon a retching pom-pom director team and A gun's crew. By the time that the commander reached the scene hoses were being unreeled and shrinking ashen-faced men with deck brooms and shovels had started to collect the remains of their late shipmates into a dreadful unrecognisable blood-drenched pile.

Falling out from his below decks action station on the A gun ammunition supply and on his way to his mess for breakfast, sail-maker 'Sails' Leslie Howes, dressed only in thin overalls, feet in plimsolls, was summoned to the pom-pom mounting to prepare his shipmates for burial. It was impossible to follow normal routine of sewing each man into his own hammock. 'Sails', shivering from the Arctic cold and the horror of the sight of the bloody debris of body remains and sea water gushing from hoses washing blood off the deck and ships fittings, knew what had to be done. With the information that five had been killed, speed was essential so that the ship's company could start to recover from the shocked numbness that gripped the cruiser. With one detailed assistant he raced below to his canvas and sailing makers store and there quickly by machine ran up five square canvas bags.

More than half frozen, Howes, still clad only in his overalls and helped by Petty Officer Ruggles, filled five bags with what remained of five men and the tops of the bags were sewn up. Volunteers moved the bags weeping blood, aft to the quarter-deck where preparations for burial at sea had been advanced. Then the final macabre act of *Curlew*'s ordeal was played out, a pipe relayed by the bosun's mate called Leslie Howes to the sickbay where to his astonishment he found that a body had been laid out in a hammock for him to sew up and prepare for burial; it was the body of the young HO from A gun and the fifth casualty. Four men had been killed on the pom-pom, he had been informed that the remains represented five. The wretched shocked sailmaker was ordered to open the five bags and with the help from the tough GI distribute the contents of one bag amongst the remaining four bags and then resew them so finally the funeral service could begin. Four pierced weighted bags and a long body shaped hammock sank from sight as the ship slowed, starboard screw stopped, her ship's company standing silent at defence stations mourning their shipmates; the commander, GI, captain of guns and crews of the quarter deck nos 9 and 10 guns, acting as funeral party.

Leslie Howes had worked at his grisly task through an endless morning; it did not occur to the commander or the first lieutenant that Sails and his helper needed a stiff drink or something hot to ease their awful task. When he finally staggered forward to his mess, the miscellaneous and special duties mess, he found that his mess-mates had not forgotten him; their morning grog issue remained on the table untouched in cups for their exhausted messmate to drink his fill. This he did, then shocked them somewhat by sitting down to eat his delayed midday meal. It was a little time before his messmates realised that he was not insensitive or overtough but rather that his senses and cold exhausted body required refuelling.

There was no time to mourn shipmates, *Curlew* like every ship already within the mountain fringed fiords and the others to follow was soon under attack from Ju87 and 88 enemy squadrons. For *Curlew* this happened as soon as she was identified by enemy agents ashore as an anti-aircraft ship moving through the fiords linking Vaags and Ofot fiords. Endless days followed with only short breaks from air attack, ammunition replacement had frequently to be embarked under way, under attack, from supply vessels secured alongside and ammunition bypassing empty magazines and going straight into gun breeches as the ship engaged dive bombers. No rating knew of the progress, purpose or objectives of the torment they were undergoing or why, in spite of the fact that with the navy holding command of the local seaways and routes back to the United Kingdom, no adequate air cover had been planned or was being provided for the fleet.

In the midst of chaos, constant attacks and hell one miracle of naval routine survived and hardly faltered. At 1100 hours the pipe 'Up Spirits' marked for the men serving in the King's ships a datum point in every endless 24 hours – the careful procedure of drawing, in the presence of an officer, from the spirit room or store the measured issue of rum for the men on the ship's books entitled to an issue of undiluted spirit or grog. The careful observed blending of two parts of water with one of spirit for issue to those below the rank of petty officer was carried out even under enemy attack; only rarely did an air raid interrupt the routine, and the issue of undiluted rum (neaters) and grog reached everyone by noon, it was a vital high point, essential for maintaining morale and a solace for men under impossible pressures.

Curlew eventually succumbed under the weight of the air attacks; the cruiser had been given the task of giving anti-aircraft cover to men of the Royal Engineers feverishly trying to construct an airfield for Hurricane fighters on the edge of Lavangsfiord close to the township of Skaanland. The enemy bombed the site ceaselessly and for three days subjected *Curlew* to a succession of concentrated assaults, until finally at 1530 hours 26th May a stick of bombs struck the quarterdeck, and the cruiser, out of control, struck a reef ½ mile off shore at Skaanland. The ship, with nine dead, sank – she was the twelfth war and merchant ship sunk over the seven days 21st to 26th May.

As a rule, men on the lower deck, were kept in almost total ignorance of what was going on as disaster followed upon disaster. But there were exceptions. One of the few early examples of a hard-pressed senior officer giving priority to keeping his men informed was *Coventry*'s executive Commander D. Norman RN. The cruiser was in constant action throughout every 24 hours of succeeding days, hounded by waves of enemy aircraft trying to corner the anti-aircraft ship in the narrow Norwegian fiords; every officer and rating was desperate for rest and above all else sleep. In this situation Commander Norman scrapped daily orders and in their place produced a daily summary of what had happened over the last 24 hours, often illustrated with a sketch plan, and then included a forecast of what the ship might be required to do over the next few days.

Forgoing his few chances of sleep and assisted by Leading Seaman Jack Crowther he produced an unbroken series of bulletins from Friday 10th May to 26th May; then the commander and his assistant finally succumbed to complete physical and mental exhaustion but they had succeeded in helping the ship to survive the worst period of the fated campaign. Commander Norman, when the ship arrived in Norwegian waters, had summed up the crucial need of internal ship communication, especially for the men below decks entombed in the ship's hull, in the boiler and engine rooms, gun control transmitting stations, electrical high and low power controls, the lower steering position and the men sealed deep down in the magazines. Here reports of what was happening were sparse, exhausted upper deck parties and gun crews could only shout the occasional, garbled dis-

jointed description of events, alarms and action down ammunition
shutes to be passed on second, third and fourth hand down to the
small brightly lit magazine tombs. Cold, clammy, stark, claustrophobic and surrounded by a honeycomb of emptying shell racks,
little information percolated down to the magazine crews.

Every variation of course and changes of engine revolution was felt
in the entrails of the ship and brought stomach-wrenching alarm and
fear. Underwater explosions, near and far, were magnified; guns
opening up and crashing in ordered control changing to and urgent
confused uproar as each gun fought its own battle against planes diving from all directions; sudden distant cries, shouts, silence; the ship
heeling under emergency helm and revolutions aggravated tension,
driving men to breaking point.

All this Commander Norman appreciated, and it was primarily
for these men, shut off from visual contact with events, that he produced an information bulletin, an essential ingredient for the
maintenance of morale. On this score he was in 1940 one of the few
ahead of his time.

The extraction and evacuation of the Allied force from Norway in
June 1940 was a masterpiece of emergency planning and subterfuge
that outwitted the enemy as well as the Norwegian army which was
to be abandoned to its fate.

Convoys sailed from Harstad bearing beaten troops back to the
United Kindom escaped enemy observation or attack from powerful
units of the German fleet quartering the Norwegian seas not far
from the convoy routes. Yet a strange paradoxical incompetence
afflicted the professional naval staff who had with a grim ruthless-
ness and skill embarked an entire Allied force in great secrecy,
then sailed with immaculate efficiency a series of large convoys of
troopships. They failed to organise air reconnaissance over the sea
areas into which the command sailed unprotected ships as independent units. The enemy battleships *Scharnhorst* and *Gneisenau*, the
heavy cruiser *Hipper* and four destroyers were patrolling the area of
routes between Vestfiord and the United Kingdom, and on 8th June
this powerful force found and sank a tanker *Oil Pioneer* with the
armed trawler *Juniper*, followed a few hours later by an empty troopship, the 20,000 ton *Orama*. That afternoon the enemy battleships
sighted the aircraft carrier *Glorious* and her two escorting destroyers
Acasta and *Ardent*. Within two hours the three British ships had been
sunk, only 46 surviving out of over 2,000 officers and ratings. The
carrier was packed with aircraft, naval Swordfish and RAF Hur-

Ajax on the America and West Indies station, 1939.

Ajax rescue team in the earthquake devastation at Concepcion, Chile, January 1939.
(Reproduced from a damaged photograph).

(*Left*) HMT *Brimness*, guns crew. (*Right*) HMT *Brimness*, 1940.

(*Left*) Upspirits — rum issue at sea. (*Right*) Rescue of German seamen from ss *Arucas*, sunk by the cruiser *York*. 3rd March 1940.

ricanes. The latter had been flown on from airfields close to Harstead by pilots who were making their first deck landings, but their skill and bravery were to be squandered. The carrier sailed without her Swordfish aircraft deployed on protective anti-submarine and surface vessel patrols and with no aircraft ranged on deck armed with torpedoes or bombs for self-protection or to deliver offensive strikes.

The three ships went down with colours flying, guns firing in puny ineffective defiance and the destroyers making desperate torpedo attacks, scoring one hit on the *Scharnhorst*, until the force was overwhelmed by the German ship's 11 inch guns. The action has been described by official naval historians as a 'splendid chapter in a long naval tradition of sacrifice and gallantry', but was it not a fact that 2,000 officers and men died unnecessarily because of professional failures? The death of these ships and their crews did fortuitously and accidentally prevent the battleships sighting and intercepting two lightly escorted convoys just over the horizon bearing thousands of troops back to British ports. The Home Fleet for some inexplicable reason was deployed far to the west chasing shadows while in the east vital troop convoys sailed virtually unprotected.

Even as the beaten troops endeavoured to escape from Norway the British Expeditionary Force with its French and Belgian allies was in full retreat in the Low Countries and northern France. Planning and preparations were in hand to mount a seemingly hopeless rescue operation by sea. The Home Fleet was deploying every possible destroyer for the task, 56 destroyers plus one cruiser backed by an armada of minor war vessels, trawlers, small craft of every description and size with numbers of merchant ships which became eventually engaged in apparently futile evacuation operations, Dynamo and then Aerial, the later operation which brought out the remainder of the British forces and the Czech and Polish units. A ghastly reality supplanted an unimaginable possibility and thousands of troops commenced being lifted first from Boulogne and Calais, then off the beaches of La Panne close to Dunkirk on 26th May and Dunkirk itself and later as the French crumbled further south from Le Havre and Cherbourg. The huge exodus brought impossible strains and maturity to the mixed crews of the HM ships, mainly destroyers who fought many eyeball to eyeball and point blank actions extracting soldiers from seemingly impossible situations. The withdrawal from the European mainland continued round the Finisterre peninsula deep south as far as the south-eastern corner of the Bay of Biscay at Bayonne and St Jean de Luz where on 26th June the last troops were embarked. A total of 558,032 fighting men, 368,491 British and the remainder Allied plus many uncounted thousands of civilians of many nationalities were lifted out of continental Europe by an armada of 850 ships and small craft with a loss of 235 from enemy naval and air action also navigation hazards. Included in the ships lost were 40 HM ships of which nine were destroyers. Most of the destroyers had fought ferocious actions in confined harbours against shore batteries abandoned by the French and manned by German gunners, Panzer tanks and supporting troops which were held back from embarkation jetties by destroyer guns fired over open sights.

On 26th June the two naval rescues of defeated armies were complete and the personnel of mixed regular, reservists and hostility only manning the ships involved had come to terms with each other. The regulars had by now discovered that their shipmates who had recently been civilians not only matched their courage but brought new initiative to life on crowded mess-decks.

When the last act of the evacuations was over the country to its surprise found that the enemy was allowing them a breathing space, so men from the fleet were able to have short spasms of leave and enjoy the overwhelming delights of hero worship directed to the men of the fleet. In the nine months since war had been declared the nation had endured two major military disasters and the United Kingdom was beleaguered, alone, facing an enemy who appeared to be invincible.

In spite of grievous losses at sea both of merchant and fighting ships, the navy had produced some successes that gave comfort to an anxious civil population: the defeat of the pocket battleship *Graf Spee*; the rescue from the *Altmark* of prisoners tranferred from *Graf Spee*. The first and second battles in Narvik's fiords and now the conclusion of two almost miraculous evacuations of hundreds of thousands of soldiers from continental Europe confirmed the island people's faith and trust in their seamen.

It is difficult to describe adequately to generations who have grown into adulthood and been born since those heady and perilous days, the very special affection, generosity and exuberant welcome, hero worship shown to sailors on leave. Simple often earthly pleasures that ranged from contact with females young and old who still touched sailor's collars for luck, an infinite variety of emotions and affection, the incredible limitless hospitality offered in the homes of strangers, pubs and clubs; most places of entertainment were free to sailors in uniform.

Blacked out London at that time was extraordinarily safe for the citizen, servicemen and women; an immense mutual bond linked the indigenous peoples of Great Britain. Scots, Irish, Welsh, the English and above all else the Londoners were still then the masters of their native city in a back to the wall situation, alone and borne up by confidence, pride and perhaps an arrogant conviction that they alone were fighting to retain civilisation against the barbarisms of Nazi German hordes.

There was an unique form of self-discipline and policing in blacked out London, impossible to imagine ever being repeated in the capital city's new and contemporary multi-racial society: looting, mugging, all forms of crime seemed to be at a low ebb. The night streets, pricked only by pinpoints of shaded blue lights from vehicles in groping traffic, were safe, friendly; unseen strangers banged into each other without fear of assault. Blacked-out double curtained doorways concealed oasis of light, pubs, restaurants, cafes, generous hospitality and entertainment.

Alas, it was to be only a short interlude in the capital's long history, something remembered with nostalgia by an ageing generation grateful to have been part of it but also saddened that their children and future generations might never understand or believe in the possibility of a united nation which for a moment, in a war of grotesque horror where millions were to die, could experience an uplift of the human spirit.

Precepts of the navy's discipline code hardly wavered in the face of the harsh realities of total warfare or in recognition of the unprecedented physical and mental exhaustions suffered by men of the fleet. Only a minority of commanding officers made concessions for the effects of the recent bloody experiences of defeat and the appalling conditions at sea, when administrating the terms of the naval discipline act. Men, who after the ordeal of war in the Norwegian fiords, the ports and beaches of France, then broke ship, overstayed leave or became involved in drink stimulated fracas ashore on return to their ship had to suffer the full severity of traditional naval punishment by warrant.

Few ships were free from the dismal ceremony to deter others, the clearing of lower-deck to listen to the Articles of War being read prior to the reading of a warrant sending a shipmate to cells or a detention centre plus other associated penalties, loss of pay, leave and privileges. The surviving anti-aircraft cruisers from prolonged periods in Norway where they took the brunt of enemy air assaults had men sent to detention quarters following their return to the UK; one cruiser, *Calcutta*, which went straight on to the evacuation beaches of la Panne and Dunkirk, then to St Jean de Luz had her share of warrants as a bizarre reward for the ship's company's part in the great evacuations. Following repairs in the dockyard the ship moved out to a buoy in Plymouth Sound. Once secured lower-deck was cleared to hear two warrants No 7 and 8 read which sent two shipmates to detention for misdemeanours ashore in the pubs of Devonport where men sought to recover their sanity.

The men in destroyers which took the brunt of the close action while extracting the expeditionary force had also to pay for the consequences of any deviation from the naval code of conduct.

Wild Swan with her sister V & W destroyers had been ordered to evacuate troops from the quays of Boulogne under direct enemy artillery and mortar fire, then to face the inferno off the la Panne beaches and Dunkirk. The ships were engaged in point blank exchanges of gunfire time and again while landing demolition parties and embarking troops. *Wild Swan*'s fire held enemy formations at bay while hundreds of soldiers clambered inboard to pack below deck spaces and crowd the upper-deck. Lieutenant-Commander Sclater extracted his ship stern first at speed still being raked by fire from ashore causing many casualties. Sclater disembarked his passengers at Dover and returned to face the same furious attempt by the Germans to halt the evacuation.

Tough, professional dedication and superb seamanship of the destroyer commanding officers never faltered and repeatedly they entered and returned from harbours dominated by enemy artillery and tank bombardment. Their unflinching commitment was reflected by their attitude to men who failed to match their same dedication. On her last return to Dover with soldier passengers *Wild Swan* was near missed aft by the bomb from a Ju87, damaging her screws and Claude Sclater received orders to proceed to the yard of Green, Silley & Weirs at Tilbury for repairs where he could also give three days' leave to each watch. A week earlier during one of the ship's rapid turn-rounds in Dover one of the ship's company broke out of ship and was missing when *Wild Swan* sailed. The individual was now being held as a deserter in Devizes police station waiting to be collected by an escort to incur retribution from his captain, and also trouble for acting Petty Officer Bob Burns:

I was just about to pack a quick weekend case, hoping to get at least three days' leave to get home, when our No 1, Lieutenant Lee (when he was an able seaman in *Resolution* in 1933, I was a boy 1st class) called me to his cabin and instructed me to leave the ship by tug to Chatham then proceed to Devizes in Wiltshire to apprehend a deserter in custody at the local nick. Naturally expecting a patrol of two AB's I was flabbergasted when he said no, do this yourself. After getting the appropriate passes, travel warrants etc, I joined a train at Chatham to London. Ten minutes after train departure I was lying in a railway ditch by the track, desperately avoiding machine gun attacks by four Messerschmitts, my number one uniform was smothered in mud. Eventually I arrived at St Pancras to be informed that there were no more trains to Devizes until 0530 on the morrow.

As darkness fell, the wailing of the sirens started, I was intending to make my way to the Union Jack Club at Waterloo for a bed, but a copper and a warden insisted and ushered me to the entrance of the Underground. I spent a terribly uncomfortable night in that humid and smelly atmosphere before getting the train to Devizes. At about noon, tired, filthy, hungry, muttering to myself what I would do to this bloody deserter, I rolled into the cop shop to be told that he had been turned over to a motor RN patrol late the previous evening.

An equally tiring return by train to London where in desperation I entered a barber's shop to improve my bedraggled appearance. I awoke in the chair to a demand from the barber for £3 (a fortune to me). Apparently in my weary stupor, I nodded my head to all his suggestions, face towels, shampoo, massage etc, etc. Eventually I reported to Lieutenant Lee at Green, Silley & Weirs to be given the final blow, he had let the torpedo gunner's mate to go on leave in my place because he felt that Liverpool was too far away for two days' leave. Throughout my service in *Wild Swan* I itched to punch the nose of that deserter who finally returned after ninety days 'over the wall'. The poor devil never survived the sinking of the ship in June 1942.

While an uneasy lull persisted before massive air raids commenced on the kingdom's cities, the war at sea in the North Atlantic intensified; there were also agonising pre-occupations over the future of the French major war vessels with the possibility that they would soon come under operational control of the Germans. This problem was resolved by the tragic necessity of naval action to immobilise units of the French fleet in their West African bases.

Men continued to prefer to join up and serve with the fleet than the army and Arthur Henry Ridout (Charlie) was one of the many hundreds:

In the early days of training, the recalled pensioners were kind and understanding to us HO's who at the time in early 1940 were mainly volunteers and all generally young. Our Chief Petty Officer at *Royal Arthur*, Skegness, CPO Doig would say, 'In my last class I had, stokers and cooks, stewards, writers and jack dusties, but you in this class you're all seamen and you're all volunteers.' Class number at Skegness (Ex-Butlin's holiday camp) was 226. We then were sent to Liverpool in June, HMS *Wellesley*.

During my training period at Liverpool we were taught seamanship, gunnery and field training to the standard that must have been much the same for seamen in the 1914-18 war period. We drilled with long Lee-Enfield rifles of the Boer War period. Still in June 1940 when fallen in for evening quarters, I heard a voice from the watching crowd call out, 'Go for it Jack, the army's had it!' This was my first thought that our country now relied on the Navy.

In general I feel that our training and background owed more to the 19th century than to the navy of pre-1946. I say this without disparagement because I think it was a great and fine tradition to be trained in. The senior AB's always made it clear that the junior ratings were of small consequence and one was taught to 'keep your place'. My proudest moment was when I returned from the captain's table rated up to able seaman and was offered sippers to celebrate from the rest of the mess.

I was only briefly in Anson block, the seamen's messes at the Royal Naval Barracks, Chatham, HMS *Pembroke*, but they were the worst. The buildings were old, overcrowded and difficult to keep clean. I asked to be sent to sea and was soon on draft leave to reduce numbers in the barracks. I joined the cruiser *Nigeria*.

At sea the main armament (twelve 6″ guns in triple turrets) was usually in two watches, that is four on and four off except in the dog watches. Since our messdeck was below the armoured deck we were not allowed to sling hammocks at sea, so we either slept on the deck above or on the mess table or stools. We slept fully clothed with life jackets on with an overcoat or duffle on top.

Many of my messmates had been boy ratings in the destroyer *Kelly* and knew Lord Louis Mountbatten. He was considered mad but a very good commander and was much looked up to. Captain Philip Vian (of the *Cossack* fame) when promoted Rear Admiral flew his flag in *Nigeria* as the flag officer Force A. He was considered by the lower-deck to be out of the same mould as Lord Louis but seemed to lack the same sense of humour. Rear Admiral H.M. Burrough was not so dashing or spectacular as the other two but his wise judgements kept our ship from many dangers and hazards.

On the messdeck, Signalman Roger Furze made drawings of some of our messmates and the mess-deck scene. He later became a noted artist and film designer, including *Henry V*.

Lack of privacy was the main strain of messdeck life. But this was surmounted. Each table which constituted a mess was a private home for its members. A member of another mess would not sit down, only if he had been invited. There was an invisible division between messes (ie, tables). Our messdeck round A turret barbette had seamen's messes on the portside and signalmen's messes on the starboard; the two divisions very rarely exchanged visits but there was no antipathy.

Immediately following Italy's declaration of war on 10th June, a reduced Mediterranean fleet braced itself to meet and deal with an unknown potential of the Italians who possessed ships of elegant line and renowned for high speed. Malta and Alexandria were the bases for the British ships which until Italy's entry into the war had enjoyed near peace-time conditions and minimum war routine at sea. Alexandria offered the full spectrum of pleasures, corruption, indulgences of the flesh, catering for every physical taste or craving of fleet's libertymen. There were also unlimited facilities for inter-ship and formation sports. Malta, the main fleet base, offered the same opportunity for savouring the fleshpots but on a smaller scale and because of the presence of the fleet's Provost Marshal, on a more controlled basis. The delights that Valetta had to offer in its thoroughfare known as the Gut was an Eldorado for generations of men who served in the Mediterranean Fleet.

In both ports the ships still retained vestiges of peacetime pristine paintwork, polished brass and steel still unstained from endless days of sea patrols and the results of enemy action. They were manned by men of sun-tanned health dressed in immaculate whites. These men were witnesses of a daily scene of unimaginable poverty and human degradation which was the lot of thousands who lived out their short lives in the great Egyptian port and to a lesser extent in the Malta colony.

Berthed alongside each ship in Alexandria was a dumb light placed there by civilian contractors so that all the ship's waste should be tipped into its noisome hold. The barges received all the food leavings and waste from individual messes, the galleys, tins, bottles, the debris thrown out by a ship's population. Under the hot North African sun the slimy oozing deposits became a malodorous cargo in the open holds. Each of these infernos held a wretched skeletal slave of the contractor, who crawled over the dreadful stinking mass picking out the bottles and tins. Sailors of the host ships with stomach-churning dismay became aware that this human being, who was often a badly deformed child, was eating the ghastly offal, at the same time selecting large unidentifiable lumps, placing the selection into tins for sale and consumption ashore.

The discipline system of the time only allowed for protests from the lower deck to be channelled via the complaint stifling procedures set out in KR and AI's. Nothing was done to stop this awful trade between the fleet and contractors, barges remained alongside for days until towed away and replaced by another frightful barge with its slave attendant, some of whom in the awful heat and stench collapsed to die in the slime. To the everlasting shame of those who commanded the fleet and individual ships the terrible practice only stopped as the tempo of war in the East Mediterranean increased and ships only remained in harbour for a few hours to store, refuel and load ammunition; the barges were no longer necessary as gash could be held inboard to be ditched at sea once the ship cleared the harbour approach channel.

At Malta a franchise for collecting gash for human consumption was given to men who had made deals with the ship's Master at Arms or, in the case of destroyers and smaller vessels, the coxswain. For a fee these men were permitted to board ships inharbour after every main meal carrying a container into which they tipped the contents of mess gash buckets as they toured the mess-decks, the ship's company and officers' galley, the wardroom and warrant officers' pantries. A few individuals from the ships, when hurrying ashore as libertymen, suffered pangs of guilt laced with disgust when they saw this awful cold mixture of plate scrapings, left-overs and galley waste from HM ships being sold from a filthy vat at the dockyard entrance, to workers and children at one penny or a half penny, arms plunged deep into the congealed food refuse.

Some reinforcements including the cruisers *York* and *Ajax* had arrived to join the Mediterranean Fleet and its embattled Commander-in-Chief, Admiral A.B. Cunningham. The *Ajax* had completed her refit and still retained many of the men who had fought in the Battle of the River Plate. *York* had come from Atlantic patrols and the icy Denmark strait. In the strait she had intercepted and sunk one of six German merchant ships, the SS *Arucas*, that had broken out of Vigo in Spain and tried to return to their German home ports.

In company with *Ajax*, *York* was soon in action with Italian destroyers which had tried to trap the cruisers on the night of 11th/12th October in the Ionian sea. Three of the destroyers were caught in *Ajax*'s defensive fire, two sank immediately and the third, the *Artigliere*, was found badly damaged and under tow then sunk by the

York. The cruiser took the Italian crew off their ship, and then sank the destroyer.

Eric Smith, after leaving *Ajax*, had completed his gunnery school courses and had a draft to a new destroyer, *Legion*, Commander R.F. Jessel, nearing completion at Hawthorn Leslie's yard at Hebburn. Commanded by a brilliant destroyer captain, the *Legion* was very soon proving herself in a number of famous sea actions and several spectacular rescues. The destroyer was at hand to help survivors of the torpedoed armed merchant cruiser *Rajputana* in the Denmark strait and in the following months she saved men from the damaged *Cossack*, and embarked 1,400 men from the *Ark Royal* sinking off Gibraltar.

Smith very soon established a niche for himself within the smaller destroyer ship's company. He was an individual with a robust appetite, always seeking ways to improve the ship diet and recorded the functioning of the canteen messing system:

One person in each mess is elected to be the mess caterer. It is his job to make out the daily menu and to order the required food from the canteen manager or the 'Pusser'. A free issue of bread, meat, potatoes, tea, sugar and milk (tinned) is made weekly to each mess. The amount is dependant on the number of ratings in that mess. Each caterer is then allowed 2s 0d per man, per day for the purchase of all the other necessary foodstuffs. It is up to the caterer to budget within his cash limit. If this is exceeded the members of the mess have to make up the difference from their own pockets at the end of each month and to make over the money owed to the paymaster (in the case of a destroyer he is usually the first lieutenant, known as Jimmy the One.) If at the end of the month the mess is in credit the sum is given over to the mess caterer to distribute evenly amongst the mess members.

In our mess the senior leading hand was a chap named Leading Seaman Hallet, who said he would take over as caterer for the first three months. In that time the only second veg we ever had for dinner was dried pussers peas which were quite cheap (about 2d per lb) but which had to be soaked in the mess 'fanny' overnight with a small piece of soda and a spoonful of sugar to soften them up and make them edible. Occasionally, and only on Sundays, he sometimes got generous and added a couple of tins of carrots from the canteen. We seldom had a dessert or a breakfast so the main meals of the day were midday dinner and the evening supper which varied greatly according to his whim. Two 'cooks of the mess' were detailed each day and it was their job to prepare whatever meal the caterer had decided on and to take the preparation to the galley where it was cooked by the duty ship's cook. It was their duty also to see

that the mess was thoroughly cleaned after each meal before turning to
for part of ship work or to go on watch.

Being a big eater in those days I was only to pleased to learn all I could
about preparing and making the various dishes, duffs, cakes etc. Learning from old destroyer hands I soon became quite expert. After a couple
of months of the same monotonous diet it was decided to have a mess
meeting to elect a new caterer. Leading Seaman Hallet was told to shove
all his pussers peas up his 'sail hatch' although Jack Spencer, one of my
messmates, protested that it was a bit unfair because 'Hookey' still had
twelve cold 'Chinese wedding cakes' (Rice puddings) to go from the day
before. Anyway Hallet was unanimously sacked as caterer and another
leading seaman took his place.

He was not too successful either, so as I always seemed to be knocking
up some gorge or other I was eventually elected in his stead, a position I
held for the rest of the commission.

Eric Smith proved to be a diligent mess caterer who was always alert
for any chance to 'acquire' victuals from any source to improve the
'gorges' he planned for his messmates and if he could achieve mess
savings at the same time so much to the good. One of these opportunities happened after *Legion* had been in commission for a year and
not long after the destroyer had sunk the Italian submarine *Adua* and
had taken *Ark Royal*'s survivors into Gibraltar.

About this time we had an outbreak of scabies onboard and my mess was
one of the worst hit by this epidemic, nineteen men out of twenty-two
having to have treatment for this uncomfortable skin complaint. Normal
treatment seemed to do no good, so 'Doc' Surgeon Lieutenant James
RNVR arranged for the whole mess to take their kitbags and hammocks
ashore by *Legion*'s motor boat, thence by Army lorry transport to the
Military hospital at the top of the rock [Gibraltar] where all our kits
would be fumigated and where we would take special soft soap baths. It
was a comparatively small hospital with only six baths, so while the first
six went in for their baths and treatment the remainder of us just waited
around smoking and chatting outside an archway crammed with packing cases. I was intrigued by these cases as from the stencilled markings
on the sides they appeared to hold army foodstuffs. Now as mess caterer
I had more than a passing interest in them.

Some of my messmates concealed me and I prised open the top of one
of the crates. To our joy we found that they contained a variety of tinned
food such as chicken, soups, tinned beef and vegetables of all kinds, custard powder and fruits. A hurried 'mess meeting' decided it was not too
immoral to borrow from the army. This question being settled, as the
first six 'de-fumigated' messmates came out of the hospital they were
instructed to cram into their kitbags as much of of the 'booty' as they

could. This continued until we had all passed through the hospital routine and then made sure that the crate lids were properly resecured. When the army transport arrived to take us back to the jetty, we loaded our gear the kitbags now being much heavier than when we set out. To the late Army Quartermaster of the Rock Hospital I offer belated apologies although you should have known better than to place temptation in the way of a matelot.

Legion was moored to a buoy in the middle of the harbour so once the motor boat had secured to the after gangway we had to hump our bags and hammocks up the ladder, inboard then to our mess. 'Jimmy the One', Lieutenant J.C. Cartwright, stood at the top of the gangway gazing down as we clambered out of the boat. I was the second man to stagger up the ladder and as I neared the top I tripped mainly because of the weight of my kitbag, it dropped to the deck with a thud and small sweet smelling wisps of powder wafted through the canvas top of the bag. Jimmy smiled, 'Looks as if you have split your talcum powder, Smith' he remarked. Little did he know that it was a 14 lb tin of custard powder that had come unshipped. When I got below I discovered that that it had covered all my kit. The whole lot had to be dhobyed out in the bathroom immediately. Back in the mess we went through our haul and found that we had provisions to last many weeks without having to buy very much from the canteen manager. We looked forward to some good living and mess savings. In fact when the next month's account came round it was found that we had savings at £2 per man.

Jimmy sent for me and asked if I felt that the men in my mess were being adequately fed. I replied in the affirmative but I could see he was not satisfied. Later he asked Doc to examine and weigh some of the mess selected at random and when he discovered that far from losing any weight they had put some on, I told Doc that it was perhaps too much 'figgy-duff' and promised to cut down on desserts. I left him a highly mystified man.

The two brothers Eric and Harold Harlow of Walmer, Kent, belonged to a family who for generations had operated a large hardware business serving a rural community. The brothers volunteered together to join the Navy but only Eric was accepted, Harold was too young and told to re-apply a year later. Eric Harlow progressed through and from the initial training establishment at Skegness, HMS *Royal Arthur*, on to additional seamanship and gunnery training. In early October 1940 he was drafted to join a destroyer, one of fifty World War One destroyers handed over by the American Government in exchange for the leases of bases in British Guiana and the West Indian colonies. They were highly unstable, lightly armed ships; none was fitted with asdic or had had a major refit before being handed over. On passage to Plymouth Eric's ship sighted and picked four RAF air crew out of their rubber dinghy.

The commanding officer was a young Royal Navy lieutenant, completely overwhelmed by his good fortune and the glory of his first command which transcended all the shortcomings of his ship. His enthusiasm and consuming desire to get his ship to sea and into action with the enemy alternately perplexed and terrified his men. He was hungry for battle and anxious to make his name and constantly exhorted his ship's company and God to assist him. He held prayers and church services at every opportunity permitted to him in KR and AI's.

His single-minded drive succeeded in getting the dockyard to complete the refit ahead of forecast. There was of course a strong probability that the dockyard managers, driven to distraction by his constant pressure, conspired to rid themselves and the yard of this 'troublesome officer'.

While at Devonport dockyard a few extra guns were added to the destroyer's puny gun armament; she was still carrying her original and not very reliable six 21" torpedo tubes in two mountings. To reinforce the single forecastle 4" gun, two quadruple 5" machine gun mountings were installed aft, to port and starboard; amidships a Hotchkiss gun was fitted. The young captain sailed in a high state of excitement in his unhandy ship overburdened with top weight, bound for Scapa Flow. On arrival the ex-American ship received orders to form part of an escort sailing immediately to protect a squadron of large merchant ships converted to lay mines. The squadron was required to fill in gaps in the minefield barrier between Iceland and the Faroes.

The lay commenced in a flat calm but with thick fog patches on the sea into which the minelayers and their escorts disappeared and then emerged at irregular intervals. Eric's commanding officer announced in triumph to his fearful ship's company that a German sea raider, the pocket battleship *Admiral Sheer*, was approaching the area of the minelaying operation. The raider was at sea but the captain's hopes soon faded; a position in a cyphered situation report had been misread. No sooner had the alarm subsided when the huge shape of a Focke Wulf Condor reconnaissance aircraft flying very low appeared out of a fog bank. With alarm bells ringing the destroyer's crew raced back to their action stations; on the forecastle the 4" gun crew were ordered to load with the captain on the bridge above yelling 'Open fire, open fire'.

The Condor lumbered out of a bank of fog crossing the bow as the crew fumbled to bring their gun into action. In the confusion and panic, the gun was loaded with the charge first, then, to add to the captain's exasperation, the gun had to have the breech reopened to remove the charge, the fused projectile rammed home, and in its correct order, the charge. By this time there was nothing but fog to fire into; the Condor out of sight continued to circle the squadron of giant minelayers. The plane came into sight again from the ex-American destroyer; this time the multiple 5″ mountings were called into action, the notoriously unreliable guns obliged, lived up to their reputation, fired four rounds each, then seized up.

Eric Harlow at his action station on the Hotchkiss-waited tensely for his turn of ignominy or glory as the ship waited for the German aircraft to re-appear. It came out of the murk astern to pass very close up the port side. Eric was ordered to open fire; he banged the firing handle but nothing happened, so he did it again. The plane passed so close that a well aimed spud could have hit it. Eric struggled with his recalcitrant weapon until a mighty blow knocked him clear of the gun and mounting. It was the gunner's mate, infuriated by the shame of his weapon failures. The GM leapt into the firing position and although the Condor was now gone he crashed the firing lever with a huge fist and half the gun disintegrated into a mass of flying gun parts and springs. It took many hours to locate the parts and reassemble the gun. On the deck below off watch engine room staff witnessed the seamen gunners' pantomime with derision and hysterical laughter.

Leslie Stevenson joined up on 22nd October 1940; he was ordered to report at HMS *Wellesley*, Liverpool:

. . . accepted for the navy. Officer says, I'll put you down as a recorder. My stepfather said, ah, you'll be on the guns recording shell-fire. I am ordered to Liverpool to join HMS *Wellesley*. Ask a policeman, tram drivers, dockies anyone I meet, where is it? They send me to Huskisson dock, Gladstone Dock, Pier Head; all over Liverpool I search for the ship. Training ship I thought, sails or something? Asked matelots. Never heard of it. What class ? . . . What do they mean? Finally, an old man, least likely, looks me up and down and says, You know the old Southern Hospital, son? No, I says. Well on that tram, ask the conductor and you will see a condemned building. Yes it was HMS *Wellesley*. Sign on!

My interviewer who accepted me for the RN must have been a Yorks/Lancs man. Decoder in his accent became Recorder! My stepfather did laugh when I told him. He died in May 1942 whilst we were on a Malta convoy. We had lots of books of codes thrust on us, and had to pass in morse, 9 words per minute. Lovely and slow for an internal buzzer they said. Missed P/T one morning, Jankers. Had to run all evening round Liverpool, then exercises on return. Some chaps dropped, big investigation. You see, our Class Z went up to 42 years of age. Some poor sods had never run since being kids at school. Murder for them. Age for this punishment later brought down to 30's.

This hostility only (HO) rating like the many thousands of HOs who joined with him had entered a war and a range of experience that would exceed his wildest dreams or nightmares. During the five and a half years between his arrival at HMS *Wellesley* and demobilisation in February 1946, Leslie Stevenson served in a number of ships and locations, which would have taxed the stamina of a highly trained regular service man but was not in fact unique for the citizen sailors.

I served as a leading writer in *Nelson*, a 35,000 ton battleship, from December 1940 until March 1944. Conditions on board were good compared to small ships, but and here is the rub, discipline was at all times very strict. Rig of the day always adhered to and woe betide any scruffy 'Jack me hearty'.

Cliff Smith joined up in August 1940 and following his few weeks at HMS *Royal Arthur* and a fortnight at HMS *Vernon* the torpedo school, as a probationary writer, he qualified as a writer; at the base HMS *Eaglet*, and was drafted to the *Nelson* on 30th December 1940.

When I joined *Nelson* as a sprog writer (HO) hostilities only, the majority of the ship's company, 80%, were regulars (RN). I recall vividly that the full-time sailors considered themselves to be far superior beings to us lowly part-timers, and we were informed that we just had got to learn the Navy Way – chop chop! This to us was very different from our civilian ways and like every other simple-minded conscript, one had to learn the hard way. I remember a callow midshipman informing me to forget all my office experience in civvy life and to start from scratch to do as *he* instructed, *The Navy Way*. Well after a lot of aggro' we all learned to live with the problem, and strangely enough, once we HOs had come to terms with the 'Andrew' we got to appreciate why we were doing our jobs their way and that we were all together in the same boat.

Broadside messes were the rule in *Nelson*. A conglomeration of writers,

Jack Dusty's, sick bay Tiffeys which included a fair number of leading hands, made up our mess. As we were all 'day men' (ie not regular watchkeepers) we had an able seaman as our messman. This job was considered as a sinecure by the holder – usually an old hand – ours was a three badge AB, vintage 1921. Harry our man was what is known as a lower deck lawyer – he knew the King's Regulations backwards.

I once asked him why he had never gone in for promotion. He told me he could make more money with his dhobying firm and barbering, not forgetting his 'Crown and Anchor' board circuit (strictly illegal) more than any chief petty officer's earnings inboard. I believed him.

He was as they say a real treasure. I well remember when I first joined the battleship, a real greenhorn, I could not sleep comfortably in my hammock – I looked and felt like a banana and suffered from horrible backache. Harry soon put me right and showed me the pusser way to sling 'an ammick' as he called it. It is surprising what individual instruction could do against class instruction, because after I had learnt from an artist, my hammock became my pride and joy, the most comfortable billet I have ever slept in. . .

When one became established in any kind of craft, large or small, various dodges and perquisites were soon exploited. For instance, being in the pay section, I never slept in our mess – the office was much better – usually four of us slung our hammocks there. This was a great advantage; we had our card schools, chess matches, wrote our letters in more or less privacy and if we ever wanted a snack or a brew we always had the wherewithal to make one. Our office was next door to the Gun Room pantry and we always kept the messman happy with his pay for services rendered in the form of cups of coffee and savoury snacks. Life is what you make it in the Navy.

Being what is known as 'Daymen' as opposed to 'Watchkeepers' we in the miscellaneous branch did not get much in the way of Jankers or other punishments that the seamen and stoker branches got. We did get one Jack Dusty drafted to us in 1942 who was a real 'Skate'. I'd never seen his like before, he was dirty, scruffy, greedy and a general pain in the neck to everybody. The leading hand of the mess, who was a regular Jack Dusty decided that he (the scruffy Jack Dusty) should have a bath. Three of us were detailed off for this dubious duty of execution and we set to with scrubber, deck cloths, mop and bucket and gave him a real going over. He was a bit of a handful and very smelly to start with, but came through his ordeal bloody but unbowed. He never changed, but we finally got rid of him to a ship bound for the Far East. Incidentally he was HO – no regular navy man could be so scruffy.

In the Mediterranean, on 9th December 1940, the British Army of the Nile launched their attack on the Italian Army who in a few days were in full retreat leaving behind hordes of prisoners of war. The ships of the Mediterranean fleet moved westward along the seaward flank of the Nile army's advance bombarding Sidi Barrani, Sollum and Bardia, escorting army supply vessels and transporting away from the battle zone thousands of prisoners who were choking the army supply routes. The Italian air force was reinforced by the arrival of the German Luftwaffe and the ships of the fleet were being subjected to Italian high level and torpedo bomber attacks and dive bombing from the German Ju87's, the highly experienced squadrons of the Fliegerkorps X who had learned their deadly skill in the narrow Norwegian fiords. The fleet began to suffer severe losses at a time when its commitment to support the army was on the increase and support from the RAF hardly existed.

Italy had invaded Greece on 28th October and advance formations of the British army were now being escorted to Pireaus, the port of Athens. The fleet were using Suda Bay, Crete, as a refuelling base and a convoy assembly port. The cruiser *York* was one of the many ships engaged in the protection of supply convoys to the Greeks, and had been present when the Fleet Air Arm had successfully attacked the Italian fleet in its base at Taranto in November.

York was commanded by Captain Portal RN, brother of the Air Marshal and the cruiser's executive commander was Commander Caspar John, later to become Admiral of the Fleet Sir Caspar John. He was the son of the artist Augustus John. This was a formidable duo, but they had a ship's company of rapscallions, many of whom were members of the Royal Marine detachment – an incident was recalled by Marine Chris Buist:

> We had several loan and tobacco barons in the ship who lived it up in big way ashore, they were all in the detachment. The ship called in to Pireaus and gave shore leave to one watch. Some of the barons when they returned to the ship which lay alongside were towing a large goat which they secured to the officers' gangway. Next day the ship had its Christmas dinner and celebrations and there was lots of booze, all the officers, except the captain and commander, thrown over the side.*

---

* The cruiser *York*'s log for December 1940 records that the ship arrived at Pireaus on *Friday 27th December* and leave was given to the starboard watch from 1315 hours to 2330 hours. The cruiser sailed at 1149 hours on Saturday the 28th.

CHAPTER THREE

1941

Another of the ex-American, four stacker, destroyers handed over in exchange for lease of bases was the *Churchill*. Sidney France had joined up in late 1939, and in January 1940 had been drafted to serve in *Fame*, launched in 1934 and one of the flotilla of *Fearless* or F class (1932 programme) destroyers. She was of the classic interwar construction of fleet destroyers, armed with four 4.7 inch guns and eight torpedo tubes. France was enraptured with his months in this fast and glamorous class of warship and was disappointed when at the end of 1940 he was discharged ashore for courses and then wrote of his endeavour to get back to sea in another destroyer. The following are some extracts of what happened to him; he called it:

Gimme the Boats – and the Bucket
. . . . Devonport Barracks was even more crowded than in 1940 and I almost camped out on the step of the drafting office until a friendly, well-spoken petty officer took me aside and in the most fatherly manner told me that when my draft came through, he'd find me, no bother, but until then, would I please stay away from the office or he would personally separate me from my breath! He did not forget me.

Although January 10, 1940 had been beautiful for me, January 21, 1941 was even better. '*Churchill*' said an expert (there's always an expert). 'That's one o' them old Yankee four-stackers, ain't it? Cor, you don't want that draft, mate. Break a leg, break the window of the Commodore's office, go to chokey, but don't go in one o' them First War deathtraps!' What a load of rubbish – hadn't I always wanted a First War boat?

I left Devonport alone and found my way to the Clyde and Greenock, where somehow in the confusion of a crowded landing stage, I found *Churchill*'s liberty boat among all the others. I boarded the ship at 2045, to be directed to 3 mess and told as I had been travelling all day, I could have all night in and join up part of ship next day.

My first impression of my new home was not a good one. In *Fame* our messdeck was on the upper-deck level and was well-ventilated (too well sometimes) but here I descended two decks to the cramped place in which I was to live for the next two years, into an atmosphere thick enough to cut with a knife. How could anyone possibly live here? In an area about 25′ x 15′ x 8′ high lived sixty men, about six square feet of deck area apiece but even that sounds like luxury living.

On the port side 2 mess, 3 mess to starboard. Each mess had a bare scrubbed table about 12′ in length with wooden backless benches inboard. Outboard of the tables a row of lockers were used as seating. The bunks were three high, the bottom one being clipped up when not in use but coming down on the lockers at night. The middle bunk during the day could be lifted and clipped back at an angle while the top one was a fixture. Between the bottom and middle bunks when in use there was about 24″ clearance. The same applied between the middle and top bunks but above the top one the clearance was just enough to allow a man to turn sideway and wedge himself against the deckhead. That way you didn't fall out. The inboard bunks of each mess were close together so it could be difficult if occupants of adjacent bunks were not on speaking terms! . . .

At the after end of 3 Mess was the gyro room, housing the Sperry Master Gyroscopic Compass and this little cage had a bunk, to which I was allocated. I spent my time petrified with fear that I would fall from my bunk and wreck the gyro, directly under me. Forward of the messdeck proper, was a small compartment which held six bunks each side, with an alleyway running through it, leading to the sick bay and to a ladder to the chiefs' mess. This compartment for some reason that nobody seemed to know was known as 'Donnelly's' and was used for those who had watchkeeping duties in harbour.

As we were almost on the waterline at that level, ports were only rarely opened and in fact were welded shut later in the commission. It's funny how we can get used to anything. On that first night, even after everybody had quietened down, I found it impossible to sleep, with all the noises of a ship around me. We were closer to the engines here than we had been in *Fame* . . . Yet, later on, that smelly, stuffy steel box was to become very attractive when I had had four hours on a heaving freezing upper deck.

At 2100, 15 minutes after I joined, *Churchill* slipped from the buoy and I had the satisfaction of knowing that minesweepers had swept a channel for us to proceed safely to sea.

The next day when I turned out, we were in the Irish Sea and out of sight of land and although she was not a Fleet destroyer, I knew that this old tub would do for me. I felt at home in her.

I had the forenoon watch and the last dog and the sunset that evening was wonderful. It was out of this world. We took over the morning watch at 0400 next day and 'Daddy', what had happened to the world? Icy rain flew horizontally along the deck, threatening to slice the skin from my face. The deck itself had become a vicious living beast, which seemed to roll both ways at once, at the same time lifting her bow and stern together, like a wild mustang trying to dislodge its rider. I found it was absolutely impossible for a normal person to walk along that crazily heaving deck and fervently wished I was safely ashore. Again and again she thrust her bow into the waves and I failed to see how she could struggle to the surface, but she did, every time. And gradually, there grew a love for that old ship that never faded; we got used to her motion.

In 1940, though, it was thought that they were simply a bit too top-heavy for North Atlantic work (we knew that – from personal experience! It was said that they still rolled in dry-dock). To cure this top-heaviness, the dockyards completely removed the tall mainmast and cut 6' from the tops of funnels 2, 3 and 4. The after 4" gun was replaced by a 12 pounder and three of the triple torpedo mountings were taken out, the fourth set of three tubes being repositioned amidships. Later, the two 4" guns on the raised deck above the galley were replaced by two single Oerlikon mountings. All this did very little good – she was a rolling bitch all her days and yet I loved her – eventually!

But on my first trip, I was not keen on her. There are three days that are just a blur in my memory, during which she lost her convoy, found it, lost it again and hammered all over the Western Approaches looking for it. Vaguely, I recall people advising me to 'get something down me' and I manfully chewed dry bread, ignoring the 'friends' who suggested swallowing a piece of fatty bacon on a string.

Somehow, I managed to keep my watch (nothing heroic about that – seasickness was no excuse for missing a watch) and I remember one blustery afternoon when Blue Watch were keeping their watch in the lee of the third funnel. Those not actually on look-out were allowed to keep out of the worst force of the weather, so long as they remained on the upper deck.

At that time, we still had the two 4" on the midship gundeck, each on the extreme edge of the deck with a low guard rail below the level of the barrel. I was face down under the barrel of the port gun, my left arm draped languidly over the low guardrail and my other arm, with my head, hanging over the side. Bob Allan sat with his feet braced against a ringbolt, his back hard against the funnel, holding tightly to my ankles as the ship rolled crazily. 'Hang on, Sid,' he shouted above the banshee whine of the wind in the rigging. 'You'll go over the bloody side!' As I lay there, admiring the pale-green substance issuing from my aching mouth thinking what a lovely shade of Eau-de-nil it was, feeling more miserable than I had thought it possible to be, I thought that this was such a good idea that I took my arm from the guardrail and let it hang down the side with the other one, saying, 'OK, Bob, let go.' Thankfully, Bob hung on.

After the worst of the weather subsided, I began to feel human again and was urged to wash and shave. Feeling much better, I made my way forward along the upper deck and as I approached the galley flat (the passage alongside the galley) the canvas dodger parted and a sailer emerged in a staggering run for the guardrail. His toothless mouth was framed by ginger stubble decorated with bits of his last meal. His bloodshot eyes glared miserably at me from the depths of their dark pits and my stomach churned afresh. I joined him at the rail, making a further joint sacrifice to Neptune.

This man was one of the many who never got used to the motion of HMS Corkscrew and he was at last sent back to depot, 'Unfit for service in small ships'. To me, such an entry on my papers would have been a shameful thing – I could never have faced Ernie Wonnacott! But it came right for this lad; I met him three years later and found he was in a cruiser and had never been seasick since leaving *Churchill*.

In later years, when I could enjoy a good meal in any weather (and keep it down) and could accept the ship's erratic progress as a man accepts his wife's irritating little habits – and for the same reason, because he loves her – I was never able to achieve the superior attitude that some people adopted towards the seasick ones. We had one old (he must have been about 35) leading seaman who himself spent the first day at sea down in the tiller flat with his head in a bucket, but after that one day was all right and made life even more of a misery for the unfortunates. 'You've gorra weak stommick, boy!' 'Whaddya mean, I'm chuckin' it as far as anyone else!' I felt that I was one of the lucky ones who had somehow got used to the rollercoaster and I only felt sympathy for those who were physically unable to appreciate the exhilaration of small ship life.

I had not yet arrived at that happy state however and I was glad when the captain decided to run into Stornoway for shelter. With the deck steady at last, I was shown the Maximum Roll Indicator which showed that we had rolled 63 degrees to starboard. With her mast laid over at an angle of 27 degrees from the horizontal, no wonder that the whaler, slung outboard on the old Admiralty Pattern davits, had scooped up a load of the Irish Sea!

The Stornowegians were glad to welcome a representative of the Navy into their lovely little harbour and they heaped Highland hospitality on us. The amount of hospitality imbibed was shown in an incident when we left after the storm abated. As we cleared the land, settling down to a course, Jimmy the One made the usual request of the man at the wheel, 'How's your head, Quartermaster?' Scouse O'Hanlon on the wheel, still feeling the effects of last night's dance at the Town Hall (bar open till midnight) said, 'Ooh, it's blurry awful, sir!' 'Not *your* head, the ship's head man!' snapped Lt Cdr Moens. . . .

Some weeks later bringing in an Atlantic convoy with every man of the escorts desperate for rest from the endless motion of their ships, *Churchill*, instead of proceeding with her sister escorts into the River Foyle, was ordered to turn back. One of the convoy ships, which continued on for the Clyde, had a man who had fallen down a hatch and required urgent medical assistance.

As watch on deck, it was our job to take the doctor over to his patient. We manned the boat, five of the watch on the oars, our PO, Taff Jordan at the tiller and Signalman Stokes, reputed to have the sharpest eyes in the ship, ready with his Aldis lamp to keep us in touch with the ship. We were lowered to deck level to await the arrival of the medical team, a surgeon-lieutenant, RNVR, fresh from medical school and Jan Luce, a leading sick berth attendant who was said to have been a surgeon's assistant at the Battle of Trafalgar. Jan rarely had a fag out of his mouth, even when dressing a wound, although to do him justice, I never saw him actually drop ash on to a patient, always blowing it away at the last moment.

They climbed into the boat, Jan nimbly and the young officer gingerly, the bag was handed in and the boat was lowered to slipping level under the eagle eye of the first lieutenant, standing on the gundeck above. He watched the sea and when he judged the moment to be right, he gave the sharp order, '*Slip*'. If all went well, the Robinson Patent Disengaging Gear fell apart and the boat was free of the falls, smoothly water-borne on an up-coming wave.

That night, as so often happened, things did *not* go well and the boat fell six feet to hit the sea with a bone-crunching thud. Taff had the tiller hard over, sending the boat sweeping away from the slip, the boatrope was slipped and we were on our own. 'Give way,' ordered Taff and we bent to the oars, sending the heavy boat across the sea. In 1940, as we stood beside that snow-buried whaler in Skegness, Mr Lamb had forgotten to tell us of the energy required to propel a one-ton boat over the ocean.

After ten minutes of heavy pulling, all of us encumbered by our 'heavy weather gear' – which meant woolly 'long johns', all the jerseys you could find, an overall suit, a duffel coat, all topped off by an oilskin coat, a couple of pairs of gloves, a balaclava helmet and a sou'wester – we were sweating buckets and yet we seemed to be no nearer to our destination. Taff gave us a break and asked Stokes to inform the ship of our slow progress. The shaded lamps blinked across the darkness and we found that the merchant ship had not yet stopped engines! We had been trying to catch up with a ship doing five knots. We knew that Blue Watch were good, but not *that* good!

The ship hove to as we approached. Down the sheer wall of her side tumbled a jumping ladder and the doctor craned his neck to look at the dimly-lighted deck, far above us. I am sure that none of his college lecturers had warned him that he may have this sort of house call to make, but after listening to Taff's instructions, he said that he would do his best.

To show him how easy it was, Jan went first. He stood on a midship thwart with Stokes steadying him, as Taff took the boat in to the foot of the ladder. As we steadied on the top of a wave, Jan grabbed the ladder and, bag slung over his shoulder, went up like a monkey. The boat drifted away as he climbed to the deck and Taff looked inquiringly at the doctor. He swallowed hard and said, 'All right, PO'.

We pulled the boat alongside again, the doctor gritted his teeth and reached for the ladder. We swept away again, so as not to crush him against the ship's side. When we looked back, he had his arms and legs wrapped tightly round the ladder and was unable to move. As the ship rolled, he was being dunked in the ocean again and again. At last the sailors bodily hauled him and ladder to the deck. It's funny, matelots love to see officers in undignified situations, but that night, nobody laughed. We all admired a lad who would try something that was not really so easy for an old shellback like Jan Luce, then do a job that none of us could hope to do.

We laid off for about an hour, while the casualty was made comfortable and having retrieved our medical party, we returned to *Churchill* at 0230. 4½ hours' hard work was rewarded by the Skipper's, 'Well done, you chaps, good show. Away you go, into the wardroom and have a drink on me!' Fancy, common sailors dripping salt water all over the wardroom carpet!

The captain's treat was followed by one on Jimmy. I remembered that Jim Robertson, a wardroom steward, had told me that officers paid 3d. a shot for spirit out of bond, but had to pay the full 10d for a bottle of beer. So – when everybody else asked for a whisky or a brandy, what did Sid say? 'Just a bottle o' beer for me, sir, thank you.' The Skipper mentally comparing 10d. with 3d. gruffly said, 'Now don't be shy, France, you can have a Scotch, you know.' 'Oh, no, sir,' I said, *so* politely, 'Beer's quite good enough for me, sir, thank you very much, sir.' Then I had the same on Jimmy's wine bill. I was a nasty little swine!

We arrived in Lough Foyle in darkness, to tie up at the oiler and replenish our tanks, a routine task. As we lay there, the usual small boats came out from Moville to trade eggs and butter for cigarettes, the rate of exchange being 20 fags for a pound of butter or a dozen eggs. Absolutely illegal, of course, but when it meant you could take fresh eggs and butter home to folks who rarely got such luxuries, who cared? Moville, although geographically north of the Lough, was in Southern Ireland and being neutral, was not bothered with rationing.

The exchange of goods was always done quickly. The eggs were passed up and the fags immediately stowed under a canvas. This quickness of trade at one time caused a little bother, because of the Clever Jacks.

Out in mid-Atlantic Convoy HX112 had an escort that included the destroyers *Walker* and *Vanoc*. The weather was atrocious – it was March 1941 – and Leslie Stevenson was still wrestling with sea sickness.

The smell of paint in the Atlantic winter, this brought on my sea sickness more than 'ogg wash' oggin or whatever. Cigarette smoke similar. . . .

Those wires fore and aft along the waist were there to hang on to in rough seas. No one told me. I was just about washed over the side going for a loaf of bread. Bows and bowels lost!

Leslie mentions the tensions that built up in the claustrophobic stinking messdecks. 'My friend Harold Thompson, I had been to his home in Wallasey, Liverpool squared up to me one night on the mess-deck. Tension, I do not know why to this day.'

Convoy HX112 formed by 41 ships, continued eastward and homeward bound shepherded by the 5th Escort group, senior ship the *Walker*, Commander I.A.P. (Donald) Macintyre, four other destroyers and two corvettes. Five U-boats had been directed to concentrate and then attack the convoy. The first attack started on the night of the 15th/16th when *U-100* sank a single tanker before the escorts drove it off. In daylight the 16th, U-boats *U-37*, *U-100* and *U-110* tried unsuccessfully to break through the screen of escorts. After dark *U-99*, Lt Commander Kretschmer, succeeded in penetrating into the centre of the convoy where he caused mayhem, sinking four oil tankers and two general cargo ships, a total of 43,815 tons of shipping.

U-99 withdrew having expended all her torpedo outfit and then was located as *U-100* approached the convoy from astern and disaster struck both submarines. *Vanoc* sighted and rammed *U-100* and *U-99* was driven to the surface, and forced to scuttle after a ferocious and accurate depth charge attack by *Walker*. Kretschmer and thirty-nine of his men were picked up by Donald Macintyre who took enormous risks by switching on his searchlight to assist in the rescue of the enemy survivors. *Vanoc* managed to collect six prisoners of war from the *U-100*. Coder Leslie Stevenson recorded:

We sank the *U-99* and took off all the crew, but their Chief Engineer was lost while actually scuttling the U-boat off Iceland . . . Commander Donald Macintyre gave his cabin to the U-boat captain Otto Kretschmer, much to the disgust of the merchant navy men we had also picked up from that convoy . . .

His crew and I lived in *Walker* together for some days until we landed them at Liverpool to be marched away to PoW camp. Pictures in all the papers, U-boat ace captured and so on . . .

HMS *Vanoc*, in company rammed *U-100*. Lieutenant-Commander Scheoke died a horrible death, jammed between the bridge and periscope . . .

Churchill was at sea in May as one of the escorts to a Halifax bound convoy while the Home Fleet and Force H from Gibraltar searched the North Atlantic wastes for the battleship *Bismarck* and the heavy cruiser *Hipper*. The first inkling of the added menace to their charges in the form of enemy capital ships at loose across the convoy routes was the heartstopping grim information that the famous battle-cruiser *Hood* had been sunk by the *Bismarck* and *Hipper*. Sid France later wrote:

> The news that the fleet had caught up with the crippled ship (*Bismarck*) and battered her to death on May 27th, made us realise how lucky we had been. We passed through the fleet as they returned from their 'Glorious Victory', among them the brand new *Prince of Wales*, her crew equally brand new and still carrying some civilians, her forward turrets out of action as she followed the rest of the armada required to put one ship to the bottom, most of them looking very shaky. . . .
>
> On the same trip, we picked up survivors of the British ship *Marconi*. At first sight in the grey dawn, there seemed to be no life in the little boat alone in the wilderness of water until a lone figure waved eagerly. As we closed the boat, it was this man who made a line fast to the boat and helped us hoist his mates inboard, refusing to come aboard himself until the others were all safe. As he finally came over the side, he cast off the line, allowing the boat to drift away into the Atlantic wastes and said, 'We don't need her anymore'. He gave me another thing he had no further use for, a spoon with which he doled out a daily ration of condensed milk to the other survivors. . . .
>
> He was a 61-year-old Liverpudlian and asked – demanded – permission to work his passage. Fitzgerald told him that he had already done that and ordered him to his bunk until we reached St Johns. All of us in bottom bunks were asked (none had to be ordered) to give them to the survivors. Mine was taken for a 17-year-old whose feet our doctor had to amputate. I can still hear that bairn crying in the darkened messdeck that his toes hurt, poor little bastard, he had no toes to hurt. Later, in Newfoundland he lost a bit more of his feet as the gangrene spread, but he did find happiness; he married his nurse.

SS *Marconi* was sunk on 21st May and her few survivors were picked up by *Churchill* on the 29th.

In the Eastern Mediterranean the brilliant gains made by General Wavell's Western Desert army, the destruction of the Italian desert army and the drive westward to Benghazi and beyond had been dissipated and virtually every gain lost because of the decision to transport seasoned desert fighters to the Greek mainland to help the

Greek army resist the Italian invasion. Within short weeks General Rommel and his German Afrika Korps had driven the weakened British army back to the Egyptian frontier leaving the port of Tobruk bypassed and under siege. In Greece the British and Greek forces were under full retreat and in a few short weeks had to be lifted out from southern beaches and ports under heavy air attack with immense difficulty and heavy losses of men, ships and equipment. The units that retained some combat efficiency were taken to Crete and landed to garrison the island, the remainder were taken back to North Africa, the operation continuing under constant air assault with an almost complete absence of Allied fighter cover.

Then followed a bloody and doomed struggle to hold Crete, which culminated in yet another evacuation of the army with appalling losses. When it was over the proud East Mediterranean fleet had barely escaped total annihilation; two battleships and one aircraft carrier were badly damaged, three cruisers and six destroyers had been sunk, three cruisers and seven destroyers damaged. In Greek and Cretan harbours thirty-two Allied merchant ships had been destroyed or abandoned, at sea twelve vital transports had been sunk.

The defeat of the British and Allied arms had been entirely due to the overwhelming enemy air power, a repeat of what had happened in the Norwegian Fiords, in France and the beaches and ports of the French coastline. The losses and results were entirely predictable even to the most junior rating in the ships of the fleet; they had seen and endured it all before. Their Commander-in-Chief, Admiral A.B. Cunningham wrote in his despatches: 'Men of the fleet were already over-tired at the start of the two evacuations and had to carry on through under savage air attack and the breaking point was very near'.

Men of the fleet put it rather more bluntly: 'Sick they were, mate, never air cover to speak of. No information to ship's company. Bullshit talks from the C in C down. "This operation will shorten the war by six months!" It never bloody well did. "Your courage and tenacity." We'd nudge each other and say, here comes the courage and tenacity bit.'

The Crete battle saw the end of the *York* in Suda Bay. A month earlier, in March, she had been critically damaged by two of six Italian-manned fast explosive boats belonging to a special services unit. The cruiser was crippled on 26th March by two of a group of Italian armed high speed launches that had penetrated the bay's boom defences. *York* was hit by two of the unmanned craft and with immense difficulty beached herself while at the same time the tanker *Pericles* fuelling the cruiser *Coventry* was struck by one of the craft that passed under the gap in the bow destroyed by a torpedo from the Italian submarine *Naiad*. The tanker sank a few days later in convoy trying to get *Pericles* back to Alexandria for repairs.

Chris Buist was out of *York* when she was hit, ashore recovering from fever in the hospital in Malame. The ship was hit at 0500/26th March; he and all other walking sick/wounded were returned to the ship that forenoon to report for salvage duties. Over the next weeks the ship was hit time and again by the German air fleet attacks until the task became hopeless and the ship abandoned. The captain and senior officers left the island for other appointments.

'My nerve was broken,' wrote Chris Buist, 'when I joined the units to fight out the island. I became part of the groups retreating south over the mountains and was lucky to be taken off at a beach I cannot remember, back into Egypt. Still a nerve case I was drafted into the MB.D1 Mobile Naval Defence organisation and entered Sicily via the *LST 420*.'

The same night that *York* received her mortal damage, *Coventry* was springing away from the tanker when one of the unmanned craft slipped under her missing bow (removed two months earlier by the Italian submarine *Naiad*) and crashed into the tanker. There was no panic in the battle-hardened cruiser, still with her original crew though her third captain; the ship was not a fashionable command. The six Italian special service men were picked up from their rafts.

With the East Mediterranean Fleet emasculated, it was not possible to fight a convoy from the east to replenish the island of Malta and so something had to be done from the West and Gibraltar. The convoy for the supply operation Substance set out from the United Kingdom in early July, consisting of six supply ships and one troop transport with 5,000 men to reinforce the Malta garrison. The escort was massive; from the Home Fleet came the battleship *Nelson* and three cruisers with destroyers to reinforce Force H. The fleet was successful in forcing the narrows between Sicily and Cape Bon, North Africa, but the cruiser *Manchester* received severe damage from a torpedo, the destroyer *Fearless* was lost and her flotilla mate *Firedrake* was also badly damaged by a bomb.

It was only a few days short of his thirtieth birthday when Thomas Henry Guard was accepted as a hostility only volunteer. He reported

to HMS *Raleigh* in March 1941 for his recruit training, moving on to
the barracks at Portsmouth, HMS *Victory*, to await a draft to sea. He
had to wait a month and then received a draft chit for the destroyer
Firedrake. Thomas Guard wrote:

> I was really appalled at Portsmouth barracks – I heard that they were
> due to be pulled down before the war started and there were so many
> thieves about – you could not leave any of your gear around. I was glad
> to get out but three years later I was to spend some time there – but I was
> far more experienced. . . .
>
> I loved my two destroyers *Firedrake* and *Fury* and of course everything
> was on a more personal basis and I did not find any hostility between
> RN, RNR etc. It was a case of we are all in this together. I was in the com-
> munications mess which was down the hatch – I never liked this very
> much but when in *Fury* I was on the seamen's mess deck – somehow I felt
> safer! I was on the after bridge when *Firedrake* was hit by a high level Ita-
> lian bomb. The captain called out, 'Have we been hit?'. I replied, 'Yes,
> sir, flag locker has gone,' only to find that there was a huge hole in our
> side and one boiler blown out! I am sure it was *Onslow* that stood by us for
> some time but eventually we made the 800 miles back to Gib under one
> boiler on our own. When we were nearing Gib the fleet lined the upper
> deck to give us a chuck up. I was told that never before had this been
> done – and never again.

The intake of men into the Navy continued unabated, D.S. Goodbrand was one of the June 1941 volunteer entries ordered to report at
HMS *Raleigh*, Torpoint, Cornwall. Goodbrand kept a log of his naval
experience and this first account covers his time, June to September
at *Raleigh*.

Scouse and others.
    Scouse was a barrel-chested Neanderthaler who believed the world
began and ended with Liverpool. So when actor Michael Redgrave
entered *Drake* hut about 8 pm one night towards the end of June, he
monopolized his fellow Merseysider with a natural ebullience in keeping
with his outlook, much to the amusement of the rest of us and the bewil-
derment of the latest arrival, if the latter's basilisk state was anything to
go by.
    There was an air-raid warning within an hour and we all trooped into
the adjacent shelter, our new entry, the famous star of stage and screen,
towering head and shoulders above everyone. A false alarm; we all
trooped back into the billet, about 30 of us and listened to Scouse extol
the virtues of his fellow citizens under real air attacks.
    Most of us had arrived four days earlier, collected by truck from
Plymouth railway station and conveyed to HMS *Raleigh*, the basic train-

ing camp for seamen at Torpoint, Cornwall. The Germans had invaded Russia two days previously. As we rolled through the camp gates derisive chants of 'Abandon hope all ye who enter here' greeted us from three-week-old veterans, with uniform collars scrubbed and bleached to a pale blue to give the impression that their wearers were long-service matloes with oceans of experience behind them. A macho fantasy.

The class of new entries settled down under the able tuition of Chief Petty Officer Tozer, a bluff Westcountryman summoned out of retirement for the duration. We were a motley crew: labourers, clerks, miners, railway workers, public servants, of all ages between 18 and 40, mostly married, mostly glad to have escaped from boring civilian jobs, English, Welsh and Scots with a tough Glasgow contingent, hard drinkers all. Dick Hughes was a merchant seaman from Anglesey, Ted Miller a train fireman from Bury, Jock Meldrum a Highland shepherd, Giddings a Wiltshire farm-hand. The class leader was Capstick, a bright athletic Cumbrian. We were kitted out, mauled by the doctor and dentist, inoculated, vaccinated, received pay and identity books and discs, drilled, lectured and royally fed. The whole induction process took less than a week. Our arms swelled from the jabs and we groaned in unison. It was the first time I had heard Scots and Welsh accents at grass-roots level. Fascinating. The course lasted ten weeks at the end of which we were to be drafted according to our inclinations (in theory) then go on ten days' leave, returning to RN barracks, Devonport to await Their Lordships' pleasure. It was a wonderful summer, despite the irascible Scouse.

Scouse occupied the lower of one of two tier beds near the door of the hut and was therefore in a favourable stance to size up any incomer before anybody else, harangue the billet on his favourite subject, the myths and legends of Lime street and Scotland road and pursue Redgrave who slept almost opposite him, with intimate questions as to the morals of his leading ladies. Redgrave would lie on his bunk with hands under his head or smoking a reflective pipe, occasionally permitting himself a non-committal remark but generally regarding his garrulous interrogator with the unwinking gaze of one who plainly discerned an unwelcome visitor from some alien planet. I don't think Scouse got much out of him. The gulf between them, aggravated by the newcomer's reserve, was impassable.

The rest of us regarded the film star with a mixture of wariness and awe. It was somewhat unnerving to have such a 'different' giant in our midst; inevitably the vaunted caste-system or some variation of it, raised its hoary head with undertones of inverted snobbery so dear to the British heart. Once during a knot-tying session in the billet, CPO Tozer, his fancied inferiority bubbling to the surface, told Redgrave that 'he needn't think he would get any special treatment in the navy just because he was in the public eye', a quite unjustifiable remark which to his credit, he instantly regretted. Imperturbably the actor continued to wrestle with the intricacies of a bowline-on-the-bight. He left *Drake* hut after four days and re-appeared as class-leader in a neighbouring hut, where he seemed to settle down happily enough. Scouse grumbled a bit, then forgot about him, finding consolation in deriding with apostolic fervour the rest of his class-mates who had been unlucky to originate anywhere in these Islands outside the confines of his favourite city, to their immense hilarity and amusement. 'I don't blame you', he would address some grinning victim, 'I blame the bloke who let you in at the door . . . ' This oracular coup-de-grâce delivered, always with telling effect as far as Scouse was concerned, he would then retire to his bunk and immerse himself in the pages of *No Orchids for Miss Blandish*. Repartee flowed fast; there was great tolerance. I remember no violence. Capstick was a Godsend.

Now and again a bunch of refugees from the Gorbals, from the next hut would invade our privacy to entertain us with macabre tales of razor-slashing in 'no mean city'. On these occasions Scouse was invariably missing for some mysterious reason.

The weeks went by, filled with sunshine, good food and Naval indoctrination. In the mornings we rushed like berserkers to divisions, were inspected by ramrod brass, dismissed to training sessions and generally took everything in our stride. We felt a certain pride in becoming ordinary seamen and being part of the naval tradition and wrote glowing letters home. It was like being in a holiday camp firmly anchored in the nexus of service to the nation.

Tall tales and rumours abounded, veining the very stuff of conversation. Actor Robert Newton was supposed to play the boozy boyo with panache and his escapades in the environs of 'Guzz' were legendary. . . . The cooks put bromide in the tea, which no doubt accounted for its abysmal taste. . . . Meanwhile the war went on in another world.

The odd thing happened. One Scotsman 'went over the wall' and took the low road back to the Highlands but was caught in Glasgow and returned by the police to Torpoint and into Jankers. Somehow he avoided the current punishment of being made to circumnavigate the parade ground at the double holding a rifle behind his neck with each arm extended outwards to balance it, and rejoined us after a few days none the worse for his exploits. And once little John O'Raw, a 35 year-old Lanarkshire miner and family man, sat down on his bed one evening, put his head in his hands and wept shameless tears of homesickness while his mates crowded round offering self-conscious sympathy or stood helplessly at bay. All perked up considerably as leave approached.

Our civvy clothes had been sent home during the first week of training, so we sallied forth resplendent in seamen's rig to sample the local pubs. This was known as 'catching the liberty boat'. We understood that shipboard terms were to supplant use of habitual English for the duration. Thus 'deck', 'bulkhead' and 'heads' took over from floor, wall and ablutions.

Single men were paid 14 shillings a week. I sent home ten shillings and kept the rest, spending most in the Naafi canteen. . . .

We drilled, fired rifles and revolvers in the butts, drilled, learned to identify enemy ships by silhouette, spliced rope, drilled, rowed in small boats, absorbed discipline, learned to salute, drilled, were rated T, G or UA, kept our noses clean, yearned for sea-going ships to savour the taste of rum and wrote home that leave was imminent. Lean and tanned, we never felt healthier in our lives.

By the tenth week transformation from civilian to naval rating was complete, saving the restrictions imposed by a stone frigate. The rough cameraderie of Drake hut was about to dissolve, but not before we bought CPO Tozer a watch. 'You're not a bad lot!' he said gruffly in valediction. I believe every class that passed through his hands ended up buying him a watch. A sterling character, like most of his kind. Then we passed out on parade, collected our railway-warrants and jammed the corridors of trains going north, east and west to savour the delights of civvy street. It seemed everyone we saw was wearing a uniform of some kind.

Leave over we returned to RN barracks, Devonport, to groan at the accommodation some said had been condemned forty years previously, slinging our hammocks in earnest for the first time and making acquaintance of a new breed dubbed 'Barrack stanchions', amiable cynics who apparently contrived year after year to avoid being sent to sea and sat the war out in the comparative comfort of 'Jago's Mansions' as we learned to call HMS *Drake*. Meanwhile we waited for the draft to catch up with us – the luck of the draw.

When it came Dick Hughes went for DEMS training, John Smith from Wishaw to submarines, Ted Millar to torpedoes, Sandy Law to gunnery and Capstick to the writers' trade. Matt Tarbert, Willy Brooks, Jim Dunlop and John Grant, all stout Glaswegians, swelled the ranks of AB's, while Scouse departed for scenes unknown, doubtless to entertain other messdecks and propagate the folly of electing to be born in any place except Liverpool. The rest of us, HOs all, vanished into steel labyrinths of lower deck anonymity, and if we saw each other again it would be a miracle.

In October I was drafted to a camp at Wembury near Plymouth to learn high angle gunnery. But, I was always keen to go to sea as a wireless operator. Before enlisting I had taught myself to receive and transmit morse at speeds up to Service standards, and at the end of December was able without too much difficulty to wangle a W/T course at HMS *Impregnable* at St Budeaux, but that is another story. Both Michael Redgrave and Robert Newton eventually returned to make films, as ordained by the man in charge of national morale, and Guzz knew them no more except on the silver screen.

Before Goodbrand made his way to HMS *Impregnable* to learn his trade as a telegraphist and then went to a sea-going ship, he spent three months, September to December 1941, at the Gunnery School and coastal battery, HMS *Cambridge* at Wembury, between Plymouth Sound and the estuary to the River Yealm.

The battleship *Nelson* had long periods during the months of January, February and March with other capital ship units of the Home Fleet patrolling the northern passages and the Denmark strait in an abortive effort to intercept outward and homeward-bound German battleship and cruiser ocean raiders.

Nelson then operated far to the south, close to the equator, and missed the search and final sinking of the *Bismarck*. In September she became flagship to Admiral Somerville who led Operation Halberd. A force of three battleships, one aircraft carrier, five cruisers, eighteen destroyers and nine submarines fought through a convoy of nine ships bearing reinforcements of 2,600 troops and stores to Malta. The passage was strongly opposed by Axis bomber and torpedo aircraft and the Italian fleet put in an appearance and engaged the fleet cruisers. Only one merchant ship, *Imperial Star* was sunk and *Nelson* was hit by a torpedo.

Cliff Smith was at his action station during this action.

The convoy was to go through to Malta at a time of very strong opposition from the Italian Fleet Air Arm. I can't say much about the Italian Fleet – I only saw them when they capitulated in 1943, but no one can cast any doubts against the bravery of Italian airmen. I know the Germans didn't think much of their allies, but during numerous convoys at that particular time the Italians gave us a lot of trouble.

One torpedo bomber made a suicidal attack on us, dropped his torpedo which struck us forrard on the port side. A huge hole was blown in our bowls and we slowed almost to a stop. The brave airman was shot down and killed, but I did not see any of it because my action station was in the bowels of the ship – the 6″ shell room. The atmosphere down there was, to say the least, tense. There was absolutely no chance for any of us to get out of our steel coffin, should the ship sink. Each compartment is battened down and has to be kept watertight. However after a couple of hours (it seemed like days) we were released. The relief of breathing fresh air again after the claustrophobic shell room, was fantastic. That was my last experience of the 6″ shell room. When our repairs were completed I was posted to a different action station-4.7″ ack-ack supply party which when you think about it could have been 'from the frying pan into the fire' – as the saying goes. 'You pays your money and takes your choice.'

Nelson succeeded in returning at reduced speed to Gibraltar for temporary repairs prior to returning to a dockyard in the United Kingdom. While there Cliff Smith was required for special and unpleasant duties.

The Jaunty (Master at Arms) came into my office and said could I do shorthand. When I said I could he told me to accompany him to his office. There he had two ratings standing at attention . . . Their crime was sodomy and they had been caught in the act! My distasteful job was to take verbatim statements of the proceedings and then type out the report. Well anyone who has served in the Navy or armed services couldn't be called prude and certainly I wasn't, but when you have to write in cold print some of the words that were said, it was crude to say the least.

The upshot of this case was that they were both found guilty and discharged straight from the service into one of HM prisons in the UK. I asked the Master at Arms what would happen to them when they had served their time (both of them were Regular Navy). I was told that they would be put straight into an infantry battalion of some regiment. . . .

I did a spell in both the captain's office and the pay office. In the captain's office I was privy to many confidential documents also the service certificates and crime sheets of all the ship's company ratings, and what tales they told. Some of the misdemeanours were hilarious, others crude, but all were paid for by various forms of punishment. Stoppage of leave and/or pay was fairly common, but at sea the principal retribution was 'Jankers' and this could be anything from doubling round the upperdeck in full kit with a rifle to cleaning out the heads. Two crimes which I've always remembered were committed by a boy seaman. Number one was in the naval jargon of the time, quote 'guilty to the prejudice of good order and naval discipline in that he did urinate in his hammock!' The second by the same boy was – quote – that was he guilty of 'slack hammock' (in other words had failed to turn out on time) and also that he was in his hammock 'wearing seaboots', which must have been mighty uncomfortable. A feature of life in a battleship was that we got many of the 'old lags' or skates as we called them, drafted to us after they had done time in a HM establishment for the correction of delinquent seamen. Believe me, we got some hard cases!

The sad thing that struck one at the time was the number of very efficient and able 'Able Seamen' we got from these places and looking at their documents, they'd done time, been disrated and lost badges many times all on account of booze! Many would sell their souls for a tot, gulpers or even just sippers, but strangely they'd never nick someone else's tot left lying unattended.

A successful evacuation of Norwegian and Russian inhabitants of Spitzbergen was carried out by a force commanded by Rear Admiral

Philip Vian during the later part of August. The force consisted of the flagship cruiser *Aurora*, the cruiser *Nigeria* with three destroyers and a large transport, the *Empress of Canada*. The force destroyed the coal-mining installations and captured three enemy colliers and other smaller vessels. Radio installations on Spitzbergen and Bear Island were destroyed by the cruisers' bombardments then the force proceeded to Murmansk to disembark the Russian civilians. While this was happening *Nigeria* received bomb damage during an air raid on Murmansk: several men were killed but the cruiser only received superficial damage; the force sailed for the United Kingdom. On passage Admiral Vian led the cruisers for a sortie on the night of 6th/ 7th September towards the Norwegian coastline close to North Cape seeking enemy shipping. In the early hours of the 7th in a position to the east of North Cape, in heavy weather and poor visibility *Aurora* and *Nigeria* found a small convoy of two troop transports, *Barcelona*, 3,101 tons, and *Trautenfels*, 6,418 tons, with 1,500 troops of the 6th Mountain Division embarked. The convoy was escorted by the German Navy gunnery training ship *Bremse*. In a confused action in darkness and violent seas the cruisers' gunpower destroyed the *Bremse* and *Nigeria* collided with the sinking wreck which caused some damage to the cruiser. Meanwhile the transports made their escape into Posangerfiord.

Aurora and *Nigeria* rejoined the British force and returned without further incident to Scapa Flow on the 10th.

Able Seaman Ridout's action station was in *Nigeria*'s B turret and after many false alarms and dawn and dusk action stations he wrote:

When we were really in action it was difficult to realise that the shells I pushed onto the loading tray were on their way to the enemy. We bombarded the radio stations on Spitzbergen and Bear Island and I did see through the trainer's telescope the fires that we had started. Night action was the usual thing in the Arctic and dawn action stations were always assumed whatever time 'dawn' happened to be. The whole ship shook violently when she rammed a German destroyer during our action off North Cape on 7/8th September 1941. We suffered little damage and made a safe journey back to Scapa Flow. That night many of us 'boys' grew into men. . . .

Air raids at Murmansk while we were at anchor in Kola inlet caused some fatal casualties and the loss of some of our messmates shook us considerably especially when I heard the 'pipe' ordering that four practice projectiles to be provided to weight their bodies prior to burial at sea.

Moving from the area of action and horror in the North Atlantic and Arctic theatres: action in the period September to December 1941 in the warmer and deceptively friendlier Mediterranean seas was just as lethal in terms of ship sinkings and casualties. The Axis air forces and Italian Fleet dominated and controlled movement in the Eastern Mediterranean basin from bases in Crete, Greece and southern Italy and to a lesser extent in the Western Mediterranean from French North Africa and Sardinia.

Legion (Commander Jessel) had been part of Force H operating from Gibraltar since late June. More recently the destroyer shared the hazards of Operation Halberd which took place in the period 24th to 30th September when the battleship *Nelson* was hit by a torpedo from an Italian aircraft. During the operation *Legion* with the *Gurkha* attacked and sank the Italian submarine *Adua*. Then followed several weeks of patrols and alarms culminating in Operation Perpetual in November when the aircraft carrier *Ark Royal* successfully flew off 37 Hurricane fighter planes to reinforce the air defences of Malta. As she was returning from this operation, the U-boats *U-81* and 205 attacked and torpedoed *Ark Royal*, and she sank 25 miles out from Gibraltar after *Legion* had taken off most of her ship's company.

The destroyer continued as part of Force H and from late November she remained based on Malta where in spite of the incessant air bombardment shore leave was granted after nightfall and some of the sailor-oriented entertainments in the Gut continued to be enjoyed by Eric Smith and messmates:

After a meal, my two oppos and myself went along to Jim Irish's dosshouse where one could get a clean bed for 6d. A notice outside read 'Old man and winger 1/-!', which included a quick cup of tea in the morning! The beds were in long dormitories, quite clean, and we would leave our shoes at the foot of our beds for José to clean during the night. It was customary to tip him when leaving in the morning, usually about 3d.

Whenever I had money on my person and was sleeping ashore, I always wore my belt round my waist next to my skin. I knew of so many instances of sailors being robbed when in drink, especially in foreign ports, through not taking elementary precautions. We three turned in in adjoining beds and were soon asleep. In the early morning hours I began to wake up and could sense a hand feeling about and searching under my pillow. I remained still until I fully realised what was happening and then suddenly shot upright in my bed, scaring the intruder out of his wits. I'm sure it was José the night attendant but it was too dark to see properly. I woke my two chums and whispered what had happened and we all went on the lookout for the man. We never saw him and anyway my money was intact. So we decided to teach him a lesson, got ourselves dressed, then mustered all the polished shoes we could find, mixed them up and tied them in pairs by their laces and placed them in a bloody great heap in one corner. We then left and made our way back to the ship.

We heard later from other of our shipmates who had stayed there, of the abuse that José had to suffer from the other matelots who awoke to find that they all had odd shoes; they all left without paying their customary tip. One occasion when crime did not pay.

This was a period of successful Italian Fleet convoy operations to reinforce the Axis forces in North Africa. There were many opposing fleet postures, some allowed the Italian fleet covering escorts to progress large convoys of troop reinforcements and supplies into Benghazi, Tripoli and several minor ports. This spasm of Italian fleet activity came to a sudden halt on the night of 13th December at 02.30 when two Italian cruisers and their escorts which had reversed course after being sighted by reconnaissance aircraft from Malta ran into the destroyers from Force H which were on passage to Alexandria to fill in a gap left by the withdrawal of Australian destroyers called to join the Far East Fleet now that Japan had attacked the Allies.

The half flotilla of destroyers lead by *Sikh* (Commander Stokes), *Maori*, both Tribal class destroyers, *Legion* and the Dutch destroyer *Isaac Sweers* hugging the coastline round Cape Bon virtually collided with the Italian squadron commanded by Divisional Admiral Toscano, his cruisers *Alberto di Giussano* and *Alberico da Barbiano* loaded with a lethal deck cargo of aviation spirit. Commander Stokes led his destroyers into a line ahead gun and torpedo attack, that left the cruisers sinking and burning as funeral pyres for Admiral Toscano who perished with 900 of his men.

We were creeping through the strait between Pantellaria and Africa just off Cape Bon. We were not at action stations although the area was a well-known E-boat alley. Suddenly from *Sikh* came a signal: 'Full speed ahead, have sighted two enemy cruisers'. Action stations sounded and all four of us revved up to full speed and tubes were trained outboard. The order was given to open fire and the next ten minutes or so was a hell of bangs and the swish of torpedoes as they left the tubes and sped on their mission of destruction. The Italian force was taken completely by surprise and offered only token return fire. *Legion* scored one torpedo hit on a cruiser and several with her 4.7″ guns; her pom-poms, oerlikons and small range weapons scoring many hits of damage on the cruisers and escort vessels. The action only lasted 10-20 minutes, but the result, one cruiser sunk, one damaged and blazing (to be finished off next morning by planes from Malta) one destroyer and one E-boat sunk or damaged. Our four destroyers suffered neither damage nor casualties. Still at action stations but 'stood down' for a breather we relaxed and congratulated ourselves on an easy victory over the enemy.

One of my loading numbers on 'Y' gun, Dizzey Gillespie, a native of Birmingham, asked Buck Taylor, captain of the gun, 'What were all those red and green light flying over our heads during the action?' On being told that they were tracer shells and that he should have worn his tin hat, poor Dizzey fainted!

So wrote Eric Smith of the action.

The destroyers' victory was soon revenged by the destruction of a British cruiser squadron which ran into a minefield trap laid by the Italian fleet. The cruiser *Neptune* was sunk with heavy loss of life and two more, *Aurora* and *Penelope*, were badly damaged, the destroyer *Kandahar* had to be abandoned. Off Alexandria the cruiser *Galatea* was torpedoed by U-boat, *U-557*, and a cruiser squadron commanded by Rear Admiral Sir Philip Vian as it entered harbour was followed in by three Italian chariot eer teams who succeeded in damaging the battleships *Queen Elizabeth* and *Valiant*, and also a Norwegian tanker and the destroyer *Jervis*. The Italian Commander-in-Chief, Admiral Iachino, was at sea with two battleships and supporting light forces covering the passage of convoys from mainland Italy to North African ports. The Italian C-in-C had a brief encounter with Rear Admiral Vian's squadron before the latter withdrew to Alexandria after passing on the auxiliary *Breconshire*, loaded with troop reliefs and stores, to Malta-based escorts which included the *Legion* and the remainder of the half flotilla which 48 hours earlier had destroyed Admiral Toscano's squadron.

For the remainder of December the Italian fleet continued to escort convoys into Tripoli, Benghazi and Tobruk to resupply the Axis North African army unmolested by British surface ships. The Japanese fleet attacked the US naval base at Pearl Harbour, and America entered the Second World War.

In the Far East Japanese army landings had commenced on the coastline of Malaya. On 13th December a second major landing of a division of the Japanese 25th Army was made from 36 transports in Camranh Bay.

The drydocks of the Royal Dockyard Singapore contained two cruisers which were now at great risk of being trapped by the rapid advance of the Japanese army. *Emerald,* first commissioned in 1926, had been badly damaged in a collision with the *Dauntless,* the second cruiser *Mauritius,* only commissioned in January 1941, was in dockyard hands for engine room overhaul and for modifications to the turret training races.

Bill Sands was still serving in *Emerald* and had forgotten his resentment of being shanghied into mobilised service after the 1939 Reserve Fleet review; now after 2¼ years in the cruiser he was part of the establishment of senior and experienced able seamen. 1940 had been spent escorting North Atlantic convoys: '20 days to cross the Atlantic – endless monotony'. Then followed a near idyllic period, 'showing the flag round South Africa and India,' calls at small ports to boost morale of English communities. Rig the quarter-deck for dancing. Runs ashore at places of great interest, Zanzibar, Madagascar and Seychelles'.

This did not last long for *Emerald* joined a scratch force of East Indies Station ships which included vessels of the Royal Indian Navy and the Royal Australian Navy, commanded by the Commander-in-Chief East Indies, Vice Admiral Ŗ. Leatham. The force carrying troops of the Indian Army entered the Persian Gulf at the end of April to deal with a *coup d'état* by Rashid el Gailani who had deposed the Regent of Iraq and his government. *Emerald* remained in the Gulf and the Euphrates estuary until the revolt was crushed and the Regent restored to power on 1st June. Bill Sands:

> landed Gurkhas at Basra then remained with the *Yarra* (sloop) at 100 mile intervals on the Euphrates to monitor our military presence. A small party from *Emerald,* a sublieutenant, an ERA and some seamen ratings commissioned an Arab tug to patrol the river. We lived Arab fashion – cooked on oil drip stove – heads, the stern rail! I had much experience of small craft handling so was appointed as coxswain. Sub lieutenant started doing things the pusser way, starboard 10-midships – port 10 – steady, but of course we had no instrumentation or a compass. We agreed best for him to tell me where he wanted to go and then leave it to me – worked very well. Overhanging bridges and coming alongside similarly constructed arab tugs caused problems, some bridges damaged. A joke that went sour; we were moored alongside a wharf upstream and ahead of the base depot ships. A bloated stinking buffalo corpse lodged itself between our hull and jetty, eased our mooring lines and let it float down to the base ship. Messenger arrived ordering us to get underway to secure a line around the corpse and tow it away. . . .
>
> After six weeks I was discharged back to *Emerald* with poisoned bites

and fever. Some 200 of the ship's company on the sick list, hammocks laid on deck under awnings, the doctor and sickbay tiffeys took all day to do the rounds. *Emerald* ordered back to Calcutta. . . .

Japanese enter the war, we are guard ship at the Seychelles for six weeks, marvellous time with sailing parties to small paradise islands. . . . ordered to join Admiral Somerville's squadron and within days in collision in the Malacca straits with *Dauntless*. Large hole in port side, the tubes were trained outboard and many of the crew were sleeping on deck. The forward set of tubes were torn off their mountings and piled onto the after set, fires, exploding ammunition, general mayhem with six dead and many injured. We were soon docked down in Singapore and the ship's company transferred to shore accommodation – very luxurious by lower-deck standards . . . still in dry dock when the Johore causeway is blown, one of the last convoys to get away. Saved from an 80 plus Japanese aircraft raid by a violent tropical storm.

Mauritius, the other cruiser in Singapore fleet dockyard, had arrived on 6th November following deployment as escort to a convoy from Colombo. She commenced immediately to to disembark fuel, stores and ammunition prior to entering dry-dock. On the 10th the ship's company moved ashore in to the relative comfort of the Fleet shore accommodation that already housed the men from *Emerald*. Working parties marched down to the ship to start work at 0730 to back up the Chinese dockyard workers who started work an hour earlier. While the major modifications to the turrets and overhaul of auxiliary machinery was undertaken, the messdecks and spaces were being repainted. The ship's company except for duty sentries and fire parties left the ship at 1530; the dockyard workmen continued for another three hours until 1830.

Sid Bark, Ordnance Artificer 4th Class, who had been with the ship while completing before commissioning gives a reason for docking in Singapore: 'because of problems experienced by the 6″ gun turrets of the cruiser *Ajax* and *Achilles* during the battle of the River Plate in 1939, armed with the same 6″ MK XXII triple turrets, we were in Singapore to make changes to the turret training races, and the top of A and B turrets had been lifted off so work could commence.'

On 24th November, *Mauritius* entered dry dock. The new cruiser had only commissioned on 1st January 1941 and following a work up period in Scapa Flow as part of the 10th Cruiser Squadron of the Home Fleet she began a series of long uneventful months at sea. She covered convoys in North and South Atlantic; then in June she was transferred to the East Indies station. Here she continued to patrol vast empty sea areas and escort large troop convoys moving towards the Red Sea and the Middle East. *Mauritius* enjoyed breaks from her long monotonous weeks at sea with generous leave in near perfect peacetime conditions. Hospitality and the fleshpots of Simons Town, Durban, Mombasa and Colombo entertained the cruiser's ship's company many times.

A strange fact, however, was that although in the ten months since being commissioned the cruiser had not seen any action with the enemy, *Mauritius* was acquiring a dismal record for the high number of men punished by warrant.

After arrival in Singapore, later on the 10th, and before the ship's company disembarked to quarters ashore, at 1010 hours, warrant number 34 was read and five minutes later a rating was discharged to detention quarters in the base HMS *Sultan* and to the real risk of being there when the city and naval base surrendered to the Japanese. The rate of warrant punishments awarded and being read to the ship's company cleared from lower-deck was already averaging a little over three a month and as the cruiser's wartime career continued would rise to an average of more than 58 per annum while other cruisers with similar war exploits and numbers of complement ran at less than 38 per annum. This fact would dog the cruiser and might have had a bearing on the problems and hardships suffered by the crew of what was after all a modern ship which did contain a few of the glowingly amenities described by Admiral James as comfort and modern lower-deck living conditions, in his foreword to *Naval Life and Customs*.

The first commanding officer, Captain L.C.A. Curzon Howe MVO, appointed to the ship, left as a sick man before the work up in Scapa Flow was complete. There was some delay before a new man was appointed so for some weeks the ship's executive commander, Commander A.R. Pedder assumed temporary command until Captain W.D. Stephens, a captain of considerable seniority, joined.

> The commander was obviously a man determined to get the maximum amount of work from the ship's company. There was what was known as 'Pedder's Hour' which was the way he introduced changes in the clock to ensure that the hands did a full day's work as well as finding time for breakfast after dawn action stations. Not every ship went to dawn action stations like *Mauritius* did, except when they were in an area of threat. . .
> Mail was obviously infrequent with gaps of three and five months which did happen to ships in the South Atlantic and the Indian Ocean. . . . the ship was in two watches and worked watch and watch for long periods.

These conditions could have made life irksome for a ship's company
who had not seen action in their new ship and therefore made men
overstay leave and break rules of discipline which in turn were coun-
tered by firm implementation of the discipline code.

Mauritius continued her stay in dry dock into December. On the
2nd the battleship *Prince of Wales*, Admiral Sir T.S.V. Phillips' flagship, the battlecruiser *Repulse* and four destroyers arrived from the
United Kingdom. On the 3rd with the repainting routine continuing
the cruiser undocked and tried to make ready for sea against a
background of several false alarm air raid warnings that scattered
the dockyard labour who then needed considerable persuasion to
board the ship again. Admiral Phillips sailed on the 8th in the *Prince
of Wales* with *Repulse* and his destroyers. *Mauritius* commenced basin
trials in an increasingly deteriorating situation as the Japanese land
forces pushed south down the Malayan peninsula. Later that day
came the mind-numbing information that the two British capital
ships had been sunk by a highly coordinated Japanese aerial bomb
and torpedo attack. The destroyers rescued 1,285 from the *Repulse*
and 796 from the *Prince of Wales*. Admiral Phillips and the
battleship's Captain Leach were among the missing.

With the threat of the enemy approaching Singapore increasing
by the hour *Mauritius* was towed to the armament wharf to embark
ammunition on the 13th. Next day the cruiser's Royal Marine
detachment that had been despatched to assist in the defence of the
island returned with several of its members wounded. Surprisingly
on the same day two members of the ship's company were discharged into the base HMS *Sultan*.

At 0502 Monday 15th December, with her armament largely ineffective, much of her auxiliary machinery still to be re-assembled and
her main engines operative only because of a number of expedients
Mauritius sailed from the naval base threatened by an imminent air
attack. W.M. Lewis, Chief ERA, wrote: 'We limped out of Singapore
for Colombo and home minus our fire fighting ring main and much of
our auxiliary machinery needing overhaul . . . we could not have
fought the ship as damage control would have been ineffective.'

The cruiser made Colombo on the 18th and remained there until
sailing on 1st January 1942. During the twelve days in Colombo harbour Captain Stephens authorised three more warrants nos, 35, 36
and 37 to be read and in fact before the ship arrived in Plymouth on
11th February 1942 having called at Durban, Simons Town and
Freetown two more warrants had been read making a total of 39 for
the cruiser's first year in service. Captain Stephens not only had

cause to discipline his sailors, but also, 16th December to log one of his officers:

> December 16th. At Sea.
> . . . Logged and admonished Mr. – Commissioned Ordnance Officer for continued immoderate consumption of spirituous liquors after previous warnings, signed W.D. Stephens.

As 1941 came to an end the East Indies station fleet and the units that served under Dutch command in defence of Sumatra and Java waited fearfully for the full impact of Japanese fleet and air assaults; in the East Mediterranean the fleet had temporarily lost the initiative after heavy losses, its two severely damaged battleships faced a long and uncertain passage to United States of America dockyards. The Home Fleet grappled with the increasing weight of U-boat attacks and sinking in the Northern seas and the endless ferocity of the storms in the North Atlantic.

As one of the thousands manning Home Fleet ships, Tom Bywater, now an able seaman, joined another ship after a spell in the battleship *Royal Sovereign*:

> I was sent to Blackwall dock, London, to join *Vanessa* (V & W destroyer) which was at the end of a refit. When I arrived I met the Gunnery Control Officer, a sub lieutenant and together we looked down into the dock and we found the ship stripped. No guns at all, so I had 14 days' leave, a pleasant surprise. Rejoining the ship, settling in and getting to know almost everyone we left for Scotland and a working up period, then down to Liverpool, Gladstone dock, to be our depot while on convoy duties. On to Londonderry to top up with fuel and into the Atlantic to rendezvous with a convoy.
>
> What a ship! – we lived forward of course. The dockyard mateys had left minute holes in the bulkheads and decks leading into the oil tanks. Into rough weather: we had 3 or 4 inches of sea water mixed with oil all over the mess-decks. A bale of cotton waste, buckets and mopping up operation while off watch was our introduction into the North Atlantic. It was mostly rough weather although there were a few calm days. Some of us got our sea legs and I don't mean with pills, cause there wasn't any. . . .
>
> The rough weather although unpleasant was a boon, U-boats were useless in these conditions. Coming off the middle watch one night in a violent sea and pitch black skies I actually was thanking God for such vile weather. Night time is so different in the bad weather of the North Atlantic and with daylight it is always a surprise to find the convoy ships still plunging and rolling their way in formation. . . .
>
> At Halifax the good people there sent out to us a load of hams;

everyone received one; we visualised going home on leave with these hams as a present to our families. Alas on the way back and entering the Gulf stream the hams started to go off! Soon there was a long trail astern of hams bobbing in the wake. . . .

I remember Scott coming off watch and being swept overboard by a big sea over the quarter-deck. One felt awful, could not lower a boat. Why didn't you go in after him, you ask yourself?

Thomas Guard, able seaman, one of the 'old men' in *Fury*'s ship's company had run into a minor spot of trouble, recorded in verse by 'Spiv' Francis.

The Disgrace of Tom!

The strangest tale that I have heard
And this is true, you take my word
Concerns Tom Guard and some japer
Who fill's Tom's locker with paper

Now Tom is quite a decent bloke
Who's always meet to take a joke
And so its hard to realize
This story which creates surprise

It seems old Tom, at last choker
With all this junk stowed in his locker
Threw the paper torn to the floor
Which act did then create uproar

'Now pick it up,' said Killick Mac,
To which old Tom did answer back
'Oh no, I think the proper bloke,
Is man who perpetrated joke.'

Now Mac got wild, said, 'Grab your cap,
Afraid you'll have to take the rap,'
Tom said, 'Alright that's Oke with me'
So both the Coxswains went to see.

It seems the charge became quite strong
Tom found himself now in the wrong
For Coxswain (much to his distaste)
Made out report of Tom's disgrace.

First Lieutenant then saw old Tom
Inquiring where charge did rise from
Then Tom of course did not deny
His awful guilt in his reply

First Lieutenant used discretion
Said to Tom, 'Let this be lesson,
In future, bear in mind each day,
Orders given you must obey.'

Tom Guard escaped lightly with a caution but even in destroyers
and smaller craft discipline was enforced by punishment by warrant
and he wrote, 'I thought the system of reading a warrant in front of
the ship's crew was quite unnecessary – I heard this twice, once in a
ship and once in barracks – but I suppose the idea was to warn others
and to show that justice had been done.'

CHAPTER FOUR

1942

New Year 1942 arrived with the Americans at war with Germany since 11th December 1941, four days after the Japanese had attacked Pearl Harbour. The tardy allies refused at first to profit from the two year lone war experience gained by the British battle against U-boats in the Atlantic. In consequence they were suffering terrible losses, their shipping sailed unorganised, with lights blazing, radio chattering incessantly and without escorts.

U-boat commanders reeling from the mid-Atlantic conflict with growing numbers of British convoy escorts had a field day experience. In the West Atlantic and eastern seaboard of America they massacred 300,000 tons of American merchant shipping in January. The toll was to grow month by month until at the end of July 1942 3½ million tons had been sunk for the loss of only eleven U-boats.

The hardened men of the British Atlantic and Western Approaches escort flotillas could barely suppress a grim form of satisfaction over the punishment received by a boastful, dollar rich, late entry ally who many suspected was playing the same WWI tactics by remaining neutral until Britain and her Empire was bankrupt and exhausted.

By now the Mediterranean Fleet consisted of only one squadron of four cruisers commanded by Rear Admiral Sir Phillip Vian in his flagship *Naiad* and about eleven effective destroyers. The Desert Army, which had during the summer of 1941 succeeded in driving the Axis army back to beyond Benghazi for the second time, was again under heavy pressure and in retreat from the German and Italian divisions that had been supplied and reinforced by convoys from mainland Italy and Greece after the Italian fleet had regained command of the central Mediterranean seas.

The reduced Mediterranean Fleet still used Alexandria as its base and although the great port was subject to bombing and minelaying aircraft raids of varying intensity they hardly affected the entertainments on offer to libertymen. Destroyer *Legion*'s men on their runs ashore were still savouring the activities enjoyed by generations of

Fleet libertymen. A shore run by Eric Smith and his mess-mates is an example:

> In Alexandria we managed to get in several runs ashore where we usually made our presence felt by painting the town red. Scoop announced that he was going ashore for a 'Haircut run'. Spike and I decided to go along and left the dockyard at 61 gate and proceeded up Sister Street to the main part of the city. Street pedlars squatting in the gutters offered their chapatis oblivious of the clouds of black flies round their heads and on their wares. The touts outside the brothels called out the many delights to be found inside. 'Inside Navy – all girls clean' – 'Any way you like, 10 piastres' – 'Inside Navy – all ship's company inside'.
>
> Leaving Sister Street behind us we escorted Scoop to the nearest tonsorial parlour whilst Spike and I searched for and found a nearby bar. Scoop seemed to be a long time getting his hair cut so we went back to the barber's shop. There was Scoop, sat in one of the chairs, a white sheet around him, his hair being trimmed by a young Egyptian maiden, whilst another, supposedly a manicurist, was kneeling on the floor at his feet with her hand under the apron. Scoop sat there with a silly grin on his face: 'Best bloody haircut I've ever had', he drooled. After his haircut? We visited a photographer's where we had our pictures taken together. We then wended our way to the fleet club for a meal, after which we went to the beer garden for a drink and a game of Tombola.
>
> Once again we were lucky and won about £5, so what had started out as a quiet run ended up as a wild evening in the night spots of Alexandria. At the end of the evening we caught a gharri back to the dockyard, the driver pulled up about 20 yards from the gate. The reason for this soon became obvious when he tried to overcharge us. Drunk or sober, 'Jack' is well aware of the charges ashore and we had no intention of being seen off by a bloody Arab. We offered him the going rate but he demanded more, which we refused to pay. On alighting, Spike accidentally(!) knocked off the lamp on the side of the gharri which brought forth a torrent of abuse and threats from the driver. We had enough of this, so in unison we upended the gharri, horse and all and made a dash for the dockyard gate; the driver, recovering, grabbed his whip and chased us, screaming threats against all Englishmen the while. We, safely through the gate, turned and gave him the 'Victory V sign' and staggered back inboard. . . .

In Bombay the old battered anti-aircraft cruiser *Coventry* was completing a six-month refit, a refit that none of her veterans of the 1940 Norwegian campaign, the East Mediterranean fleet battles against overwhelming air power, the Greece and Crete operations and evacuations, had dared to hope would happen, they had expected the fate predicted by their Commander-in-Chief. *Coventry* had been torpedoed in the bow by an Italian submarine, *Naiad*, on Friday, 13th December 1940, off Bardia. She had been allowed only time for a temporary blanking off of the destroyed bow – the first patch fell off at sea, but her presence was so urgently required that Admiral A.B. Cunningham ordered, '*Coventry* is to be repatched and then run as long as the ship is capable of floating and steaming.'

She survived against all odds, frequently having to run before storm and sea to avoid sinking yet staying at sea through the transfer of troops to Greece and then after Greece fell to Crete, followed by the battle for the island and the final evacuation. Her Petty Officer John Sephton was awarded a posthumous Victoria Cross, the first to the WW2 Mediterranean fleet. She was present when her sister anti-aircraft cruiser *Calcutta* was sunk and then with her third captain of the war played a vital part in the campaign to neutralise the Vichy French forces in the Lebanon and Syria.

Then, to the cynical astonishment of her ship's company, *Coventry* received orders to sail for Bombay and a major refit. This was now, at the beginning of 1942, almost complete and her ship's company, who had been living ashore in HMS *Calabar* and a bug-ridden hotel, moved back into a fumigated ship and prepared to return to an uncertain future in the Mediterranean. Captain Carne had gone and a fourth captain, R.J.R. Denby, was in command. Her unconventional, eccentric executive commander, the gin-connoisseur Dalrymple Hay, who had held the ship together during the Crete debacle, a period where fortuitously he was temporary captain, had gone. His relief was Commander J.M. Robb RNR who had been recently promoted. 'Robbo' Robb had been with the ship since re-commissioning in August 1939; he was a solid individual, courageous but lacked the imagination, panache and initiative of his predecessor and very soon the lower-deck was less disposed to tolerate without complaint the awful overcrowding, spartan facilities and poor ventilation aggravated by the tropics. Leslie Stevenson joined the cruiser while she was still in the Mediterranean and before the start of the Lebanon and Syrian conflict. His comments are probably less inhibited than the recollections of the majority who had served in *Coventry* through two years of action and disasters. He writes of the daily working parties and the re-occupation of the ship on completion of the refit:

> Hot weather work was a mixture of athlete's foot, dhoby itch, hands to bathe and iced drinks before starting, then at a cafe close by, hot corned beef. The duty watch and fire parties slept on deck under the stars. . . . I

found that the stokers envied us seamen our cushy number, who could blame them for that? Similarily they envied their officers and their larger living quarters, gin, women inboard. Loathed that British so pompous accent, promotion seekers. Some Captains Royal Navy glory-seekers. I've sat in the mess opposite listening, agreeing quietly. . . . When there was a gin or a party of women, we were kept out of sight; it wasn't for us lower-deck scum.

Crossing the Indian Ocean then into the Red sea, the cruiser exercised continuously to recover her skills as an efficient and highly effective anti-aircraft cruiser; but there were irritants:

. . . evening quarters at 1600 in the Red Sea! All in the rig of the day despite the heat. Whites, which we stripped off when it was over and had to dhoby. Those on watch came off at 3 minutes to 1600 to get into the rig and left 3 minutes after whilst his relief changed or arrived below . . . was it something to keep us occupied or just to annoy the lower-deck?

George Sims, able seaman, RNVR, a member of the cruiser's AA unit wrote:

Our next stop was Suez and shore leave was given. Some of the ship's company received invitations to a dance organised by the WRNS. During the evening we were surprised to learn that the Wrens knew a good deal of *Coventry*'s past and that she had arrived from Bombay. Even more astonishing, the Wrens prophesied that the ship would soon take part in an operation to Tobruk. While making the canal transit, those to whom the future had been revealed pondered the truth of the forecast, and when it would take place. Arriving at Alexandria, we saw the familiar landmarks but were well aware that considerable changes had taken place, as regards the war situation during our absence.

The depleted Mediterranean Fleet at great risk and without more than token air support had continued to fight through small convoys from the east to the beleaguered garrison at Tobruk and to the fortress Malta. These convoys had to run the gauntlet of continuous daylight air attacks from enemy-held airfields to the north in Crete, Greece and Italy and to the south along the North African coast from El Alamein to Cape Bon. After one of these operations the destroyer *Legion* remained at Malta to reinforce Force K and was still there when Rear Admiral Sir Phillip Vian set out from Alexandria on 20th March to fight through a fast convoy of four ships including the Fleet auxiliary *Breconshire*, which had made several successful runs to

Malta. The convoy was loaded with 26,000 tons of supplies urgently required by the besieged island.

The convoy escort and covering force consisted of four cruisers and ten destroyers and were joined later from Malta by the Force K cruiser *Penelope* and the *Legion*. Rear Admiral Vian's flagship was the *Cleopatra*; his previous flagship, *Naiad*, had been torpedoed on 11th March when returning from an abortive attempt to intercept two Italian escorted convoys to North Africa. Most of *Naiad*'s ship's company were saved and included the London RNVR anti-aircraft unit who had been sunk in their previous ship *Curlew* during the Norwegian campaign in 1940.

Admiral Vian's force and convoy were intercepted by units of the Italian fleet, one battleship, three cruisers and seven destroyers at 1500 on 22nd March in the Gulf of Sirte. The four-hour engagement that followed became known as the Second Battle of Sirte and a classic naval action where light cruisers and destroyers, using smoke and torpedo attacks, held off a superior force. The result of the battle was that Admiral Iachino in his flagship, the battleship *Littorio*, and his cruisers damaged four of the British covering force ships and prevented the convoy arriving at Malta under cover of the night. The Axis air forces were then able to sink two of the convoy ships; the other two were so badly damaged that less than 6,000 tons was unloaded or later salvaged from the original 26,000 tons that set out from Alexandria.

Official reports on the action with some reluctance acknowledged: 'The Italian tactics did delay the convoy which was consequently exposed to further attacks from the air next day before entering harbour; to this extent the Italian manoeuvres succeeded.'

The following account of the battle comes from the narrative written by the gun-layer of 'Y' gun on *Legion*'s quarter-deck, Able Seaman Eric Smith:

We joined up with Vian's force on the 22nd and during the afternoon Savoia torpedo bombers came into attack. They were beaten off with only slight damage to our ships. At 1427, Captain Bush, *Euryalus*, reported to the Admiral in *Cleopatra* that enemy ships had been sighted to the north-east. The convoy and close escorts turned south-west, whilst the cruisers and destroyers closed the enemy fleet making smoke the while to screen the convoy from the Italian ships. The convoy was again strafed by Ju88's and the close escorts had a hell of a job holding them off. Like *Penelope*, *Legion* had not received a copy of the Admiral's intention for battle and on joining the area we joined Captain Poland's division of

Mediterranean 1941. *Ark Royal* with *Fury* as rescue destroyer. *Nelson* in background.

(*Centre*) Battleship *Nelson*.

(*Bottom*) Mediterranean 1941. Italian bombs mask convoy ships.

1941. A downed Italian bomber.

1941. *Firedrake* with Italian bomb damage being chec by the fleet returning to Gibraltar.

Mauritius on the East Indie station.

destroyers. At 1640 the whole Italian force came into sight to the north-east. It consisted of the battleship *Littorio*, one heavy cruiser, two light cruisers and four destroyers. The 5.25" guns of our cruisers and the 4" and 4.7" of our destroyers were up against the might of the enemy's 15", 8" and 6" armament. Vian's cruisers opened fire at extreme range whilst the destroyers were laying a smoke screen between them and the convoy. *Cleopatra* was hit by a 6" shell from the *Banda Nere* killing 15 bridge personnel. *Littorio* opened up with her 15" and splinters hit the *Euryalus*. At about 1800 the cruisers were under air attack and at 1850 the Admiral turned into the smoke screen followed by the other cruisers. The enemy's 15" guns could be heard and shell splashes could be seen all around the ships. *Havock* received a near miss from one of the 15" shells which damaged a boiler and killed two officers and five ratings. She was sent to join the convoy. *Sikh*, *Hero* and *Lively* opened fire on the *Littorio* but the range was too great and the smoke prevented them seeing the enemy. The Italians were gaining on the convoy but by this time the weather was deteriorating.

At 1815 the cruisers and destroyers were ordered to attack the Italians with torpedoes using smoke cover. We were about eight miles from the enemy on parallel tracks. *Sikh* made a complete turn to lay a new smoke screen between us and the enemy and then 10 minutes later turned south-west. We were now in position to launch our torpedo attack. *Jervis*, *Kipling*, *Kingston* and *Legion* now turned west to bring our ships in line abreast. Speed was increased and all destroyers opened fire, we in *Legion* holding our fire until we were within 4,000 yards from the targets. I remember looking through my gun-layer's telescope during the action and we seemed to be right alongside the battleship.

At about 1850 all four of the enemy's larger ships came into view and Vian's cruisers kept up their fire on the enemy for some 20 minutes whilst we were carrying out our first torpedo attack. The range was now under three miles. At this moment some Savoia torpedo bombers chose to launch an attack and we had to turn away to miss the tracks of their torpedoes. This delayed our strike, but all the destroyers again turned into line abreast in order to pursue attack. Eventually the range was reduced and the second enemy ship in line made smoke and turned away from us. *Legion* being last in line could not see the rest of the division for smoke (they had fired 25 torpedoes) and on coming out of the smoke we were only 2,000 yards from the enemy. We got all our torpedoes away without seeing what damage if any had been done to the Italians. *Kingston* had been hit by a 15" shell which passed through the ship and exploded outside. The upper-deck, pom-pom, oerlikon and searchlight supports were badly hit and one officer and twelve ratings were killed. Shortly after this the *Littorio* was seen to have a fire aft from a shell hit and more hits were seen as she withdrew. . .

As the enemy ships turned away for home, the British ships regrouped and steamed to rejoin the convoy ten miles distant. . . In growing dark-

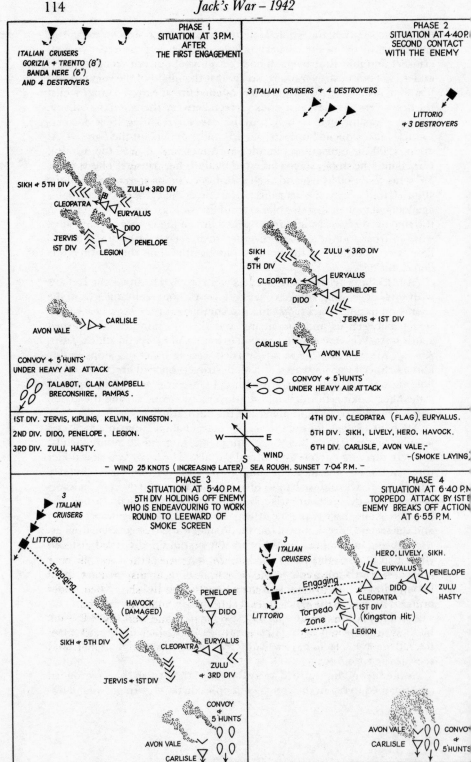

PHASE 1
SITUATION AT 3 P.M.
AFTER
THE FIRST ENGAGEMENT

ITALIAN CRUISERS
GORIZIA & TRENTO (8")
BANDA NERE (6")
AND 4 DESTROYERS

SIKH & 5TH DIV

ZULU & 3RD DIV

CLEOPATRA

EURYALUS

DIDO

JERVIS
1ST DIV

PENELOPE

LEGION

AVON VALE   CARLISLE

CONVOY & 5 HUNTS
UNDER HEAVY AIR ATTACK

TALABOT, CLAN CAMPBELL
BRECONSHIRE, PAMPAS.

PHASE 2
SITUATION AT 4·40 P.
SECOND CONTACT
WITH THE ENEMY

3 ITALIAN CRUISERS & 4 DESTROYERS

LITTORIO
& 3 DESTROYERS

SIKH
&
5TH DIV

ZULU & 3RD DIV

CLEOPATRA

EURYALUS

DIDO

PENELOPE

JERVIS & 1ST DIV

CARLISLE

AVON VALE

CONVOY & 5 HUNTS
UNDER HEAVY AIR ATTACK

1ST DIV. JERVIS, KIPLING, KELVIN, KINGSTON.

2ND DIV. DIDO, PENELOPE, LEGION.

3RD DIV. ZULU, HASTY.

N
W   E
S   WIND

4TH DIV. CLEOPATRA (FLAG), EURYALUS.

5TH DIV. SIKH, LIVELY, HERO, HAVOCK.

6TH DIV. CARLISLE, AVON VALE,·
–(SMOKE LAYING

– WIND 25 KNOTS (INCREASING LATER)   SEA ROUGH. SUNSET 7·04 P.M. –

PHASE 3
SITUATION AT 5·40 P.M.
5TH DIV HOLDING OFF ENEMY
WHO IS ENDEAVOURING TO WORK
ROUND TO LEEWARD OF
SMOKE SCREEN

3
ITALIAN
CRUISERS

LITTORIO

Engaging

HAVOCK
(DAMAGED)

PENELOPE

DIDO

SIKH & 5TH DIV

CLEOPATRA

EURYALUS

JERVIS & 1ST DIV

ZULU
& 3RD DIV

CONVOY
&
5 HUNTS

AVON VALE

CARLISLE

PHASE 4
SITUATION AT 6·40 P.M
TORPEDO ATTACK BY 1ST
ENEMY BREAKS OFF ACTION
AT 6·55 P.M.

3
ITALIAN
CRUISERS

HERO, LIVELY, SIKH.

EURYALUS

PENELOPE

Engaging

DIDO

ZULU

CLEOPATRA

HASTY

LITTORIO

Torpedo
Zone

1ST DIV
(Kingston Hit)

LEGION

AVON VALE

CARLISLE

CONVOY
&
5 HUNTS

The Second Battle of Sirte

ness the Admiral decided that he could not refuel or ammunition at Malta and withdrew his forces and returned to Alexandria. . . .

The convoy reassembled on route for Malta with *Glen Campbell*, slowest of the four ships tailing astern. *Carlisle* (anti-aircraft cruiser) and the Hunt class destroyers formed the close escort with *Penelope* and *Legion* leading with the damaged *Havock* and *Kingston* on either flank. At 1000 *Pampas* was hit by two bombs that did not explode. *Talabot* was not so lucky and was hit and disabled and taken in tow by *Penelope*. . . .

One Ju88 came suddenly out of the sun at our stern and dropped a stick of bombs which straddled us, almost alongside my Y gun mounting. One engine was damaged also the feed water system to the boilers. We were only twenty miles from harbour . . . so we shaped a course for Marsaxlokk on one engine. . .

There we stayed for two days while repair work was done to the feed system sufficient to risk steaming to the dockyard. We were of course attacked by bombers most of the way. We made it into Grand Harbour and secured alongside prior to de-ammunitioning and going into dock. . . . That night and all through the following morning Malta dockyard was subjected to the most fearful bombing up to that time. On the afternoon of 26th March, having beaten off earlier attacks, the enemy struck yet again and we were hit in the forward magazine and there was a violent explosion. *Legion* quickly went down by her bows until her forefoot touched bottom. The order to 'abandon ship' was given but failed to reach one of the gun crews and they had to swim for it. We lost eight killed and a few wounded who were later hospitalised. Most of the dead were members of the damage control party, who were down below, stokers and torpedo-men. One of our asdic operators, Jock Warwick, who had been a boy with me at *Ganges* was in a bad way, pinned by his legs. Commander Jessel who had been wounded in the heel endeavoured to reach him and support him but was unable to do so. By now the ship was sinking slowly and poor Jock drowned.

The ship gradually disappeared; those of us who had survived stood around on the jetty, sad and forlorn, hardly able to realize that we had lost our home of the past 17 months. The *Legion* had been a happy and efficient ship. The hostilities only ratings who had joined as 'Greenhorns', in 17 action-packed months had become battle-hardened veterans. Commander Jessel, our captain, was one of the finest officers I have ever served, always cool and calm under fire, an inspiration to all of us who from time to time watched him handle his ship when under attack. He enjoyed the greatest respect from all who served with him. . . .

Later that afternoon we mustered on the jetty and were given £1 each by 'Jimmy the One' who shook hands with us as we were paid (from RNBT funds I believe), as did the few other officers who were there and we were told to go ashore for the night and report back to the jetty the following morning. So, away went Spike, Scoop and myself together with a few other of our messmates, booked ourselves a bed each, and then proceeded to give a sailor's farewell to the Gut. The following morning, Spike who had been foraging around where we had been sunk waved to us excitedly. He had found the three photographs, water stained, but otherwise OK washed up on shore with other debris. The photograph that we had taken in Alexandria months earlier. [See facing p.129] How they had appeared from our separate 'ditty boxes' is still a mystery. . . .

We were detailed off for different ships and split up. Scoop went to a submarine for passage home, Spike and I went to the *Aurora* which had just come out of dry-dock only partly patched up, some went to the *Penelope* and others with our captain to the *Havock* . . . *Havock* foundered off the North African coast and her survivors including Commander Jessel were taken prisoner by the Vichy French. . . .

Penelope was continually attacked by aircraft all the way to Gibraltar and had so many shrapnel holes in her funnels and sides that she became known as HMS *Pepperpot* . . . In *Aurora* we were luckier. We beat off two air attacks but were hit in the bows by one aerial torpedo that did little damage; the rest of the trip was without incident. At Gibraltar we survivors were kitted out with a basic kit at the base HMS *Cormorant* and then lent a hand to re-ammunition ship, we then sailed for Liverpool where *Aurora* was to dock. We arrived early in an evening and we 'passengers' were allowed ashore before being warned to be at Lime Street station by 2300. Most of us had a bit of cash left and we spent a couple of hours remaining to us in the various pubs around Lime Street. No one wanted to be adrift, we reached London at 0500 on Easter Monday morning to find the Underground entrance locked so had to wait around for an hour until it opened. We then made our way to the Union Jack club in Waterloo Road for breakfast and from there on to HMS *Pembroke* at Chatham where we received the remainder of our kit replacements, were paid, then were sent off on 14 days' survivors leave.

The situation in the Pacific and Indian oceans was grave; the Japanese fleet had gained a number of naval victories. In the Battle of the Java Sea against a force of British, Dutch and American ships under the command of a Dutch Admiral the cruiser *Exeter* was one of the several Allied ships sunk. *Exeter* still had many in her ship's company who were in the ship for over four years and had taken part in December 1939 in the Battle of the River Plate.

In the Atlantic, the Americans continued to suffer horrendous losses of merchant ships from the guns and torpedoes of U-boats operating in the West Atlantic.

Convoys to northern Russia, which had commenced in August 1941, had up to March 1942 operated relatively unopposed by the enemy; one ship had been sunk out of 110 sailed in twelve outward-bound convoys and again one in the returning convoys of empty ships. The greatest danger was the round the clock darkness, ice, snow, hurricane winds and mountainous seas which took their toll of men, losses made more poignant when through a failure of drill or a mistake. Tom Guard remembers one incident when *Fury* was covering a Russian convoy;

> We were with the *Victorious* in terrible weather and a torpedo watchman was swept off the stern. His name was Gordie Boyes and his 'oppo' reported 'Boyes overboard!' There was some confusion on the bridge because they thought that a buoy had gone. Of course man overboard should have been the report.

Outward-bound to Russia, Convoy PQ13 of nineteen ships departed from Iceland on 21st March 1942. The escort consisted of the fleet destroyers *Fury* and *Eclipse*, one Hunt class destroyer *Lamerton*, three armed trawlers which were to be handed over to the Russian fleet and two rescue trawlers. The Fiji class cruiser *Trinidad* with a main armament of twelve 6" guns in four turrets escorted by the destroyer *Oribi* formed the close cruiser support.

On the fourth day out the convoy ran into a NE gale of tremendous ferocity and over the next 72 hours the convoy became scattered over a distance of 150 miles. As the gale blew itself out and in very poor visibility the captain of the *Fury* as senior officer of the escort from his bridge searched in vain for a sight of his charges. On the 27th *Trinidad* arrived in the area, reinforced by her flagship, the cruiser *Nigeria*, to help in the search for and rounding up of the deeply laden and scattered merchant ships. While this was going on a German reconnaissance BV 138 aircraft sighted the disorganised convoy and then followed for the rest of the daylight hours, air attacks on the unprotected merchant ships by Ju88's of the 111 Bomber Group 3. By the evening two ships, *Raceland* and *Empire Ranger*, had been sunk.

Fury ordered the trawler *Blackfly* to rescue the survivors but in the fog banks and rough seas she failed to find any. On the evening of the next day, 28th March, the convoy ships had been marshalled into two untidy groups but at the same time three German destroyers ordered out from Kirkenes to intercept PQ13, sighted a boatload of survivors from the *Empire Ranger* which were picked up by one of the destroyers. Shortly afterwards another of the German ships, the *Z26*, found a convoy straggler, the SS *Bateau*, and after taking off the crew sank the freighter by gunfire and torpedo.

In the continuing bad visibility made worse by the dense banks of fog the German destroyers, the *Z24, 25* and *26* searched for the main body of the convoy. *Trinidad* with *Fury* steaming east at 20 knots to round up a group of four ships at 0843 hours ran into the German ships. In the mêlée that followed the cruiser scored gun hits on the *Z26*, then tried to finish off the destroyer with torpedoes but had the misfortune to be hit by one of her own rogue torpedoes and came to a standstill badly damaged. *Fury* dashed off into the fog in pursuit of the *Z26* which was seen to be on fire aft. In the fog *Fury* charged into the other group of eight merchantmen and the *Eclipse*; in the confusing fracas that followed *Fury* twice opened fire on the *Eclipse* but fortunately caused no damage. Then *Eclipse* sighted the damaged *Z26* and engaged while *Fury* returned to standby and assist *Trinidad*. *Eclipse*'s guns and torpedoes brought the larger German to a stop and sinking and as she prepared to finish her off with her last torpedo the *Z24* and *25* appeared on the scene and drove off the British ship. The conditions were appalling; huge freezing seas crashed over the destroyer bow's submerging forward guns and swept the bridges of the combatants. As *Eclipse* retired at top speed into the shelter of a fog bank she was hit twice above the waterline but suffered no vital damage.

Z24 and *25* turned to their sinking consort, took off 96 survivors and returned to Kirkenes. *Trinidad*, with a bad list and managing only to make 10 knots, with *Fury* in company limped into Kola inlet on the 30th, while the convoy in two loosely formed groups straggled into port running the gauntlet of a group of four U-boats waiting off the port approaches. Two freighters, the USA ship *Effingham* (6,241 tons) and the British ship *Induna* (5,086 tons) were sunk. The convoy of nineteen ships that had set out from Iceland lost five ships, which was the heaviest loss suffered by a convoy to Russia up to that date.

In *Fury* one of the characters of the forward mess-decks was a London Cockney radar operator who answered to the name 'Spiv' Francis. Spiv recorded in verse much of the ship's daily incidents and fragments of what had occurred in action with the enemy. The battle of 29th March did not escape his pen, or the shells fired at *Eclipse* and the antics of a sub-lieutenant who had not established a rapport with the men he commanded:

Our Subby
One day whilst out on convoy bound
Three German ships our lookouts found
'Action Stations' then was sounded
On what took place our story's founded.

Subby was in charge of 'B' gun
Which was manned to fight the Hun
But vision now was very poor
Target hidden! How could they score?.

But Subby puffed with ambition
Failed to grasp this new position
'Fire now!' he cried though ships were hid
But crew did not do as they were bid.

Subby stormed at this rebuff
'Fire now!' he cried (this in a huff)
Still the crew held back their fire
Despite our Subby's rising ire.

Layer turned about and said
'Snow so thick, can't see ship's head'
'A direct order to you! Fire!'
Said Subby, temper rising higher.

Then on the ocean just ahead
A friendly ship was seen instead
Layer realised that this was silly
So fired that gun just willy-nilly.

'At last! At last!' our Subby screamed
'Has come to pass that which I dreamed
'Always it's been my desire
'To hear gun bang when I say "Fire!".'

Fury was fated to be one of the escort for the first homeward-bound convoy to be the focus of the increasing enemy attacks on the sea supply line to Russia. Convoy QP10, sixteen ships, sailed from Murmansk on 10th April with an escort of seven destroyers, four minesweepers and two trawlers. The convoy was under heavy attacks from the air and U-boats throughout the first three days of passage. The ships SS *Empire Cooper* and SS *Harpalion* were sunk by Ju88's of the 111 Coastal Group 30 and SS *El Occidente* and *Kiev* by U-boat *U-435*. The escorts and convoy ships shot down six German aircraft. Tom Guard, able seaman, remembers:

> The Harrison cargo boat *Harpalion* was put out of action – her rudder damaged – and we rescued all the crew who came across in a lifeboat and heavily bombed all the way. I remember at the time I thought this was very unsporting!

By the end of July 1942 the Americans had at last introduced a full convoy system and shipping losses in the West Atlantic were beginning to go down. In Africa and the Mediterranean the Axis land forces had been halted at El Alamein but Tobruk, garrisoned mainly by South African troops, had surrendered. In June a supply convoy of six ships set out from Gibraltar with a massive escort, Operation Harpoon, to bring supplies to Malta. Only two merchant ships managed to survive the strong opposition by the enemy air, submarine and surface forces.

A complementary convoy of eleven ships, Operation *Vigorous*, set out from Alexandria. One merchant ship and several ships of the strong escort were sunk and the entire force had to retreat back to Alexandria in the face of heavy air attacks and the approach of the main Italian fleet of capital ships. The joint operations to fight through seventeen supply ships to the island fortress only succeeded in getting two ships into Grand Harbour, Malta.

The old anti-aircraft cruiser *Coventry* formed part of the large escort force in the Vigorous operation, recalled by Able Seaman George Sims:

> We took on extra ammunition and 200 bags of mail. One of the mail bags burst and those of us gathering up the letters noticed that they all bore Malta addresses. The ship's company were thus informed of the impending operation. We veterans of the Mediterranean hoped that our extra oerlikons would make a big difference. . . . By evening we were again at sea with three merchantmen on the starboard beam and destroyers busily patrolling. Next day was sunny and pleasant, all the more so because we were covered by two RAF fighters. Towards evening however, RDF reported enemy aircraft and the alarm rattlers brought us to action stations. RDF reported more closing aircraft formations though our spotters scanned the skies in vain, the scream of wind through the dive bombers' rigging and the shriek of falling bombs announced the attack. We were in the act of turning to port when three Ju88's placed a stick of bombs either side of us. Running into a welter of spray and steel splinters, we were lucky in having no casualties. Then we noticed something wrong with the *City of Calcutta*; a bomb had damaged her so she had to run into Tobruk. . . .
>
> That night we heard the engines of the Luftwaffe, shortly after their flares were dropping into the sea to illuminate where we were to pass, we did not oblige by opening fire. . . Next morning the seas were rising and we hoped that a storm would develop. . . . From tea time onwards we meet seven attacks from large groups of Ju87's and Ju88's. We had never known such continuous shooting. Now and then a stick of bombs fell close from a direct attack, but the Luftwaffe concentrated on the merchantmen and at 6pm *Bhutan* was sunk. *Potaro*, damaged shortly after-

wards, was able to keep up with us. We saw two corvettes hastening to pick up *Bhutan*'s survivors . . . just before sunset *Pakenham* just avoided a torpedo. A broadcast made minutes later informed us that a group of six enemy torpedo-boats escorted by fighter air-craft had been reported. . . Darkness was welcome though the Luftwaffe again made an unsuccessful search with flares.

We were not told that Admiral Iachino had left that afternoon from Taranto with the battleships *Littorio* and *Vittorio Veneto*, the 8″ cruisers *Gorizia* and *Trento*, the 6″ cruisers *Garibaldi* and *Duca d'Aosta* and twelve destroyers. The fleet was estimated to intercept the convoy at 9 am next morning. At the time we knew nothing of this danger. . .

Cruising through the night we relaxed from the day's alarms and the turning back was noticed by very few of the ship's company. Just afterwards the guns' crews heard a muffled explosion. Our cruiser *Newcastle* had been torpedoed by an enemy motor boat. Fortunately the damage could be made good and she stayed with the convoy. Before the end of the middle watch came another violent shock through the water accompanied by a louder explosion. A torpedo boat had sunk the destroyer *Hardy* . . . grey dawn broke the night sky and the light grew stronger. Near breakfast time the convoy made another reverse turn. Admiral Vian was making renewed attempts to reach Malta. Soon the RDF began its reports of enemy aircraft. The Luftwaffe made constant attacks on all classes of ships in the convoy and escort. Where to store the empty brass propellant cases was becoming a problem. . .

In *Coventry* we noticed another change of course at mid-morning. Once again we had turned east as Admiral Vian saw no prospect of getting his convoy past the oncoming Italians. If the morning air attacks had been persistent, those in the afternoon threatened to be overwhelming. Convoy and escorts were constantly taking avoiding action as bomb loads dropped towards them and all the time at least one escort was shooting. At half past three we saw the destroyer *Airedale* hit by an avalanche of bombs which sank her . . . the battle raged on and at 6pm the destroyer *Nestor* was hit . . . most ships had expended 75% of their ammunition and were using up the remainder fast. Whilst we continued back to Alexandria air attacks were unrelenting. There was one moment of satisfaction when an approaching torpedo bomber was converted into a harmless cloud of smoke. . .

Dusk was welcome, and darkness doubly so. Darkness brought defence stations and recuperation after the day's alarms. We had survived the worst period of constant bombing to date, but it was a new and depressing experience to be turned back by the enemy. Halfway through the middle watch two explosions announced further disaster. A submarine had torpedoed the cruiser *Hermione* which sank in twenty minutes. Only 88 survivors were picked up.

By morning light we were almost within RAF protection. There was the melancholy necessity of scuttling the Australian destroyer *Nestor*.

Soon we had RAF cover and reached Alexandria Harbour by evening. It was 16th June. Out of seventeen ships leaving Gibraltar and Alexandria with stores for Malta, only two had reached the island. . .

The official historian verdict of the Vigorous operation was, 'The enemy's success was undeniable and no further attempt was made to run a convoy from Egypt until the Army had driven the Axis forces out of Libya.'

The Axis land forces were held up at El Alamein, a mere 60 miles from the Mediterranean Fleet base, Alexandria. Day and night air raids on the port and installations by bomb and land mine were frequent by German and Italian squadrons flying from forward desert airfields. Naval staff and stores had moved east and been dispersed along the canal zone, the fleet destroyer depot ship *Woolwich* and six destroyers with the fleet repair ship *Resource* had sailed south through the Suez canal. The ships of the fleet had scattered to Port Said and Haifa, the 1st Submarine Flotilla was now based on Beirut. The 14,500 ton submarine repair and depot ship *Medway* was to sail on 29th June.

Sam Connor, ERA 4th class, had been in *Medway* since March 1941, on a recent evening run ashore he had witnessed the aftermath of an explosion of a land mine in Sister street, the heart of the Red Light district close to the dockyard:

> The darkness was filled with the dust of collapsed buildings and the cries and screams of the injured and men and women trapped in the wreckage of cafés, brothels and clubs. The street was blocked with overturned trams, gharris, parts of horses and human bodies were everywhere. There was a terrible panic and confusion for a long time.

Medway got clear of Alexandria, bound for Beirut but off Port Said the great ship was torpedoed and sunk by *U-372*. The U-boat commander believed that he had sunk a transport ship and it was some time before the enemy knew of the true value of the sinking. The depot ship in addition to all her special equipment and facilities for maintaining submarines contained the entire torpedo replenishment stocks for the East Mediterranean-based submarines and the sinking marked the nadir of the East Mediterranean Fleet fortunes. Sam Connor, ERA:

> The ship went down fast and I had to swim for it, most of us got clear, there were not many casualties. One of the destroyers picked me up and I was taken to Haifa.

The Home Fleet was also approaching its own nadir of shame, the dispersal of the largest convoy to Murmansk which resulted in only eleven ships out of a total of 36 reaching north Russia ports. Convoy PQ17 made up from 36 mainly American freighters set out from Iceland on 27th June. The convoy had a strong escort, and its passage was protected by a mixed British and American cruiser squadron and the Home Fleet, with the Commander-in-Chief in his flagship, the battleship *Duke of York*. For the first few days up to 4th July the convoy sailed through calm seas and scattered banks of dense and protective fog banks. It had been heavily attacked by torpedo bombers and U-boats, but only four ships had been sunk and there were confident expectations that the convoy would get through without serious losses.

Through an error of judgement and faulty intelligence interpretation, Admiralty in London, thousands of miles from the operational area, gave orders over the head of the Home Fleet Commander-in-Chief direct to the escort and cruiser squadron commanders to withdraw from the convoy and to concentrate ready to meet a threat of attack by the German battleship *Tirpitz* wrongly believed to be at sea. At 2215, 4th July, American Independence Day, the convoy ships were ordered to scatter and make their separate ways to Russian ports. From that moment and over the next few days of round the clock Arctic daylight the unprotected ships were massacred by German aircraft and U-boats. Only eleven ships survived; the last made port on 29th July.

The battleship *Tirpitz* in company with the pocket battleship *Von Scheer*, the heavy cruiser *Hipper* and six destroyers did sail the day after the convoy was ordered to scatter, but returned to Altenfiord after a few hours, leaving the convoy ships to the aircraft and U-boats.

Men of the British escort ships were ignorant of the reasons why their ships left the convoy and it was to be many weeks before they became aware of the fate of the ships they had abandoned and it would be years before they would know why the disaster had occurred. Convoy PQ17 was to have long term repercussions in the relationships between the American and British allies and the Fleet commanders.

Fury was one of the destroyer escorts and for a long time the only memory of the convoy that stood out from the usual air and U-boat actions that were the norm on Russian convoys was the first torpedo bomber attack that developed on 2nd July. *Fury* shot down one of the

He115's; the damaged aircraft remained afloat and as the destroyer raced to rescue and capture the aircrew another seaplane dropped alongside the wreckage, plucked out the airmen and took off again. Tom Guard wrote:

> One enemy plane was shot down and did not sink immediately and the two man crew launched their dinghy. We and another destroyer ahead of us were racing to the plane and firing when another seaplane landed beside the damaged one, took the crew on board and flew off. I know most of us said, 'Bloody good luck to 'em'. I have a picture which I took.

Not every ship of the fleets in Home and Overseas Commands was having an arduous war; there were cruisers patrolling the great ocean wastes seeking enemy commerce raiders, their supply ships and protecting long haul troop convoys and their routes. The main enemy of their ship companies was boredom and sometimes outdated and uncompromising discipline norms of the men in command.

Frobisher, a heavy cruiser of the Hawkins class armed with seven 7.5 guns, had been built during World War One. She was being extensively refitted soon after the outbreak of war in 1939 and it wasn't until January 1942 that the cruiser was recommissioned. Her commanding officer was Captain J.F.W. Mudford, a torpedo and mining specialist, and *Frobisher* was his first wartime sea command. His previous war appointments were at the torpedo and mine training establishment HMS *Vernon* and at the Admiralty. Now after 2¼ years of war he came to his command and for his first contact with reservists, RNVR, volunteer and conscripted hostility only ratings. Many of his officers were RNVR or RNR. He had little appreciation that many of those men had considerable seagoing and action experience in a great range of ships and operations in home and overseas waters.

Frank Risdon was an RNVR who had seen much action in Norway and the Mediterranean and painted a word picture of his new commanding officer:

> *Frobisher* was commanded by Captain Mudford RN, a naval officer of long experience and who was mature in years, who represented the old school of naval discipline, a martinet in the view of many, but nevertheless a first class officer . . . he was a large handsome man of commanding presence and he had very mixed feelings as he surveyed his ship's company on the day of commissioning, but he was determined to bring the ship to the peak of efficiency without delay and embarked on an intensive series

of drills, manoeuvres, immediately after leaving harbour and these continued on the long voyage to round the Cape.

The cruiser had completed her work-up period in April and departed from Plymouth to join the escort of a large convoy to Cape Town via Freetown. Frank Risdon continues:

> The ship now settled down to a routine of patrol and escort duties in the Indian ocean, mostly between Mombasa and Colombo, but also occasionally calling at Durban and the beautiful islands of this vast ocean paradise. For many onboard, who had already lived through two years of hard fought campaigns in Norway, Greece, Malta and Crete, the tranquillity of this cerulean blue sea disturbed only by the occasional shark and enormous blackfish should have a welcome relief, but HMS *Frobisher* was not a happy ship. The reason for this was not easy to define, but it could have been a combination of a number of factors which when brought together produced a cumulative effect.
>
> Firstly there was the unrelenting discipline of Captain Mudford which filtered down through the various levels of command of the officers, petty officers to the lower deck. Secondly, the shore leave attractions to the sailor of ports like Mombasa were very limited, quite unlike the hospitality extended to the officers by the colonial residents of Kenya and this was noticed and resented. This treatment was in marked contrast to the reception given to the sailors on the few occasions when the ship called at Durban where always the whole ship's company was fêted by the generous people of South Africa. . .
>
> There was also a growing awareness of a deep gulf in social status between officers and men and whilst division is essential to maintain discipline there was an increasingly changed attitude as more and more civilians swelled the numbers of the fleet. Finally, and this was probably a more powerful influence than anything else, the ship was not seeing action, as one idyllic voyage followed another.

The cruiser received orders to proceed to Mauritius, Port Louis to arrive on the 27th July.

> The commander prepared an extensive programme of 'spit and polish' operations with the first lieutenant and large sections of the ship's company were engaged in cleaning, scrubbing, painting, wire brushing, holystoning, polishing and generally bringing the ship to a state of immaculate pre-war perfection. Even the brasswork on the upper-deck was polished [forbidden in wartime] to ensure that no blemish marred the overall effect . . . the Royal Marine band rehearsed their extensive repertoire and the Royal Marine Guard of Honour drilled to perfection.

The whole ship's company worked hard and long under the tropical sun
. . . and even the commander was at last satisfied. . . .

But there was one area which still caused dissatisfaction to the higher
command and that was the state of the jetty at the landing stage in Port
Louis whence the Governor would embark and the commander decided
to do something about it. The jetty was undoubtedly in a parlous state by
Navy standards; it was battered, untidy and dirty. There could be no
doubt that some of the untarnished effect on the various ceremonies
would be spoilt by the bad impression at the departure point to all the
forthcoming occasions. The commander therefore had a working party
mustered with buckets, scrubbers and other cleaning appurtenances and
with a duty petty officer in charge was detailed to proceed ashore to clean
up.

This was a mistake. The ship's company had worked long and hard to
bring *Frobisher* to pre-war standards and had reached a point where they
had 'had enough' and this was the last straw. Amidst much grumbling
and muttering the working party was despatched ashore, where under
the broiling sun they scrubbed down, cleaned and polished the
approaches and the jetty. The jetty was transformed but whether sailors
should have been employed on this exercise is questionable. They were
further humiliated by the presence of laughing and jeering local lay-
abouts who were unused to seeing sailors in this role. The mood of the
working party on return was ugly to say the least and they gave full vent
to their feelings when they eventually arrived between decks and met
their messmates. In hindsight it would have been better to have hired
some locals for a very small sum and to have merely tidied up the jetty.

The governor made an official call on the captain in the late forenoon
to be received by the full ceremonial accorded to his rank–guard and
band. Later in the evening a dance and reception was to be held and
attended by the governor, the island dignitaries and their ladies. The
quarter-deck awning had been spread.

Most men onboard had not experienced a ship's dance before and
despite the fact that only the officers would be attending, there was no
shortage of interest and curiosity in the general arrangements. Bunting
was liberally draped around the quarter-deck and the Chief 'Sparks' was
busy with his various floodlights. As the sun began to move closer to the
horizon, trestle tables were set up and the chief steward began organising
the drinks and buffet. At last all was ready, the band assembled on the
quarter-deck again, the stewards discreetly moved around in their sharp-
ly laundered drill and gradually the officers, resplendent in mess dress
and cummerbunds began to appear on the upper-deck. . .

The guests started to arrive, the men in evening dress and the women
in long gowns. It was a sumptuous sight with the background of purple

hills and twinkling lights ashore, the floodlight quarter-deck was a riot of vivid colour, reflecting the lights of the ladies' gowns and the coloured bunting in sharp contrast to the brilliant white of the officers' uniforms. . .

Little heed was paid to the growing crowd of seamen amidships, who were first attracted by curiosity to see what the visiting women were like and also to witness the ship's dance band at first hand, the men were growing increasingly sullen and resentful at the too obvious gulf between themselves and the officers. They were still mindful of all the work they had put in to make the dance possible, the humiliating experience on the jetty, the general current of discontent grew in direct proportion to the enjoyment on the quarter-deck. . . It was when the party was at its height that the most unexpected diversion occurred. . . A shower of missiles assailed the startled guests and officers, temporarily scattering them in all directions and creating untold confusion. The missiles were composed of rather odorous potatoes, turnips, yams and other vegetables; it was obvious that the 'spud locker' on the upper-deck had been raided. . . Just as suddenly as the attack had started out of the gloom and midship semi-darkness so it subsided and officers hurried to reassure their guests and restore order and the band began to play again.

The outburst died away as quickly as it had erupted, but it might not have done so. If an officer had been struck whilst remonstrating with the seamen or charges made on the spot, a chain reaction could have developed leading to a full scale revolt.

The outcome of this incident was that no charges were brought against anyone; only the unfortunate second officer of the day who was a sub-lieutenant RNVR lost three months' seniority. His senior officer, the RN officer of the day, received no recorded penalty. The ship's fair log for the visit to Mauritius on 27th, 28th and 29th July makes no reference to the holding of a reception and dance in the ship. The log has no entries to record a large number of civilians visiting the ship or that it was illuminated and floodlit in an area where Japanese submarines were known to be on patrol. The log book only records that on 28th July HE Governor and family visited the ship and stayed for one hour and a half. The events recorded by F.H. Risdon have been authenticated by other members of the ship's company, officers and ratings. A similar account of the seamen's protest was published in the magazine *Ship's Monthly*.

On 15th August the cruiser was again in Kilindini, Mombasa and warrant number 36 was read, the ship had been in commission for less than eight months. *Frobisher* was gaining a reputation for punishment warrants to match and even exceed the *Mauritius*. It so hap-

pened that *Mauritius* was also in Kilindini; her refit in England had
been completed in March and since then the cruiser had been again
on long ocean patrols followed by stays of many days in harbour.
Perhaps because of the treatment of her sailors by the colonials of
Mombasa, in August warrants 54, 55 and 56 were read. Like
Frobisher, the *Mauritius* had not as yet fired a shot in anger or taken
part in any form of offensive action.

While the men in the cruisers at Kilindini during August fretted with
boredom, frustration and the irritations of peacetime routines and
discipline ships were fighting and men dying in the Far East, Atlantic, the Arctic and the Mediterranean.

From Gibraltar a further effort to resupply Malta was being
attempted. On 10th August a convoy of fourteen merchant ships
entered the straits from the United Kingdom protected by a massive
fleet, two battleships, four aircraft carriers, seven cruisers, 32
destroyers and four corvettes. The entire force and Operational
Pedestal was under the command of Vice Admiral E.N. Syret with his
flag in the battleship *Nelson*. The convoy's progress was strongly
opposed by German and Italian submarines, Italian E-boats and
German and Italian squadrons of bombers and torpedo aircraft. In
the battle which lasted for two days and nights, 11th, 12th and 13th
August, nine of the convoyed merchant ships were sunk, the covering
force and close escort also had severe losses. One aircraft carrier
Eagle was sunk and a second *Indomitable* was badly damaged. Two
cruisers, *Cairo* and *Manchester* were so badly damaged that they had
to be sunk, two other cruisers, *Nigeria* and *Kenya*, were also damaged
but succeeded in getting back to Gibraltar. The destroyer *Foresight*
was sunk.

The old anti-aircraft cruiser *Cairo* had been in Operation *Harpoon*
two months earlier when only two of the convoy ships reached
Malta. In this operation *Cairo*, which led the convoy in its final dash
through the Sicilian narrows with her destroyers, challenged and
fought a strong Italian squadron of two cruisers and five destroyers.
She had been hit several times by Italian cruiser shells, and had suffered dead and wounded. Now with her sinking the third of the four
anti-aircraft cruisers which had commissioned in 1939 with units of
London RNVR gunners had been sunk.

Shipwright artificer George Male's action station was with the
action repair party aft in the wardroom flat, the same station and
party he was with when they repaired shell damage in the stern dur-

Chipping ice off 'A' gun and
...nting during Russian convoy
...s.

voy PQ17. Escort destroyers
...ng the convoy, 4th July 1942.

...a. Ships company with some
...ssian alongside the ship.

Fury.

Legion. Alexandria 1941,
photograph taken of 'Scoo[
'Spike' and 'Smudge' in 'Si[
street. Photograph recove[
after the *Legion* was sunk i[
Malta on the 6th March, 19[

(*Left*) *Mauritius* escorting [
troopship convoy in the In[
Ocean, 1942.

(*Below*) *Mauritius.* Aband[
ship exercise in Manza ba[
East Africa.

ing the Operation *Harpoon* battle. He wrote of the moment that *Cairo* received her mortal damage,

At approximately 1930 there was a lull; our action station was in the after flat. I said to the chief shipwright, if I could get a breath of fresh air after being below so long, he said yes, don't be long and if anything starts again, be right back. It was only just at the top of a ladder by the after screen.

I was just inhaling some lovely fresh air looking at the *Nigeria* on our port side when all of a sudden, under a cloud of smoke, spray and flash she got a fish midships. I immediately took a dive down the ladder to my action station; as I hit the deck, it was just as if, with a terrible explosion, we had jumped a hurdle or other. It had blown off our stern (including the steering gear etc, wiping out Y gun and crew 'Royals' and the after action station crew mainly CPO stokers and tiffeys. It was decided that it was useless to try anything in these conditions and we were sinking fast – so we were taken off by the *Wilton*, a Hunt class destroyer. She now had a light cruiser's wartime crew plus her own Hunt class complement in one little ship. Where you got aboard and stood, you stayed for three days; there was not an inch of room to move. I'm sure that it was the most marvellous trip I have ever had in my life. Got to Gib: put aboard the *Rodney* and took passage home to Rosyth which to me was equivalent to a round the world on the *Queen Mary*; it was de-luxe!

Cairo had been in action since the early east coast convoys in 1939, the Norwegian campaign, then to Russia, Atlantic convoys and Mediterranean convoys. In the 2½ years she had two captains and while they had not lowered their standards of naval discipline only 45 warrants had been read, a record that contrasted strongly with ships of similar complement numbers, which had not seen action.

After the tragic débâcle of Convoy PQ17 in July the Admiralty held back from sending another convoy through to Murmansk in the summer period of 24 hour perpetual daylight, but eventually under overwhelming political pressure, 40 ships had been loaded and made ready to sail in Convoy PQ18. The convoy sailed on 2nd September with a very large close escort of an anti-aircraft cruiser, two special anti-aircraft ships, an escort aircraft carrier, 26 destroyers, minesweepers and corvettes. The destroyers had been organised into three fighting destroyer escort units with special provision of extra tankers in the convoy to refuel. Rear Admiral R. Burnett was in overall command of the escort with his flag in the AA cruiser *Scylla*.

The Germans, with confidence high after the massacre of PQ17 but without understanding why the escort had been withdrawn, began ferocious U-boat and massed bomb and airborne torpedo attacks on the convoy during the 13th and from then until the convoy's arrival at Murmansk, 13 ships were sunk.

Leading Signalman Jack French served in the 5,150 ton anti-aircraft ship *Alynbank*. The ship was armed with eight 4″ high angle guns, eight 2-pounders and six 20mm guns. With her sister ship her station was within the convoy columns.

Jack French describes the sinking of the American freighter *Mary Luckenbach*;

> A flashing light from a merchant ship in the column to starboard of us diverted our attention from the *Scylla*. She asked us if, in view of her having a cargo of 4,000 tons of TNT, she could be allowed a position nearer to the centre of the convoy. The captain was on the bridge at the time. 'What ship is that, Signalman French?' 'The *Mary Luckenbach*, sir.' He looked across at the ship, wondering. 'Make a signal to the commodore stating that the *Mary Luckenbach* requests a station towards the centre of the convoy. Give him the details of the ammunition,' and aside, 'I can't see him agreeing to that at this stage.' The reply from the commodore was negative. Events took a macabre turn.
>
> The first air attack came in the afternoon of the 13th. It was by 28 Ju88 bombers in two waves. Thirty minutes later forty plus He111 torpedo bombers, after releasing their torpedoes ahead of the convoy, flew, as an escape route, between the columns of the ships below bridge level.
>
> Eight merchant ships were sunk in the attack, which was bad enough, but added to this was the inevitable strafing of ships by other ships in adjacent columns as they fired on the planes passing through. In my position on the bridge/wireless office telephone, I was in an exposed position, the telephone mounting was shattered by a machine-gun bullet. Fortunately for me the telephone flex had allowed me to be, at that moment, several feet away.
>
> During this attack by torpedo bombers three of the four ships in the ninth column were sunk, leaving *Mary Luckenbach* on her own. The commodore signalled to this sole survivor to take station in our column (the eighth) astern of the leader *Dan-y-Bryn* and ahead of *Virginia Dare*, thus lengthening our column to five ships. The captain said, 'I feel a bit safer, Ridds, with her distanced from us. I'll be in my sea cabin if anything further happens'.
>
> Next day at 1230 twenty Ju88's attacked us from the port side and eight from the starboard, followed at 1300 by a further attack which lasted over an hour. At 1430 we were attacked by 22 He111 torpedo bombers and eighteen Ju88 bombers. During this attack the Heinkels again after dropping their torpedoes ahead, made their escape through the columns of ships. Several hits were scored on them and one belching flame and smoke, losing height, crashed into *Mary Luckenbach*. The effect was

instantaneous. A vivid flash of colour, streaks of red, blue, orange, yellow and green shot into the sky. There was no bang; just a terrible whoosh as though an enormous rocket had suddenly been launched. One moment there was a ship, the next a small patch of smoking debris on the water. The tidal wave caused by the explosion was enormous. The *Virginia Dare* next in line ploughed through the vacant space dipping her bow, all 7,000 tons of her, into the hole, for that is what it looked like, and then rearing up as her stern wallowed deep down, she passed through. We followed, experiencing almost the same effect. I think we, on the bridge, were all struck dumb by the awesome spectacle. We stared amazed. Only the voice of Lieutenant Riddelsdell broke the silence as he spoke into the voice-pipe, 'Watch your head, helmsman, it might be a bit tricky here!'

While Convoy PQ18 and its escort fought a way through the Barents sea to Murmansk, in the blue warmth of the east Mediterranean the last of the anti-aircraft cruisers commissioned in 1939, *Coventry*, with two magnificent tribal class destroyers, *Sikh* and *Zulu*, was sent to senseless destruction. When *Coventry* returned to the Mediterranean in April after her refit in Bombay, the ship's company had been startled by hearing of her future operations being discussed in public and that she was to be part of an operation at Tobruk. The desert port was then in British hands, but now it had been captured by the enemy and lay 270 miles behind the Axis land forces front line at El Alamein. The sea route to Tobruk was dominated by enemy desert airfields and there was no possibility of effective RAF cover or protection and in these circumstances an operation was conceived to capture and hold the port with a force of 500 Royal Marines. During the many months that the Allies held the port it had required a garrison of 30,000!

The planning had been completed before the arrival of the new commander of the Eighth Army, Lieutenant-General B.L. Montgomery. He was informed of the operation a few days before its planned start; when it failed he was highly critical of its whole concept, but had made no move to cancel it.

Operation *Agreement* was common knowledge in the bazaars and cafés of Alexandria; the men in the ships became aware of the total lack of secrecy when dhobymen came hurring inboard with laundry and pressed for immediate payment with great urgency. When questioned, the *fellaheen* told the uneasy sailors, 'Officers' baggage go to the Fleet club, you go to Tobruk', and in fact officers' trunks were going ashore, as they spoke.

It was an operation, described by the lower-deck, as another senior officers' 'honour and glory, shit or bust' operation. It was another foreseeable failure of a kind that the naval staff seemed unable to resist or refuse, and especially in the case of *Agreement* the plan was known in a city crawling with Axis sympathisers and agents.

Coventry sailed on the 12th with the two Tribal destroyers and eight hunt class, the fleet destroyers carrying 350 Royal Marines. A further 150 Marines were embarked in 21 MTB's and ML's which had sailed earlier and were hugging the desert coastline. On the night of the 13th in a strong on shore wind and sea the doomed enterprise met its nemesis. The landing to capture the Tobruk coastal defences was expected; many of the Royal Marines were drowned as the craft overturned in the rough sea, those that got ashore were killed or captured by the waiting fully alert defenders; *Sikh* and *Zulu* caught in searchlight beams were subjected to merciless fire from the shore batteries, *Sikh* damaged and stopped drifted ashore and sank. Those of her crew and the Royal Marines still in the ship not killed or drowned were taken prisoner, half of the MTB and ML flotilla was also sunk.

Next morning *Coventry* waiting to give anti-aircraft cover to the retiring ships was caught by a combined force of German and Italian aircraft. The cruiser was still at defence stations and 'Up Spirits' had been piped. George Sims records the cruiser's end:

The sunshine was brilliant now, and last night's choppy sea subsiding. Most of us shocked by the disaster at Tobruk, overestimated our own security, and were looking forward to dinner. The solemn ceremony of grog issue proceeded. The usual gaiety was absent and there were conversations in low tones about the captain's broadcast. Many doubted that the *Zulu* would be still afloat when we reached the rendezvous. . . .

Defence stations gun crews had been alerted on a radar report that enemy aircraft were in the vicinity. The guns were following director and had a distant snooper in its sights. Able Seaman Sydney Foster noticed this, anticipated action stations and went into the messdeck for a lifebelt which he should have been wearing all the time at sea. . . .

On the bridge the Fight Direction Officer was intent on a Beaufighter that had just broken out of a cloud, he then yelled, 'Enemy aircraft astern', fifteen Ju87's were plummeting down onto *Coventry*, the scream of rigging and the shriek of falling bombs with the roar of engines, galvanised us who started for action stations spurred by the crackle of the oerlikons. Quickly one oerlikon was silenced. Spike Sullivan, scalped by cannon fire from a Stuka, slumped to the deck.

Exploding bombs made the sea boil under the ship as on many other attacks. A searing flash and a sickening jolt shocked us. Next came a vast outpouring of black smoke. Four times in quick succession the ship shuddered – in a way never felt before by those who had time to fall flat on the deck. Sydney Foster got to his feet groping through the smoke from the galley flat to the upper-deck. His action station was on one of the oerlikons. The smoke began to clear and he made out twisted and shattered wreckage, he guessed that several must be killed. Outside there was chaos. Twisted girders, broken cable, bent steel plates showed through drifting clouds of smoke and steam . . . fires were blazing and somewhere ignited small arms ammunition was exploding. . . .

One bomb had hit the fo'c'sle square in front of No 1 gun; from the waterline all that remained was twisted metal licked by roaring fires. There had been another eruption at the base of the tripod main mast, breaking two of the struts and tearing platforms and ladders. Finding an intact ladder to the gun deck Foster made for it and noticed Sticks Hancock the seaman bugler lying as if unconcerned on the deck. The man who had called us to action stations hundreds of times since our first shoot in 1939 would never sound a note again. . .

Leading Seaman Eric Skelly, off watch and walking cheerfully from astern to collect his mess's grog ration, was galvanised into action by the screaming Stukas and the shriek of bombs. He saw a line of small evenly placed water columns rapidly moving towards him and leapt through a bulkhead door for cover. The deck heaved up beneath him and colliding with a heavy object he was flung helpless across the deck, conscious only of the oerlikons firing over the roar of aircraft engines. Recovering he was aware of the First Lieutenant calmly saying, 'Away you go to action stations'. . . .

Leading Seaman Carter's action station was below decks to assist in damage control . . . he came to a sort of crater blasted through several decks. Sunlight filtered through the smoke and he fell over a naked turso burned by flash and hurled against a stanchion. Three minutes before twenty men had been active in the control, now there was only silence and a cloud of steam. *Coventry*, the intelligence centre and succour for the raiding ships, had been completely eliminated. The fighting ship was now a drifting burning wreck. The Stukas had attacked in pairs, diving so low that one collided with a radar aerial and went into the sea. Spike Sullivan's oerlikon which destroyed one Stuka was the only retaliatory action from the ship, but Beaufighters shot down five of the Stukas. The first bombs missed but the cannon fire was lethal. Then four bombs hit along the centre line destroying the fo'c'sle as far as No 1 gun, the lower steering platform, the main mast base, radar transmitting office and the boiler room below. . .

A group remained on what remained of the fo'c'sle tending three shipmates grievously wounded and laying them on stretchers. Captain Donald Peyton Jones, Royal Marine, appeared and helped the party take to the sea. Already he had told survivors to throw overboard life rafts and floats. The boats had been stove in by blast and splinters. The Captain Royal Marines organised search parties to comb every accessible part of the ship and to bring out trapped and wounded men.

The rescue of survivors during an air attack was always a hazardous business, the rescuing ships had to defend themselves until there was a lull in the air action. We knew from our Crete experience that it was frequently impossible to pick men out of the sea until after dark. . .

There were of course a large number of men able to swim towards one of the destroyers and Eric Skelly was one of them. By the rail he noticed several rows of boots and shoes carefully placed by those who had jumped before him, placed as if they expected to return. . .

Abandon ship was a ragged affair. The destroyer came bows on to the stern of *Coventry* where a large group was gathered on the quarter-deck. Men scrambled over quickly, followed by Captain Denby, carrying ship's papers and confidential books. . . . Men from the fo'c'sle were in the sea for half an hour before a whaler from the *Dulverton* picked them up.

Leslie Stevenson remembers getting away from the stopped cruiser:

Captain Denby stood by my side; he said, 'Abandon ship, lads, good luck, every man for himself', his very words. After dumping the CB's I ventured towards the blazing inferno, I knew his decision was right. . .

George Salisbury, Coder, was in swimming with me when he saw Telegraphist Downes, a non-swimmer, in difficulties. He gave him his life-belt. George had been on our messdeck when the bombs fell, he lifted up a broken ladder to let the lads up from below. . . .

I jumped and swam towards one of the lumps of material I had chucked overboard; it carried me away from the bulk of the men in the sea. Thought no one would come to rescue me, an isolated bloke. I turned back to the main body, then swam with them to the *Dulverton*. Climbed up a rope ladder, got half way up and my strength went, fell back into the 'oggin under the *Dulverton*, thought I was near the keel. Surfaced, was pushed up the arse by a matelot who had climbed down and held the bottom rung. Near the top two arms reached down and catapulted me onto my back on the deck like a bleeding whale. A glorious feeling. Crawling aft I watched *Coventry* being fired on to sink her, then saw some of her ammo' going up, then I shook like a jelly.

Zulu after extracting herself from the shambles of the Tobruk assault arrived on the scene with a cloud of Ju87's diving like angry hornets on the speeding jinking destroyer. The aircraft withdrew as she joined six Hunt class destroyers sadly circling the burning *Coventry* manned only by her many dead. The Hunts could not sink the tough old WW1 cruiser with their 4″ guns, so *Zulu* drew off and despatched her with two torpedoes. The group set off back to Alexandria as another wave of Stuka bombers arrived overhead.

In a short deadly attack on the writhing, jinking destroyers trying to shake off the Ju87's, a bomb drove down into the vitals of *Zulu* and blew out part of her ship's bottom. She struggled on under tow but after dark, with her decks awash, her crew was taken off, she sank shortly afterwards.

During the return to Alexandria, four of *Coventry*'s survivors died and watched over by their shipmates were buried at sea in the waters where they had fought for so long. With the exception of a few replacements, the ship's company had remained intact over three years of unremitting action; because of her specialist role as an anti-aircraft ship she was with her sister ships at the heart of every desperate campaign, and now the four original AA cruisers had all been sunk.

Coventry until the gross incompetence of Operation *Agreement*, the Prime Minister 'for all his admiration of offensive intentions, was gravely concerned', had previously suffered few casualties although she had been damaged many times, and only once had retired from the war to refit and rest her crew. One of her gallant ship's company had been awarded the Victoria Cross when the ship saved the hospital ship *Aba* against overwhelming odds during the evacuation of Crete. Now she was gone with three officers and 69 ratings dead.

For long periods of her three years the war seemed hopelessly lost, the homeland was under intense aerial bombardment, mail from home was non-existent and every day at sea or in harbour could be the last. Yet within the claustrophobic, comfortless messdecks there existed a close intimacy of shipmates who shared private uninhibited fears of death, the rare moments of exhilaration during runs ashore, grief, the Dear John letters, money and the solace normally found within a close-knit family. In this seemingly endless total world war the comradeship of a fighting ship was the only security in a maelstrom of constant danger and sudden death or dreadful wounds. Now for the men of *Coventry* after three years it was gone.

George Sims wrote her epitaph: 'It was ironic that after a successful defence with her own gunnery system and skills for three years, she should fall victim on the first occasion she placed reliance on the new techniques of fighter direction cover. So ended an epoch.'

The survivors of the three ships were landed at Alexandria and sent to Sidi Bishr transit camp; there they found that long service in the Mediterranean did not earn many of them a draft home for foreign and survivors' leave. Most were drafted to ships in the east Mediterranean, to a wide variety of jobs ashore including manning a detachment of three wireless vehicles flying the white ensign in the western desert, acting as radio links between bombarding warships and the army.

Leslie Stevenson describes arrival at Alexandria and the reception camp;

> Landed at Alex, Bishop did a war dance on the jetty – no room at the inn – we were marched to Canopus II. Soup, then issued with bedding. Bitten all night, only when I got up into the desert on a quick draft I found myself covered with 'crabs'. No treatment available, used disinfectant, took skin off my balls, a bloody nightmare, I wasn't the only one. Kit re-issue was poor, cotton kitbags, hammocks and mattresses secondrate, officers alright they had their kit, landed before we sailed.

At home one of the hundreds of ships of war and merchantmen that came off the slipways was a new 'O' class destroyer, *Obdurate*, the sixth of her class and flotilla of eight ships. Her commanding officer was Lieutenant-Commander Claude Sclater. His last command, the *Wild Swan*, had been sunk in the Bay of Biscay on 17th June after receiving damage from a German bomber followed by a collision with a Spanish trawler. He had been awarded the Distinguished Service Order and Bar for his unflinching determination during the 1940 evacuation of the British Expeditionary Army from France, and later in U-boat engagements in the northern Atlantic. *Obdurate* was commissioned on 3rd September 1942 and it was soon clear that some of the officers and senior ratings did not measure up to their tough captain's uncompromising standards. By the end of October, *Obdurate* had three first lieutenants and Claude Sclater had acquired a semi-humorous, not entirely justifiable, reputation with his brother flotilla commanding officers, of eating his No 1's.

After an extremely tough workup period in Scapa Flow where appalling weather conditions defeated even Sclater in his endeavour to work up his new ship to fighting efficiency, *Obdurate* was on operational duties. At Iceland waiting to join her first convoy to Russia, Telegraphist Donald Goodbrand recorded his captain's determination to enforce the rum regulations.

Rum-Rats

You drank your rum ration there and then, at table, with the midday meal. That is the law. But some bottled theirs secretly for later celebrations of birthdays, to solicit favours or placate oppos, hiding in kit-lockers or in shipboard nooks and crannies known only to themselves. Rum was an accepted currency of the lower deck in HM ships, just as tobacco is in HM prisons. Sometimes the wardroom got wind of these goings on and all hell broke loose.

All non-duty hands were piped to muster on deck and lined-up near the torpedo tubes, marshalled into some sort of order by grim-faced bossy petty officers and leading hands, shivering in the arctic air and whispering buzzes nineteen to the dozen. Each mess was deserted, illegal brag and pontoon sessions ruthlessly interrupted and cards left strewn over mess tables as the snap search got under way.

The skipper, face taut with anger, was observed stalking forrard with his entourage of Jimmy the One, Coxswain and the Buffer, wrapped in his duffle coat against the keen wind.

The sailors craned forward, watching the ominous party vanish below. Minutes passed. Old hands groaned at inconvenience and malefactors inwardly rejoiced in the expertise of their concealment.

Down on the messdecks men's lockers were systematically rifled for evidence of the demon rum. A queer feeling of expectancy and foreboding pervaded the silent ranks of guilty and innocent alike freezing on the upper deck. When the inspection party reappeared it was obvious from their dispirited air that the search had been in vain. The sailors relaxed, innocent and guilty alike. The skipper went aft, the crew back to their quarters. Sly whispers, furtive looks; the last dog watch was piped, tension lifted. Card-games and letter writing, uckers and book reading commenced where they had left off. Somewhere in an Aladdin's cave the relieved yet complacent mirth of a master cut through the babble of new-found conversation.

On 23rd October the Eighth Army launched a counter-offensive at El Alamein and broke through the Axis defence lines to commence an advance that would continue until the German and Italian armies surrendered in Tunisia in May 1943. On 8th November a combined American and British force landed in French North Africa, Operation *Torch*. An armada of Anglo-American warships, landing and supply ships, 828 in all, carried the American and British troops who landed simultaneously at Casablanca and Port Lyautey in the west and in the east at Oran and Algiers. During the nights, 5th, 6th and 7th November over 400 ships, of the British part of the operation, passed through the straits of Gibraltar. During the assault phase of the operation sixteen merchant ships were sunk and amongst the warships lost was a Black Swan class sloop *Ibis* torpedoed off Algiers. Eric Harlow was a survivor and later when he got home on survivors' leave he wrote to his younger brother Harold, who had now been able to join up and was serving at sea in the destroyer *Obedient*:

12.12.1942

Dear Harold,
            Home once more and for Xmas too, if only you could get leave it would be perfect.

I expect you are having a pretty rough time at the moment, but it will all end one day.

Stev is coming on Monday if all goes well, I'm sending him a wire this morning.

I expect you heard the news of the *Ibis*, I didn't as I was on watch at the time, we were then two days out from England.

We started off in October on the job and escorted the troopers all the way and as it said on the wireless there wasn't any sunk, one was hit but it didn't go down.

We arrived at Algiers during the night and the landings started at 1 am. Everything went according to plan, we were doing the asdic screen at the time and we came across two invasion boats which had broken down. We spoke to them and got the boats alongside. They were British Commandos and looked a tough lot.

When morning came everything was silent except for one shore battery which still kept firing.

All that day the ships were unloading and nothing happened out of the ordinary. There were a couple of Jerry's over that evening but no bombs were dropped near us.

The next day we went to action stations in the afternoon and as evening close about 50 bombers came over. There were a couple of Spitfires but the air seemed full of Junkers 88's.

We opened fire at about 4pm with our three twin 4″. Three bombers came down at us and everything we had was fired at them. I got some good bursts in and everyone was firing like hell. All their bombs missed us – just – and we brought one down.

We were then attacked by single bombers every five minutes or so but miraculously missed the lot and brought another plane down and a possible third. That was the finish for that day and we were patting ourselves on the back. Dawn next morning a couple came over but not very near to us and we didn't fire.

It was getting dark that evening when enemy aircraft were reported. A couple of bombers dived at us, missed astern. Then two torpedo bombers came in on the starboard side and it was while we were driving these off that three came in on the port side, all torpedo bombers. The close range opened fire, but we could hardly see them as it was almost dark. One of these was brought down but a second afterwards there was a big bang and the ship seemed to jump out of the water.

We listed to starboard immediately and the skipper said she wouldn't take it and gave the order to abandon ship.

We managed to get a couple of flotta nets over but then the ship started to roll over and we all made a jump for it. I had my lifebelt on luckily, always kept it handy, Harold. Many a good swimmer was lost because he didn't have one. It was completely dark now and we had no idea where any the ships were. The lights on the flotta nets works and some fellows had torches – another thing I will always have with me in future.

After about two hours of swimming towards where we thought the shore was (10 miles off) and then back towards the ship which was now bottom up but still on fire where the hole was, we saw a cruiser and dug out like hell towards it. I was doing everything – overarm – back stroke – side stroke – breast stroke but didn't seem to make much headway and then suddenly I seemed to be very near and a whaler was about fifteen yards away.

They hauled me in and that was the first time I felt cold. It was the tremendous amount of oil fuel which kept us warm. We were smothered in it from head to foot.

There isn't a lot more to tell now. We had a bath and a tot of neaters. A crash – woke up next morning to find that we were 125 miles east off Algiers and Bougie. That made things a bit grim and that night or rather dusk, we were attacked again in the same fashion only there were not so many planes. An aerial torpedo exploded in our wake and made us all s. . . , but next day we were on our way to Gib and very thankful too.

The 100 survivors from *Ibis* and 50 from the *Hecla* sailed an old sloop home that had been rammed and patched up.

She only had one boiler going but got 10½ knots out of her which was not bad and we came most of the way in convoy.

We got lost a bit after we left the convoy for somewhere in SW England. We managed to hit Land's End and not Brest which everyone thought we were going to do . . . Back to depot and the joining routine and now 16 days' leave which means until the 28th.

Well, Harold, I hope everything is OK with you and that we shall soon see one another. I had a letter from Joan when I arrived saying how glad she was that everything was OK and she thinks that they ought to give you leave as we haven't seen one another for nearly two years. They don't know the Navy, old pal, do they?

Let's hope that it turns out that way, I shall do some wishing on a star I think.

All the best Harold, look after yourself. Will write again soon.

Eric

The last destroyer of the 'O' class, 17th Destroyer Flotilla, the *Obe-*

dient had been commissioned on 30th October 1942 at Dumbarton. George Elson remembers his three years in the destroyer with considerable pride;

> It was a ship of grand lads, but we had one or two odd men out. We had one who rarely visited the bathroom and when he did, he'd button up his overalls to his neck and at the wrists before he wet what was left. In the end he stank so much that Len Cross with some others from his mess dragged him below to the bathroom, stripped him, then gave him a long painful public scrubbing. It didn't cure him and he had to go. . . .
> We had another odd ball, the Sick Bay Tiffey, who drank surgical spirit laced with lime juice. . . .
> One day three of us had a spot of luck sitting on the deck in the flat outside the Supply Petty Officers office, having a burn waiting to go on watch. We found three 'empty' rum jars, when we shook them we could hear some rum slopping about inside – quick as a flash the gash rum was drained into mess cups, then away into a hideaway rum bottle.

Within a very few weeks *Obedient*, with other ships of her flotilla, was to gain a place in naval immortality in the Barents Sea Battle of 31st December.

The year 1942 was ending with resumed increase of U-boat activity in the North Atlantic, off the west coast of South Africa, the north coastline of South America and the south-east coast of South Africa. In the Arctic, no further convoys to Russia had been run since the convoy PQ18 in September.

In the Far East the Battle of Guadalcanal had been fought with a victory to the Japanese enemy followed by another defeat of American cruisers and destroyers in a night action, the battle of Tassafaronga. In Russia, the Russian counter-attack had begun at Stalingrad. The siege of Malta had been raised in November with a successful convoy of four ships, Operation *Stoneage*. The Eighth Army continued to advance across Libya.

The new area of activity for U-boats off the south-east coast of Africa had not intruded on the long monotonous patrols and convoy escort duties of some of the cruisers of the East Indies Station; they had escaped the actions with the Japanese fleet off Ceylon earlier in the year. The dreary business of maintaining discipline by awarding punishment by warrant was still being administered by some die-hard captains.

On 17th December at sea on passage to Diego Suarez, warrant number 59 was read in the *Frobisher*. Captain Mudford's cruiser had been in commission for less than ten months; it was a sombre unhappy record. The captain, to be fair to him, did not spare his officers. On Christmas day, at sea, he logged one of his officers who was 'admonished for negligence of his duties as officer of the watch'. This was not all, later in the day he logged no less than seven more of his officers including his commander, 'For lack of control and ward-room discipline' and 'entertaining ratings in the wardroom at sea'.

Captain W.D. Stephens was also carrying out a strict regime in his ship *Mauritius*. Sunday 1st November at Port Victoria, Seychelles, immediately following church on the quarter-deck, warrant 62 was read. On the 23rd of the same month, at sea and bound for Bombay warrant 67 was read. In December after warrant 70 had been read, a rating was landed at Bombay, discharged for detention at Yerawaa Central Prison at Poona. The cruiser then had the misfortune to have a rating on Christmas Day afternoon fall from the starboard pom-pom deck, hit a projection on the ship's side, then fall into the out-going tide as the ship lay alongside at Bombay. A search by the motor boat failed to find the body. Able Seaman A.E. Ham was log-ged 'missing presumed killed or drowned'.

In a totally different world of darkness, mountainous seas, ice and snow blizzards Convoy JW51 was about to be sailed in two parts. JW51A with 16 ships sailed from Loch Ewe on 15th December with an escort of seven destroyers (including *Fury*) two corvettes, one minesweeper and two trawlers, the convoy and its escort were watched over by two cruisers, *Sheffield* (flagship to Rear Admiral R. Burnett) and *Jamaica*, with two destroyers *Opportune* (17th Flotilla) and the *Matchless*. Apart from the perils of the continuous Arctic darkness, bad weather and poor visibility, the convoy passed through unscathed, arriving at Kola Inlet ten days later, 25th December.

The second part of the convoy, JW51B, fourteen ships, sailed also from Loch Ewe, on 20th December. The convoy sailed from Scotland with an escort of a minesweeper *Bramble*, two corvettes, *Rhododendron* and *Hyderabad*, also two trawlers. They were joined from Iceland by five destroyers of the new 'O' class flotilla, *Onslow* (Captain R. St. V. Sherbrooke), *Oribi*, *Obedient*, *Orwell* and *Obdurate*. There was a sixth destroyer, *Achates*.

The convoy followed the route of JW51A and it was also covered by the distant presence of Rear Admiral R. Burnett's cruisers *Shef-field* and *Jamaica*. On the 28/29th *Oribi* had a gyro compass failure, lost touch with the convoy and with great difficulty in bad visibility located the Norwegian mainland, then groped her way to Murmansk having no further part to play in defence of the convoy.

On the evening of the sixth day on passage, between Jan Mayen and Bear Islands the convoy ran into a fierce gale which separated five ships of the convoy and one trawler, *Vizalma*, from the main body. Captain Sherbrooke detached *Bramble* to find the missing ships. A U-boat, the *U-354*, had sighted the convoy on the 24th and had remained in contact and undetected for six days. On the 30th, *U-354* reported that the convoy was in disarray and was only lightly protected. On receiving this information a strong German surface force put to sea from Altenfiord at 1800 hrs, commanded by Vice Admiral Oscar Kummetz. The admiral's orders were to destroy the convoy, to avoid action with a superior force, not to waste time rescuing crews and to prevent the enemy doing so and to capture a few captains for interrogation.

The German admiral sailed with his flag in the heavy cruiser *Hipper*, the pocket battleship *Lützow* (formerly *Deutschland*) and six destroyers of the 5th Destroyer Division.

Admiral Kummetz divided his force into two divisions, *Lützow* with three destroyers was to sail east and search the estimated convoy route from ahead, *Hipper* and the remaining three destroyers were to search from astern of the expected position of the convoy, the two divisions were to turn and sweep a lane fifteen miles wide towards each other. His plan worked: the convoy was sighted by one of *Hipper*'s destroyers at 0715 hrs, 31st December.

By this hour Captain Sherbrooke and the convoy commodore had re-established order in the convoy, but two ships remained missing out of the formation. The trawler *Vizalma*, five miles to the north of the convoy route, had located one of the ships and was trying to shepherd the straggler towards the convoy. The minesweeper *Bramble* was still searching for the other straggler. Claude Sclater's destroyer *Obdurate* sighted *Hipper*'s three destroyers and alerted Captain Sherbrooke in the *Onslow*.

The action commenced at 0930, and for the next two hours the British destroyers, following a plan outlined by Captain Sherbrooke to his captains before they sailed from Iceland, outwitted and out-manoeuvred their powerful adversaries. With *Achates* zig-zagging across the stern of the convoy laying a dense smoke screen behind which the convoy commodore continuously made course alterations away from the enemy ships, the four 'O' class destroyers laid smoke between the merchant ships and the enemy, then dived in and out of the smoke making feint torpedo attacks at the enemy ships. They were outgunned by the German ships and their own guns were hand-icapped by heavy spray turning to ice and making gunfire irregular and at times impossible to maintain at times. Captain Sherbrooke's strategy was to threaten, but to avoid at all costs firing their torpedoes, if they did they would be at the mercy of the capital ships which were shy of destroyer torpedoes.

The strategy worked: the Germans stood off and fired whenever the British smoke screen allowed; first *Onslow* was hit several times by 8" shells from *Hipper*; the destroyer was badly damaged with both guns forward knocked out of action and many casualties. The time was 1030. By 11.15 hrs the *Achates* had been hit repeatedly and was sinking but continued to make smoke and maintained her task of masking the convoy's stern. *Obedient* and *Orwell* had received shell splinter damage and command of the destroyers had shifted from *Onslow* where Captain Sherbrooke had been critically wounded in the face and one eye, to *Obdurate* and then *Obedient* which had been temporarily out of communication because her aerials had been shot away. Still the vastly superior enemy force held off from attacking the last three effective destroyers. *Hipper's* destroyers had encountered the *Bramble* which they sank in an avalanche of fire; there were no survivors. The few flashes of defiance from *Bramble's* single 4" gun did, however, spell the end to the unequal conflict, for the flash was spotted by Rear Admiral Burnett's cruisers which were in doubt where to find the convoy which they knew was under attack. Admiral Burnett brought his cruisers at high speed out of the blackness of the northern darkness and caught the *Hipper* on her disengaged side and crashed in several salvos before the German flagship realised what had happened. *Hipper* broke off the action and shortly afterwards the two British cruisers at full speed found two of *Hipper's* destroyers and sank one, the other escaped into a snow shower reinforced by her own smoke.

Pocket battleship *Lützow* which had fired a few tentative salvos at the convoy while shrinking from a possible torpedo attack from the remaining three effective British destroyers, followed the retirement towards base by the German admiral. The convoy was intact and its fourteen ships entered Kola Inlet on 3rd January 1943. The escort had lost one destroyer, *Achates*, and a minesweeper *Bramble*; *Onslow* had been very badly damaged and both *Obedient* and the *Orwell* had numerous splinter holes. The British escorts had suffered 250 dead and many wounded but it had been a famous victory and a classic destroyer action. The battle of the Barents Sea had been fought against greater odds by five destroyers and two cruisers, than that faced by the five cruisers and sixteen destroyers of Rear Admiral Vian's force in the second battle of Sirte.

Captain Sherbrooke's convoy of fourteen ships and their cargoes had arrived intact, whereas only 6,000 tons of the material carried in the Malta convoy survived the enemy action in the Gulf of Sirte and the approaches to Malta. Colin Watson, signalman, was on watch in *Obdurate* when the enemy ships were first sighted on the morning of 31st December:

> On the upper-deck, with every wave that broke inboard the ship was covered in ice. The wind was bitterly cold with heavy snowstorms. We had been issued with Arctic clothing but it never kept us warm and after a short time on watch we were numb with the cold. Life lines were permanently rigged on deck. Below on the messdecks the deckheads dripped with condensation and the bulkheads were covered with sheet ice. The deck was under two or three inches of water which seeped into our lockers. Our hammocks were kept slung and we slept in our clothes, ready to go back on watch when action stations sounded which was frequent.
>
> *Obdurate*'s station was on the starboard quarter of the convoy, *Obedient* being ahead of us on the port bow and *Onslow* out of sight leading the convoy. I had just relieved my oppo, a young Scotsman, for the forenoon watch. I was keeping an eye on *Obedient* for signals when a lookout reported sighting unknown ships. As far as I know the person responsible for the sighting was a CPO probably the Buffer.
>
> Looking through my binoculars I saw two large destroyers and a larger ship which looked like a cruiser emerging through the mist about two miles astern, looking almost like ghost-ships in the dim light. Action Stations sounded and the CO ordered me to make a first sighting signal to *Onslow*, which I sent by aldis light: 'Two unknown destroyers, one unknown cruiser, bearing and distance . . .' via *Obedient* as Captain D was out of sight; time of origin 0830. The reply was one word 'Investigate'. The CO altered course towards the unknown ships until we were about a mile distant. I made the recognition signal. There was no reply.
>
> We kept on course when I suddenly saw a ripple of red flashes on the unknown ships. There followed a screaming noise of shells and fountains of sea-water higher than the mast rose alongside *Obdurate* as she received a near miss. We had encountered the German heavy cruiser *Hipper* and three large destroyers.
>
> We zig-zagged at full speed back to the convoy under constant heavy fire, but though we had several near misses we did not receive a direct hit.

During the action *Obedient*'s aerials were shot away; a jury aerial had to be rigged by two telegraphists, Fred Barber and Fred Little:

...us. Christmas day 1942,
...eck scene.

...us. Embarking the first
...m home in six months.

...Christmas day 1942 in
...yers mess-deck.

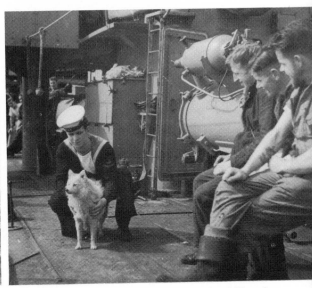

(*Left*) Destroyer Leader *Jervis* picking up survivors off Cape Bon following the sinking of enemy shipping, January 1943. (*Right*) *Jervis*. Leading seaman Jacobs (Ship's postman) and the mascot 'Snowball'.

(*Left*) *Jervis*. Motor cutter coxn Bill Skilling and stoker. (*Right*) *Jervis*, mess-deck scene. 1943.

Our captain, Commander Kinlock was reputed to be capable and able at shell dodging – he confirmed his reputation as salvo after salvo fell around or straddled us fired by the *Hipper* and her destroyers, but he could not dodge the splinters. These splinters caused casualties and brought down our aerials. With Fred Little I was ordered out of the warm brightly light W/T office by 'Pots', our PO/Tel. The sickbay flat outside the office was dimly lit and filled with groaning wounded shipmates and blood as the Doc and sickbay Tiffey tended them. Without protective clothing we forced a way out onto the upper-deck through the darkened ship screens, we cowered back terrified by the cold, snow, smoke pouring from the funnel and gun fire. We stumbled back to the W/T office, where we were driven out by 'Pots' swearing terrible oaths and threatening to shoot us.

Somehow we climbed the mast, terrified by the heeling ship at full speed, smoke and gunfire. Somehow after what seemed hours we managed to rig and hoist an insulated jury aerial on a flag hoist halliard scrounged off the Yeoman. . . .

Obedient left Murmansk alone and returned at speed to Rosyth with some of the wounded from *Onslow* and the *Achates*. Those who were able to get around insisted in standing a watch while we were on passage.

At Edinburgh on the Sunday night, after our arrival and news of the battle had appeared in the press and given out on the radio, a theatre gave two rows of seats for us. Only two of us went, all the other libertymen went to find clubs for booze. During the show the lights went up and the audience were told that naval heroes were there and were asked to stand up in the spotlights which showed just two of us and two rows of empty seats, awful and embarrassing.

On the bridge of the flotilla leader, *Onslow*, one of the signalmen was Philip Vine, just 20 years of age, who had been with the ship since commissioning in October 1941:

New Year's Eve arrived for me with the rattlers and clamour of action stations, I was dressed in the usual destroyer collection of 'long johns' covered by many jerseys and a sheepskin coat. I made my way to the bridge, my action station. Our Chief Yeoman of Signals was already there who said to me, 'Stay on the port side aft and keep your eye on the next astern'. He was a big man, ex-boxing champion and had been called out of retirement and was delighted to get a Captain D's ship, leader of the 17th Flotilla. It appeared that we had received an 'Enemy in sight report', two large ships and some destroyers, we had heard that '*Hipper* & Co' were at sea.

From my position I could not see over the forepart of the ship, but could see all the officers who were excitedly taking bearings and ranges on the compass platform.

Something was sighted astern to port, we dropped astern of the convoy as Captain Sherbrooke evidently wished to get between it and the enemy ships. All I know is that suddenly from some outline on a horizon wreathed in fog and snow showers, sparkled flashes for brief seconds then a noise like rushing wind over our heads. A terrific bang came from the forepart of the ship. A shell had landed more or less on B gun and most of the crew were killed. Another shell entered the seamen's messdeck on the port side and had burnt out the CPO's mess above it.

B magazine was flooded immediately but some cordite caught fire, which was soon extinguished. Another crash aft at the rear of us and I saw that the 285 radar hut was completely smashed along with part of our funnel. Tom Braithwaite, the Killick of our mess, was in the radar hut.

Quite a commotion on the compass platform and I saw Captain Sherbrooke turn to Torps (Lt/Cdr T Marchant) and he said, 'I am going below for a minute.' The other officers were trying to persuade him to stay below as he had a wound in his face and as it turned out had lost one eye.

There was little for me to do now as we were leaving the convoy and I went to the lookout sponson to have a chat with the young able seaman, I found him slumped over his binoculars and very still, then I knew he would 'spread no more buzzes'. 'Chief' I called, but the Chief Yeoman 'Nancy' Dawson had already called for a stretcher party.

'Can I go below, Chief?' I said. It was now almost noon and we had been up here many hours and seen much and could hear plenty of movement below, and I was starving. 'No, lad, not yet' and placing a hand the size of a football foot on my shoulder he said, 'You must stay here until I say so and you will thank me for it later, so be patient, son.'

That evening as I stood on the quarter-deck and placed and recovered a grubby White Ensign over 23 bundles sewn in their hammocks as they were consigned to the pitch black sea, I knew what the Chief Yeoman had saved me from seeing on the messdeck, sickbay and sickbay flat. Those old CPO's were like fathers, even mothers, to us young and green ratings.

CHAPTER FIVE

1943

A Sailor

He knew the icy loneliness and saw
The dread affinity of sea and sky
Close grey upon him; heard the weird wind's cry
Shrilling mad descant to the brass of war:
The cold white latitudes of despair that freeze
Blood, dreams, enlightenment in the Arctic day
Called, down the thunderous corridors of spray,
His flesh of youth bruised by irreverent seas,
No fame or ribbon sing of those whose graves
Like his, litter the ocean, though he flung
The sea his breath and had no more to give:
Only the immortal and unfeeling waves
Moan his wild threnody. He was so young,
He died before he began to live.

D.S. Goodbrand, January 1944, Russia.

The next convoy to Russia, JW52, fourteen ships, sailed on 17th January and arrived safely on the 27th. The ocean escort of seven destroyers contained two from the 17th flotilla, *Onslaught* (Commander W.H. Selby) senior ship of the escort and *Offa*. The convoy had been favoured by good weather and immensely powerful units of the German surface fleet, which included the battleship *Tirpitz*, did not stir from their base in Altenfiord. Only the U-boats made several unsuccessful attempts to penetrate the convoy's screen. There were no losses of men or ships of the escort.

In the Atlantic although the Allied escorts were gradually being equipped with improved radar equipment and new weapons, the U-boat sinkings of ships in convoy continued to be serious. Heavy air attacks had commenced on the the Bay of Biscay U-boat bases and on outward and homeward-bound submarines. In the Far East the Japanese had been driven out of Papua. In the Mediterranean with the raising of the siege of Malta, cruisers and destroyers again based on the island had virtually cut the sea-borne supplies to the Italian and German armies in North Africa. The Eighth Army had captured

Tripoli and had entered Tunisia while the East Mediterranean fleet kept pace with the advance bringing supply ships into captured ports as soon as they were cleared of blockships. The ships still faced intense air bomb and torpedo attacks.

In the Western desert W/T vehicles manned by Royal Marines and Royal Navy Telegraphists and coders supplied advance base communications for light forces, flotillas of MTBs and MLs and ship to shore wireless links. Leslie Stevenson was still with the unit and other survivors from the ships, *Coventry, Sikh* and *Zulu*:

> I was issued with a rifle, not a clue how to use it! Still covered in crabs. Only six of us and the truck frequently broke down. No real food, only dog biscuits and other army hard tack. Lost weight and interest. No mail. Mother thought I was dead. Later upon my return to Sidi Bishr transit camp got put into the rattle for wearing khaki shorts. . . .
>
> While in the desert, when the radio sets worked I did cyphering and coding with and without help. Decyphered my own recall to Alexandria after six months to join the *Hyacinth*, also a signal from the Admiralty.
>
> 'Find out why Stevenson has not written to his mother since the *Coventry* was sunk; she fears that he is dead!' I got a bollocking. But I had wrote and wrote. My stepfather had died, mother was berserk, my brother was in Burma. Why had none of my letters got home? Six months of desert diet, I was low in morale. The officer did not accept my word, yet him or some other bugger had censored all my letters.
>
> In Sidi Bishr camp conditions under canvas were horrible, fly infested heads, trenches surrounded by torn sacking screens, brown hand and arm of heads wallah comes under screen to change excreta cans while we sit on the poles.

A few months earlier in 1942, to quell fleet unrest caused particularly by the many weeks without mail from home, Anthony Eden, the Foreign Secretary, had flown out to the Middle East and addressed lower-deck representatives gathered in the beer garden of the Fleet Club in Alexandria. He had a hostile reception; he was angrily told of an Air Force that could not find planes to support the ships at sea or to fly out mail but could transport ministers and senior officers to and from the United Kingdom. It took a very long time before the promises of improvement were fulfilled. The seemingly endless patience and loyalty of the lower deck continued to be taken for granted.

Ronald Bone, able seaman, had joined the service in April 1939 as a Boy 2nd Class at the training establishment HMS *Wildfire*. By the end of the year he was in his first ship, the 'J' class destroyer flotilla leader *Jervis*. After a little more than a year in *Jervis*, he served in two more destroyers *Hotspur* and *Vivien*. Now in 1943 as a senior and experienced able seaman he was in his fourth ship:

> There was trouble from the start; all the ratings were from the UK, whether hostility only or active service, but the officers except for the navigator were all Australians and shits. The navigator was a New Zealander and the only decent officer in the ship. The others, Australian VR's, hadn't a clue how to run a ship or to treat men. Nobody knew where they were and were used as if they were dirt. By the time we reached Algiers there was real trouble, almost mutiny. We refused to turn to for part of ship work, we would only do watches, no extra work or cleaning duties. We manned the guns and took the ship to sea, nothing else. The Australians did not know what to do, nobody was charged. At Gibraltar a couple of AB's were sent ashore on draft, the remainder of us had stoppage of leave while the ship was there. A few weeks later I was also chucked off at Gibraltar.

In the fleet most senior able seamen aspired to be detailed off for a special watchkeeping duty that excused them from all the mundane and routine part-of-ship tasks. Not all wanted to be boat crews but of those who did some enjoyed the challenge of being coxswain of the 16ft motor dinghies which were fast and spectacular and known generally as the 'skimming dishes'. To drive a 'skimming dish' in anything but a flat calm could be a hair-raising experience. The single intrepid passenger crouched, often soaked and miserable, in a small canopied sternsheet or cockpit behind the single crew member. At speed in a wind and seaway, the craft except in the hands of an expert, careered about in an alarming way and when moving slowly could be very nearly unmanoevreable. It was frequently used by commanding officers as their personal runabout and because they were fast and economical in manpower, other ship's boats required a minimum crew of three men.

For Bill Sands to be 'skimming dish' coxswain was the fulfilment of his 'Yen' to have a watchkeeping duty and a boat of his own. He later, after joining a destroyer, was detailed to be coxswain of the motor cutter with a crew of three, but it never had the same excitement of the 'skimming dish'.

Thomas Bywater joined the battleship *Royal Sovereign*:

> When we joined in a new draft, the Buffer called us all 'Pink Tits' all us hostility only ratings and other junior ratings. He did not realise that

some of us even though we were HO had seen two years of sea action in the Atlantic and elsewhere. . . .

Bywater was lucky, even though he had been classified as a 'pink tit' seaman by the Buffer; he got the job as one of the 16ft motor dinghy coxswains.

> It was a special duty, but we were often left struggling in a bad seaway standing off for long periods because our COs and other officers would not tell us how long they were going to be. So we could not secure to the ship's boom and clamber inboard for a cuppa until we were called by the bosun's mate. . . .
>
> I liked my job as Jolly boat cox'n, I drove in the ice floes of the St Lawrence River in Canada to the warm harbour waters of Alexandria harbour. In Alexandria, because he insisted on my boat, I took the Commander-in-Chief, from the *Royal Sovereign* back to his flagship *Warspite*, flying his flag while the fleet stood to attention and the screeching of bosun's pipes and bugles.

In June 1943 a dramatic change came in the North Atlantic U-boat battle, all convoys to and from Russia had been suspended and the escort deployed to the Western Approaches to form special Support Groups to hunt U-boats away from convoys and to reinforce escorts. There were still many sinkings but in May and June 37 U-boats had been sunk and for a while all German submarines were withdrawn from the North Atlantic. In the Pacific the Americans had won a number of major sea victories and Allied landings had been successful on several islands. In the Mediterranean the Axis armies had surrendered on 13th May in Tunisia. In the west the Allies had captured Tunis and Bizerta, and the first through convoy since 1941 had passed from Gibraltar to Alexandria.

In Bougie, Able Seaman W.F. Larham DSM experienced a breakdown of discipline. He was a member of the Royal Naval Patrol service:

> I was working in a pontoon construction party called the Party Chain Gang. There were about 150 of us, 75% of us barely 18 years old. We were put in three watches, Red, White and Blue. We were billeted in the *LST 408*. The food was not all that good then either; Blue or the White watch went on strike. They made a scapegoat of one of the lads. He was sentenced to 90 days' detention. We had all to fall in and an officer read out the 'Riot Act' to us. We were then taken off the *LST 408* and put in shore barracks in Bougie, North Africa.

There had been a change of command in the cruiser *Mauritius*: Captain W.W. Davis had relieved Captain W.D. Stephens on 22nd March. The cruiser finally left her peaceful cruising area in the Indian Ocean at the end of May. After passing through the Suez canal she arrived in Alexandria harbour at 0700 hrs on Saturday 5th June. The ship was urgently required for bombarding tasks in Operation *Husky*, the invasion of Sicily. Immediately after breakfast, the ship's company began embarking large quantities of 6″ ammunition; the magazines were filled to over-capacity, and 6″ shells were stacked in every available space in the ship's passageways and flats. Extra torpedoes and provisions were also embarked.

The ship prepared for sea and a fast passage to Malta, slipped her buoy at 2110 and was immediately in trouble; she ran foul of the moorings off a merchant ship, SS *Taiposhan*. After letting her starboard anchor go *Mauritius* got clear at 2121 but was quickly into more serious trouble. Outside the harbour entrance and turning into the Great Pass, the cruiser ran aground on the Hydrographer's Shoal.

Chief ERA W.M. Lewis was in the engine room:

> We had sailed after dark and under normal circumstances we would have used the lights to pick up the channel marker buoys, but Alexandria was under an air attack at the time. . . . Failing to pick up the seaward channel we grounded, fortunately on sand, at 12 to 15 knots. We were firmly embedded from the bow to about level with B turret. . . .
>
> There was talk of having to remove the 6″ turrets and the ship being written off. There were no tides to help us but a clever salvage officer finally succeeded after some days. The ship was bent during the operation and from then on we always had to compensate with 3 degrees of helm to keep on course.

Royal Marine Bandsman Ian Connel had been in the cruiser since February 1942 and took part in the attempts to get *Mauritius* off;

> The incident was pretty bad, we had to de-ammunition all night long, this was made worse by the fact that we had a lot of extra ammunition inboard for Malta and other ships. We lost one of our petty officers who was astride the wire to one of the tugs attempting to pull us off. We were all on the quarter-deck jumping up and down when the wire began to sing. We all pulled back off the quarter-deck but it snapped and took both his legs off. He did not die but was taken to hospital.

Able Seaman J.E. (Nobby) Clark was on the fo'c'sle securing for sea when the cruiser struck:

I heard Mr Anderson the cable and Fo'c'sle officer informing the bridge that the clump foot was twisted at an angle. We spent the remainder of that night and the most of the next day lightening ship and putting all that would move into lighters alongside. I remember two tugs took our largest towing hawser aft from the towing slips on the quarter-deck at the same time two destroyers made as much wash as they could to rock us. The wires started to scream and the first lieutenant shouted to us to stand firm. Everyone ducked and the petty officer that got knocked off the towing slips got two broken legs.

The cruiser refloated at 1225 hrs 6th June and entered dry dock. Damage was considerable and it was not possible to undock and commence restoring and to embark ammunition until the 15th. She sailed for exercises and to Port Said but had to return to dry dock on the 24th. *Mauritius* eventually sailed for Malta on 6th July, having spent 14 days in dock and read warrants 89 and 90.

The ship received her first experience of action when dive bombers attacked in the morning of the 13th; in the afternoon *Mauritius* commenced bombarding enemy coastal batteries south of Catania. This was to be the start of a long career as a bombarding ship in four invasions: Sicily, Salerno, Anzio and Normandy.

A few of the destroyers taken from the Arctic run to Murmansk to form support groups in the Atlantic battle against the U-boat, strayed into warmer climes; one of these fortunates was the *Obdurate*, a moment in the war recorded by Telegraphist Goodbrand;

> To those who had seen something of the Northern seas it was like Paradise.
>
> Waves cathedral high en route to Iceland, ice-pack, sea-sickness (even sparkers were known to keep radio watch with a bucket between their knees) duffel-coats, balaclavas, enemy bombers and U-boats, messdecks awash with a slurry of swirling sea-water mixed with gash food, sea-boots, socks, broken crockery and all the shipboard chaos fuelled by Arctic gales – all this faded into the background as we entered the harbour of Horta in the lushly green island of Fayal in the Azores. . .
>
> 'What are we doing here?' 'Only the skipper knows.' 'Who cares? We're here, aren't we?' was said as the CO and his party went ashore to confer with local officials. On his return leave was granted, tiddly-suits donned and the watch left the ship with pockets full of escudos. . .

This verse tells of delight squandered by shame in a short interlude at a neutral port untouched by the stain of war.

Ports of Dreams

After duels of the Barents Sea,
The ice, the Arctic gales, the messdeck sludge,
The sluggard convoy, wolf-packs strategy.

Our boat turned south away from bomb and gun
And sped we wondering to remote Azores,
Fated to rendezvous with the healing sun.

Fayal the isle, Horta the dreaming port
Which drove Northern capes far from our minds,
Bowered in greenery we long had sought.

Tied up, we roamed ashore with gleaming eyes
And paced old-fashioned pathways into town,
Each scented breeze telling of paradise.

Gardens were there and folk of olive face
Who on the fringe of war made us forget
The black streets and slag-heaps of our race.

Pipe-smoking fishermen in simple guise,
Contented farmers with their ample crops,
Cheap wine and senoritas with dark eyes:

All these we saw, the lotus-eating, woke
The worm that nestles in Arcadia's bud,
And soon the liquored gangs all restraint broke.

Young women, modest, fled the incautious word,
Aghast shopkeepers laid their loud complaint –
The Mayor and Skipper hastily conferred.

Wrathful, the Skipper's writ foundered our ease,
And with shamed faces we rolled back to the ship
Under the pale gaze of the Portuguese.

Five days we swung off that forbidden shore,
Hangdog and yearning for our port of dreams
Like Bounty tars torn from Tahitian lore,

Then slung our hook. . . But this I know:
Paradise is not in some Shangri-la
Nor where sweet winds o'er Avalon do blow –

Long lost, it lies, and ever shall, for me,
In Lovely Fayal's isle in far Azores,
When we were young, in Spring of '43.

D.S. Goodbrand.

For those serving in the older cruisers and battleships in 1943, it was a good bet to assume that life would be quieter, safer and probably very monotonous with long patrols in ocean wastes guarding troop convoys from enemy ocean raiders. Tom Guard, now qualified as a leading radar operator, received a draft to the WW1, Royal Sovereign class battleship *Ramillies*.

> Then I got a draft to *Ramillies* and at the time they said the barracks would fall down because all the 'stanchions' were going, and a few skates as well! We were out off Scotland and I was outside the radar cabin when some sort of landing craft let off a few rounds and hit about six of us – some seriously but I only had shrapnel in both thighs and knee. Spent a few weeks in hospital in Kilmacolme, Scotland and then went back to *Ramillies* and out to South Africa. We called at Casablanca – the *Jean Bart* was there having been shelled by us (a few months earlier in *Torch* operation) – there was a bit of a riot ashore – this cheap wine, leaving for the next watch, the next day was cancelled and we got blamed! Quite a few were sent straight to cells when they got back on board but I'm pleased to say that I just made it to the mess.
>
> We called at Freetown and Mombasa and had shore leave – with the usual warnings but even so one bible punching type in our mess was soon in 'Rose Cottage' afterwards! *Ramillies* was never meant for tropical waters and we suffered from lack of water and terrible heat on the messdecks – for example we had to go down three decks to our lockers and by the time you came up from there having put on clean shore kit you were wringing wet. Also all the bulkhead doors had been fitted with 'Flood walls' (after the *Prince of Wales*' sinking, I believe) and the result was like a hurdle race, exhausting with the risk of cracking your head on the bulkhead opening. I well remember during a sudden tropical storm all the ship's company stripped off on the upper-deck and had a bath. Most of us slept on deck and you had to give your relief a diagram to find you – often he shook the wrong man!
>
> We had an Admiral's inspection and he picked out a chap in our mess, 'Taffy', and told him to report to the doctor. It was found that he had galloping consumption and was removed to an isolation hospital. As a result I became Killick of the mess and was ordered to have the whole mess disinfected – I never understood what good that did. One chap refused to do it and that was the only time I ever put anyone into Jankers.
>
> It was with some surprise that I heard that I was to be put ashore in South Africa for a petty officers' course (Radar). I must say that I was very glad to leave *Ramillies* except that I had two very good townies on board.

The corvette *Hyacinth* which in July 1942 had attacked and forced the Italian submarine *Perla* to surrender off Beirut was now able in July

1943 to pass through to the western part of the Mediterranean and here she had another encounter with a submarine:

> We chased a submarine along the neutral coastline of Spain, forced it to beach and we lobbed shells at the crew running to shelter in the hills. We did not go close enough to see if it was German or Italian, but beat it out of these neutral waters. The event was covered up, we were trespassing!

So wrote Leslie Stevenson. He had joined the corvette in April after returning from his six months in the western desert. He continues to describe some of the coder's actions in the W/T office of a small ship;

> Secret cyphers, we used to de-cypher some ourselves to get the early 'gen'. Frightened us to death a few times, passed the signal on to the officer with shaking hands after ironing out the creases of the signal paper so he wouldn't know we'd discovered what he had yet to know.

The invasion of Sicily, the joint Anglo-American Operation *Husky*, commenced on 10th July 1943. The British naval share of the operation was the majority, the total Allied seaborne forces for the operation were 2,590 ships of war and merchant ship transports and supply ships, the British share was a massive 1,614 craft including six battleships, two fleet aircraft carriers and ten cruisers. The largest American ships were five cruisers.

The invasion on the night of 9th/10th July was preceded by an air drop of 1,200 highly trained and experienced British paratroops that became a shameful disaster of incompetence or the politics imposed on the operation planning directives. The paratroops embarked in Horsa and Waco gliders left North Africa, towed by 35 British piloted Albemarles and 109 American C 47's commanded by American pilots, some still with civilian status. When the air armada neared Cape Passero on the south-east corner of Sicily the inexperienced Americans became confused by the force of an unforecast gale and the tracers of anti-aircraft fire from the Cape area; in panic they released 115 gliders into a tumultuous sea where hundreds of élite fighting men burdened by their battle equipment drowned.

As *Mauritius* approached her bombarding station in the dawn of D-day the cruiser steamed through groups of dead and drowning soldiers. Bandsmen Ian Connel remembers the day;

> Some of our paratroopers had fallen into the sea around us. A Chief Petty Officer dived over the side to save some. When he hit the water he

remembered that he could not swim so had to be rescued with the others.

The Allied forces succeeded in establishing firm beach-heads supported by intense naval bombardments. Enemy opposition was patchy and air strikes on the invasion fleet were on the whole ineffective. The Italian fleet remained in port, only the German and Italian submarines made serious attempts to disrupt troop convoys and to harass the bombarding warships. Their losses were heavy, three German and nine Italian submarines were sunk.

In the three weeks following D-day the submarines had only sunk four merchant ships and two LST's and damaged two cruisers, *Cleopatra* and *Newfoundland*.

The Italian submarine *Asihangi*, which had torpedoed the cruiser *Newfoundland*, was quickly sunk by the destroyer flotilla leader *Laforey*. Petty Officer Bob Burns was now serving in the *Laforey* after doing gunnery courses following his draft from the *Wild Swan*;

> As *Newfoundland* limped towards Malta we were with other destroyers carrying out, off Syracuse, an anti-submarine patrol. Our starboard lookout, in a dead flat calm, reported torpedo tracks to starboard. Captain D, (Tubby) Hutton, gave a helm order of 'Hard a Starboard,' followed the tracks and after only two pattern depth charge attacks sank the Italian submarine *Asihangi* and collected a motley smelly group of about forty of her crew. Look-out training and skill was paramount with Captain Hutton, this skill saved our necks on many tight occasions. Captain Hutton, in his quiet unobtrusive way, never failed to show his appreciation; in the *Asihangi* incident, the young HO Geordie lookout, Ordinary Seaman Childs was presented with a can of beer when we got back to Malta, and more important a 'thank you' from the man we all adored.

Against strong Axis opposition the Allied ground forces began to make progress across the island of Sicily, the Americans crossing to the north and then east towards Messina. The British army with the same goal moved through the centre and along the east coast and round Mount Etna. The Axis began to evacuate the island on 3rd August and by the 17th it was complete; 62,000 Italians and 39,570 Germans escaped across the straits of Messina into the toe of Italy. The evacuation had been covered by numerous and powerful coastal gun batteries and anti-aircraft defences. The British cruisers, destroyers and MTB's had a perilous time trying to neutralize the coastal batteries and on many occasions found themselves in action against German panzer tanks.

At Alexandria in September two British corvettes, *Hyacinth* and *Primula*, were handed over to the Greeks. Leslie Stevenson was detailed to remain in the ex-*Hyacinth* as a coder in the British communication liaison team:

> After the Greek crew arrived and moved in to my ship, a Greek Orthodox Church bishop blessed the ship and renamed her as HHMS *Apostolis*. With the Greeks the first thing to fall apart wase the ship's company heads. They would not/could not use the seats; soon the deck was awash with excreta, we stood in the doorway and dropped our pants until even that failed. Became constipated until the liaison officer spoke to the Greek Captain and we were allowed to use the officers' bog. . . .
>
> I fought with the Greek PO Telegraphist in the corvette's W/T office over some trivial matter. I had lost interest. . .
>
> With the commissioning ceremony we were handed over with the ship, two coders, two bunting tossers, one radar rating, one leading telegraphist and one liaison officer. We were not volunteers except the liaison officer who no doubt got the job because he could speak the Greek lingo.

One of the bunting tossers in the *Apostolis* was Ray Lerigo:

> I had recently completed a successful course in HMS *Canopus*, for leading signalman and I was waiting a draft. My thoughts centred on the possibility of joining *Dido* or *Cleopatra*, maybe *Euryalus*. Then again perhaps *Jervis*, it would be a bit special if I landed up in one of the Hunts. I had already served in two.
>
> How was I to know that Their Lordships had decided to hand over the corvettes *Hyacinth* and *Primula* to the Royal Hellenic Navy after distinguished records in the Med. The fateful day I remember well, when 'Drafty' requested my company, I swear with a smirk on his face, he announced that I was to put all my recently acquired knowledge at the disposal of His Hellenic Majesty and join HHMS *Apostolis*.
>
> What a come down, but still anything to get out of *Canopus*, so off I went. I joined six other RN ratings, including a Kiwi radar rating and a lieutenant RNVR, the liaison officer, to make up the British Naval Liaison Staff in *Apostolis*.
>
> Anyone who has served in a Flower Class corvette would agree that they are pretty basic. The Greek crew made nonsense of that assessment, because in the time taken for the RN ratings to stow their gear in their appointed mess, the ship had been turned into a floating pigsty.
>
> Life shared with the Greeks was totally alien to life in a ship of the Royal Navy. One concession to the liaison staff was the permission to use the officers' heads. The Greeks used 'general' messing and Friday was garlic day and didn't we know it! Every few days or so they decided to

have a clean up and after they had finished *Apostolis* resembled what we had been used to in the past, but alas not for long.

We were finally ready to join the 47th Escort Group with the former *Primula*, now HHMS *Sacktouris*, so we did have the consolation of knowing there was another group of RN ratings in the same pickle as us.

We RN ratings in *Apostolis* got on well together and I recall that we seemed to get on well with the Greeks. There was a language problem to some extent; the Greek language is not an easy one to learn. Some of us managed to pick up a few phrases. We made friends with a number of Greek ratings but by and large in our off watch times, we kept ourselves to ourselves because it was difficult to communicate. The crews of the British ships in the group regarded us with some pity and usually either *Apostolis* or *Saktouris* ended up as the canteen boat.

We were now on a regular run Port Said to Gib with convoys. Cushy really and in spite of everything, we managed to do our share.

In Alexandria Leslie Stevenson and his friend Allen risked a run ashore with some of their Greek shipmates.

We meet a couple of Greek merchant navy men, they convey the message, 'Come with us.' We have it made with Greek 'Up Homers'. Arrived at house, lovely girl gives us all supper. 'Where is mine?' says Leslie. 'Ah well she will come to you in bed,' they replied. Two hairy Greek merchant navy men only came to our room!

September 1943 saw the U-boat wolfpacks return to the attack in the North Atlantic. The U-boats had improved radar search receivers, they were armed by acoustic homing torpedoes and improved anti-aircraft defensive armament. They were however under increasing pressure from Coastal Command aircraft fitted with Leigh Lights which trapped increasing numbers of U-boats on the surface at night.

In the Arctic, convoys to Russia had not been resumed as escorts were still deployed in the Atlantic U-boat battle. The battleship *Tirpitz* in Altenfiord was damaged by British midget submarines. In the Far East the American pressure on the Japanese Sea, land and air forces continued to increase and more landings on Pacific islands had succeeded. This eased the enemy pressure in the Indian Ocean and the Eastern Fleet had been able to move back to Ceylon from Kilindini and shipping losses in the Indian ocean had declined. In Russia the German divisions had retreated to the Dnieper river.

The Eighth Army landed on the heel of Italy on 3rd September and commenced a slow advance north against strong German opposition. On the 8th Italy signed an armistice with the Allies and ceased fighting. On the 9th the American and British allies landed at Salerno with the intention of linking up with Eighth Army for a joint drive north to Naples. By the 14th the Allies at Salerno were in serious trouble with a strong German panzer counter attack down the Sele river threatening to drive the troops back into the sea. German aircraft fitted with a new guided bomb were creating havoc amongst the shipping crowded into the Gulf of Salerno.

Battleships *Warspite* and *Valiant* were rushed at high speed from Malta and during the 15th and 16th with their 15″ turrets firing at pointblank range they had begun to break up the German tank counter-thrust. The battleships were under constant attack from the German bombers and torpedo attacks, and the great ships' counter-fire put the destroyers, which provided them with anti-submarine protection, at great risk. This was of course an occupational hazard for fleet destroyers protecting fleet capital ships, and many officers and men had died in escort ships from shells fired by the ships they protected. In the Gulf of Salerno the destroyer *Petard* was hit by a shell from *Warspite*; the destroyer had been damaged on many occasions in her long series of engagements in the Mediterranean. On the 16th, a 6″ shell from the battleship, incorrectly fused, entered *Petard*'s portside of the forward upper messdeck and reduced the supply party to A and B guns to a bloody shambles. Two men were killed and six badly wounded. Jack Hall, an asdic rating and able seaman, later wrote from a field hospital near Syracuse:

I was in the forward messdeck passing shells from the top of the magazine hoist, up the shute to A gun on the fo'c'sle deck, when there was an explosion, a terrific flash, a shower of sparks and then complete darkness. I knew that we were hit of course, but by what and the extent of damage I didn't stop to think. I heard moaning and wondered if we were to sink and be caught like rats in a trap before we had a chance to get out. I darted into the port passage, which still had emergency light burning at the far end, blowing more air into my life belt as I did so. Imagine my horror when I saw blood bubbling from a hole in my chest as I blew into my life-belt; I made my way into the sickbay where the MO treated my wounds, shrapnel had torn a groove across my back, another piece had entered my chest at the side and had come out at the front. Some more lads arrived with shrapnel wounds and one had to be transferred to a hospital ship in the area for immediate emergency operation. I met him later at base hospital from where he was medically discharged.

I felt no pain at the time until later when the effects of the morphia I had been given began to wear off. Later I learned that two of my shipmates had been blown to pieces and volunteers were asked to collect their remains to be placed into their hammocks for burial. No one would volunteer for the awful task, two were detailed and given a double tot of rum.

Petard's commanding officer, Commander Rupert Egan, constantly pressed his ship's doctor for news of progress of his wounded men and used all his influence and contacts to ensure that they had maximum care and an early return to the United Kingdom. He wrote personally to them all and to their families.

Jack Hall spent six months in hospital at Algiers before being sent home in a troopship. He reported to the Asdic school at HMS *Osprey* at Portland:

> My kit had been left in *Petard* and I had not been able to retrieve it; when I reported I was promptly accosted by the Master at Arms who shouted at me for being improperly dressed for wearing battledress. I told him that he should get out there and find out what it was all about, and cease being a barrack stanchion. I was promptly put in the captain's report and treated as a defaulter, much to my indignation. The captain was sympathetic and I was issued with a new set of kit to go on leave with, but managed to borrow a Mediterranean blue one to replace the issue navy blue (rookie) one.

Eric Smith, able seaman, arrived back in the East Mediterranean in early September. Following the sinking of the destroyer *Legion* he had returned to the United Kingdom and had his survivors' leave. He had attended a course at the gunnery school at Chatham and was now qualified as a Gun Layer Class 2, LR 2, promptly drafted to a new destroyer *Quadrant*, he was in her long enough to do one Russian convoy before falling sick. By the time he had recovered, *Quadrant* had sailed for the Far East. Smith was soon on a troopship bound for Cape Town; it was a miserable passage in an American ship with appalling food and great discomfort. From Cape Town he and others were sent by train to the naval holding base HMS *Assegai* not far from Durban. After a short spell here and the opportunity to enjoy the fabled pleasures of Durban he embarked in the troopship SS *Stratheden* with many hundreds of South African naval and army personnel. While in *Assegai* Smith met up with a boyhood friend, Jim Hawkins, who had joined up in the Royal Navy. Together they travelled in *Stratheden* for the Middle East with a draft to join the base HMS *Nile*.

On arrival at Alexandria we were taken to yet another transit camp by

. Starboard pom-pom
acuse landings. August

. Some of P2's 4″ guns
reak from action.

. 4″ gun supply party,
Syracuse landings
943.

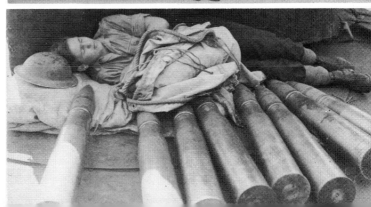

. Off Sicily, 'flakers'
lull.

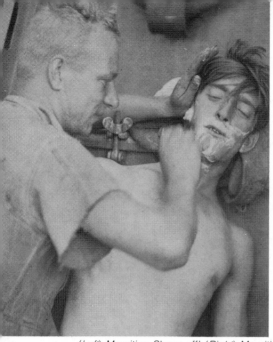

(*Left*) *Mauritius*. Shave off! (*Right*) *Mauritius*. Water rations, half a fanny between two.

(*Left*) *Mauritius*. Tot time off Syracuse and a lull in bombarding. (*Right, from top to bottom*) *Mauritius*. Left, centre and right guns crews of 'A' turret.

lorries. About five miles from Alexandria was a very large strip of desert dotted with tents and a few wooden structures. This dump was HMS *Nile*, and dump was the only name to describe it. The whole area was surrounded by a six foot high barbed wire fence. On the far perimeter were the heads, primitive in the extreme, a wooden slatted fence covering the WC's which consisted of deep trenches with slates running fore and aft on which ratings had to sit. These disgusting latrines were cleaned out twice a day by the local *fallaheen*. Flies were everywhere and more so than in the mess-halls where we had to eat. There was always a long queue for the morning sick call from patients suffering from stomach complaints. I was hospitalised for four days with a high temperature and a mysterious illness cause by an obscure bug. The whole place was a disgrace to the Royal Navy. . . .

Jim and I were only there for just over a fortnight before we were drafted but during the time we worked in the Bosun's party, mainly employed repairing tent guy-ropes; we also did 'duty watch' one evening in four. On one of these occasions I was detailed off for Town Shore patrol. About 30 of us with Leading rates and Petty Officers were taken by lorry into Alexandria where we were detailed for a variety of duties. . . .

A few days later I was drafted to the Hunt class destroyer *Rockwood* (Lieutenant S.R. Le H. Lombard-Hobson) whilst Jim went to a fleet destroyer *Eclipse* although he was expecting a draft home as he had been overseas for three years. He was told it would not be for long as he would be going home soon. . . .

It was a Saturday evening when I joined the ship and I was surprised to see her sides full of shrapnel holes. On reporting to the coxswain I was informed that I was a replaceman for the Director Trainer who had been recently killed. . . .

I made my way below to find only a few men in my mess, most having gone ashore. There was an old 'Stripey' and I asked where the ship had been to get so badly knocked about. He told me that they had been engaged in ferrying troops to the Dodecanese Islands in the Aegean, shooting up any German shipping they came across en route. On all these trips they were continually attacked by German aircraft, very little cover from our own forces being possible, our bases being far from the scene of action so gave our own fighters only a few minutes action time with the enemy before having to return to base. On their last trip to the Aegean, *Rockwood* had been heavily attacked; the Director Trainer had been one of those killed. This information cheered me up no end!

Rockwood was one of a small number of destroyers and cruisers that had been committed to a doomed and senseless campaign. It had started immediately following the Italian surrender and Armistice and the subsequent failure of Italian garrisons in the Greek Dodecanese Islands to disarm and control the German forces in the islands. In some islands, Leros, Cos and Rhodes, the Italians had assumed temporary control with some British army support but they were quickly under heavy attack from the Germans. Already two Allied destroyers, the Greek *Queen Olga* and the British *Intrepid*, had been sunk at Leros on 26th September and the Germans had recaptured Cos and Rhodes.

The Americans who had assumed the dominate role in the alliance did not support and were indeed suspicious of the British plans to drive through the Balkans via the Aegean and Dodecanese islands to outflank the German war machine. To prevent this happening they withdrew all air support for operations in the Dodecanese but in spite of this embargo and ignoring all the terrible experience gained in these same waters during the Western Desert, Greece and Crete campaigns and defeats, the British naval Commander in Chief Levant was committed to a bloody and prolonged torture with inadequate naval forces and no effective air cover. The Germans in the Dodecanese could have been left to 'wither on the vine' while the main thrust of the war bypassed them. But to satisfy political vanity not only were men to die for no purpose and many ships be lost, but the campaign was to increase the suffering of innocent Greek islanders who had endured Italian occupation, followed by the Germans; now many more would die as victims of the Dodecanese conflict.

Casualties of men and ships trying to hunt down and sink German-controlled shipping and to land troops to recapture islands became so bad because of the strength of the virtually unchallenged German air squadrons that the commanding officers of the Levant Command destroyers made a joint protest at the stupidity and useless product of the task given to them. This followed the sinking of a Hunt class destroyer and serious damage to her Greek-manned sister ship and the horrendous loss of life in a particularly horrible mining incident at night.

Two nights later the destroyer *Eclipse*, with Commodore P. Todd, embarked seeking first hand experience of his destroyer's ordeal, and *Petard* left Alexandria for one of their many excursions into the Dodecanese archipelago, the two ships loaded with stores and two companies of men of the Buffs. Passing between two islands approaching Leros in darkness to avoid the ever present Ju88's patrolling the moonlit sea, *Eclipse* blew up on a mine with very nearly total loss of life of the ship's company and the battle-equipped soldiers of the HQ company of the Buffs. The dead included Commodore Todd and Eric's friend Jim Hawkins.

Many men of the Levant force had fought for years in these waters and recently had experienced the heady successes of victory over the Axis in North Africa, Sicily and the advance into Italy. They were now back into the first years of the war when they and their dead shipmates had fought against overwhelming odds of the Greece and Crete campaigns in these same waters. They knew that elsewhere the Allied airpower was at last greater than the German enemy and that they were being sacrificed for a political face-saving policy and that they had again been let down by the professional establishment of the armed forces who would not stand up to the politicians.

When the futile exercise of death was concluded six Allied destroyers had been sunk, three were damaged. Four cruisers had been damaged, one beyond repair. Two submarines had been sunk and eight coastal forces craft were lost. The army suffered very many killed and taken prisoner.

Rockwood, three nights after the sinking of the *Eclipse*, was on another abortive sweep with her senior ship, *Petard*, looking for German invasion craft. Both ships had concluded a successful bombardment of the small harbour on the island of Kalymnos, when in brilliant moonlight a guided bomb hit and immobilised *Rockwood*. Under air attack and fire from shore batteries from Cos, *Petard* towed *Rockwood* into Turkish neutral waters in the Gulf of Kos. There she was left while *Petard* escaped south before dawn out of the archipelago and returned to Alexandria to load for another foray.

Eric Smith became involved in a bizarre incident which was the result of days of uncertainty, lying at anchor in Turkish waters, buzzed each day by a German plane and visited by a succession of Turkish officials of various uncertain rank and authority. The ship's company, starved of any information whatsoever, became apprehensive over their future; many believed that they would be interned for the remainder of the war.

Towards the end of the first week we were getting low on food and none could be procured locally. The ship's company cook did wonders with what he had. We soon ran out of bread but Jock made a sort of bread out of yams and a small amount of flour. There was no information for us. Apart from the routine part of ship work and maintenance duties there was nothing to do, shore leave was impossible and the ship's company was getting bored stiff. One morning, working in the DCT the Gunnery Officer poked his head in. . . .

Taking the plunge, I asked, 'Any truth, sir, that the Turks may intern us shortly?' He replied, 'The captain will I am sure inform the ship's company when negotiations develop.' I had to content myself with that.

Mess-deck rumours gained intensity as on the following morning two Turkish Officers came inboard and were closeted with the captain for some time. Shortly after this one of the officers returned with a well-dressed civilian. By evening the buzz was that we would all be interned and that all we had to look forward to was a period of confinement until the end of the war.

While some were openly gleeful at this possibility, there were others like myself who did not relish the thought of such a fate. Six of us discussed the chances of slipping ashore and endeavouring to make our way back to Alexandria. 'Tancey' Lee was a bit dubious. 'We could be regarded as deserters', he said. One or two others agreed with him. My new 'Oppo' Jimmy Green disagreed and said, 'If we leave a signed statement setting out our intentions, in the light of no definite information about our situation from our officers, I don't think that we could be charged with desertion.' As a senior able seaman I was inclined to agree with him. After all, we aren't running away from the war; we are trying to get back into it! In any case I don't fancy having to stay two or three years in this bloody country. The others agreed although with some misgivings. . . .

We set to and compiled the statement and arranged to leave it with a trustworthy shipmate. We decided to wait for one more day. The following morning the two Turkish officers and the civilian, this time accompanied by two soldiers carrying rifles, came inboard and all were ushered into the captain's quarters. We were now convinced that internment was imminent, so we decided to make a break for it that night. We obtained a boat's compass, some food, water and tobacco plus some miscellaneous ratings' shirts, jackets and trousers which when badges of rank were stripped off could pass as civilian dress.

We stowed the gear in the cable locker aft, midnight was to be zero hour which we thought would give us five hours to get far away. A Carley raft had been moored astern for use by the ERA's to inspect and repair the hole in the ship's side. Just after midnight Jimmy Green, Tancey Lee, Jan Stewart, Dusty Miller, Mick Logan and myself silently left the messdeck and clambered quietly over the stern, collecting the food and clothing en route, slipped the painter and quietly paddled ashore. Once inshore we secured to a small wooden jetty, folded and labelled our clothes stowed them at the bottom of the raft. Donning our civvies we struck out on a north-west course.

I have always liked walking so it was no hardship for me but a couple of the lads got fed up after a couple of hours and demanded a rest. The terrain was rocky and hilly with little vegetation, so after a short rest behind some boulders for a smoke, I urged them that it would be to our advantage to continue as fast as we could before daybreak. I said, 'Any stragglers will have to be left behind. In any event it might be best if we split up into pairs tomorrow anyway.'

By the time that dawn was breaking I estimated that we had made about 15 miles when suddenly Jan Stewart pointed out what appeared to be a cave. It was decided that it might be a good idea to rest up for the day and continue our journey at dusk. We were all tired and hungry anyway. Entering the cave, which was quite large, we were surprised to find that it appeared to have been lived in from time to time, there were some straw beds around and the cold remains of a fire. We set off in different directions to the nearest hillocks to spy out the land and then report back on anything that could be seen. There was no sign of life except for some sheep in the distance, 'It's probably some bloody shepherd's caboosh,' Jim suggested and I agreed and decided that we might as well take a chance and get some kip. I said, 'Keep well back in the cave and near the walls, we won't be seen so easily if anyone comes along. Hope none of you bastards snores.'

We settled down and were soon all asleep. I must have awoke once and thought I saw two men whispering near me, but I was worn out and thinking that I was probably dreaming I fell asleep again. Once more I awoke to find Tancey and Mick Logan in conversation with a young lad, obviously some kind of a shepherd, neither party could speak or understand each other's language. A young woman was kneeling some distance away placing twigs on a fire. She was joined a little later by an older man who gazed at us suspiciously. We were all now wide awake refreshed after our sleep and gathered round the fire; we offered the younger man some of our tobacco which he shared with the old man. He seemed quite friendly and after a while he went to a cavity in one of the walls of the cave and returned with a couple of bottles of Greek Ouzo and two battered tin mugs. For our part we fished out some tinned sardines and ships biscuits and soon we were all appeasing our hunger and thirst. The old man still seemed suspicious of us; we explained as well as we could that we were English. This seemed to satisfy him, but he left us pointing to the fire before his departure and said what sounded to be, 'Meat, meat'.

When he had gone I motioned to the young lad to come outside with me. Pointing into the distance I said, 'Egypt, yes?' Shaking his head he pointed in the opposite direction, gesticulating as well. I couldn't make much sense out of him and went back inside to the Ouzo which soon began to affect us all. We rearranged our makeshift beds a little closer to the fire and soon burred off again. The time was about 1100 hrs. At about 1600 I was awakened by someone poking me in the arm, I opened my eyes and found that the object I was being prodded with was the muzzle of a rifle held by a soldier. Another soldier was waking the others and behind him stood a Turkish officer. There was no sign of the shepherds or the girl. Getting to our feet, we tried to explain to the officer that we were British sailors. To our surprise he smiled, nodded and pointing to the mouth of the cave said, 'Come, Come – ship, ship.' We followed him outside, the two soldiers bringing up the rear.

The girl and two shepherds were standing about 40 yards away gazing at the scene. Silently we followed the officer until we reached a dirt track on which stood an Army vehicle. Motioning for us to climb inboard, the two soldiers joined us in the rear of the truck. We offered them our cigarettes and were soon nattering away speculating what would happen to us next. 'Oh well,' said Dusty, 'at least we've had some kind of a run ashore.' 'I've a mouth like the bottom of a bird cage after that hooch,' said Jim. The truck pulled to a halt some time later and we were told to dismount. To our amazement we found that we were back at the wooden jetty where we had landed the night before, with *Rockwood* right in front of us.

Pretty soon the ship's motor boat came inshore to collect us and, rather sheepishly, we embarked. The Turkish soldiers did not accompany us but waved and smiled as we left. 'You bunch of twits,' said the leading seaman who was coxswain of the motor boat. 'You'll all get 90 days each. The skipper is doing his nut over you lot'.

Our spirits were low when we scrambled inboard onto the small quarter-deck, the officer of the day and coxswain were waiting for us. We lined up at attention before the OOD. 'Off Caps' barked the coxswain (we hadn't got any). Our names, rating and official numbers were read out and we were charged with 'Breaking out of ship. Improper possession of ship's stores. Unlawfully using a Carley float. Improper possession of naval uniform clothing', and other charges that I have forgotten.

We all remained silent when asked by the OOD if we had anything to say? 'Very well, Captain's report' – 'Captain's Report,' intoned the coxswain. 'On caps, right turn, double march, report to your messdecks.' Our mess-mates laughingly questioned us and we answered them quite happily embellishing the tale of our small adventure quite monstrously.

The following morning brought the biggest surprise of all. Standing before the captain, we were all given a severe dressing down, this was expected. 'I have read your letter that you addressed to me and I am satisfied that none of you intended to desert your ship in the normal sense, that is why you are being charged with the lesser offence of breaking out of ship. What you did was serious and stupid; it could have caused an international incident.' Pointing at me and Jimmy Green, 'Both being regular serving ratings you should have known better. . . . For breaking out of ship, you will all have 14 days leave stopped and 14 days' No 11 punishment'. The Captain paused. 'For your information we hope to be leaving this place soon, I shall be addressing the ship's company this afternoon.' This was the first time that I had got away with anything in the RN!

A few nights later, escorted by three destroyers, *Rockwood* under her own steam slipped past German searchlights guarding the approaches to the Gulf of Cos and returned to Alexandria without further incident.

Back in the main theatre of the war, the Mediterranean central

basin and mainland Italy, the Allied armies had broken out of the
Salerno beach-head and Naples had been liberated. Now in October
1943 the Allies were making slow progress north of the Volturno
river against very strong enemy opposition. *Mauritius* sailed from
Naples to assist two destroyers *Laforey* and *Lookout* which were giving
the army support on the sea flank and who had suffered casualties
from repeated Ju88 bombing attacks.

The *Laforey* was no stranger to damage from bomb and shell, off
the beaches in the Gulf of Salerno, during the first 48 hours of the
landing, the destroyer had been hit five times by shells from German
artillery and the ship bore many scars from bomb splinters.

This time, off the estuary of the Volturno river, a bomb had hit the
gun shield of A turret mounting; the ship had also been raked by
splinters from near misses. Some crew members had been killed and
others wounded. Petty Officer Bob Burns remembers the wounding
of his friend and mess-mate:

> We were attacked by ten Ju88's after bombarding to assist troops trying
> to cross the river. We had several dead and wounded particularly in A
> turret when 'Blondie', captain of the gun, lost a leg. It was the first time
> that I witnessed direct blood transfusions as we limped back to port.
> Captain Hutton sustained neck and back shrapnel wounds but refused
> medical aid until all the crew wounded had been attended to. His duffel
> coat was saturated in blood. It never ceased to amaze me how he carried
> on, he must have been feeling so weak. . . .
>
> (Blondie) Petty Officer Horace Soder was one of our finest specimens
> of fitness and physical proportions; a day or so earlier at a 'Hands to
> bathe' we all admired his perfect dive from the top of the motor cutter's
> davit head, and then when Air Raid warning Red sounded, the speed
> and perfection of his crawl in the race back to the ship and action sta-
> tions. . . .
>
> The ship's company idolised Captain Hutton – his quiet, orderly, effi-
> cient handling of *Laforey* through countless actions inspired a pride
> amongst his officers and men. There were casualties of course, but even
> at its worst moments the confidence of the ship's company remained
> unshaken. I never knew him to lose his temper in spite of many provoca-
> tions. He never forgot to congratulate or thank even the most junior rat-
> ings for a job well done. . . .
>
> When he left the ship, *Laforey* was for days like a ghost ship; no laugh-
> ter and general all round depression.

Mauritius, after her first eighteen months of no enemy action, had
now been thoroughly baptised in fire. During July, August and September she had been continuously in action, mainly bombarding

shore targets in support of the Allied armies and had successfully
defended herself and given anti-aircraft fire support on innumerable
occasions without suffering any casualties. The strange paradox
about this obviously highly effective ship of war was that she had a
ship's company who in retrospective memories of their service in the
cruiser are firm in their conviction that she was a 'Happy Ship', yet
in October the dreary business of punishing men by warrant continued. Fourteen were read during the month to reach a total, for a
commission of under three years, of 120 warrants. *Mauritius* visited
Malta twice during October and on each call to restore and ammunition, men were discharged to detention quarters. Others spent time
in the cruiser's own cell block.

Royal Marine Bandsman Ian Connel writes of this period;

> The very first man to get a medal in the ship was the Bandmaster . . . a
> DSM. We could not understand this, but he said that he got it for the
> whole band who spent so many hours in the transmitting station during
> the bombardments. One member of the band said he should cut it into
> fifteen pieces. . . . The Band Corporal by the name of Cook was Men-
> tioned in Despatches.

October saw the climax of the Atlantic battle between the U-boat
Wolf packs and Allied aircraft, the convoy escorts and support
groups. 26 U-boats had been sunk. After this victory in the convoy
routes the U-boats never again recovered their grip and dominance
in the Atlantic although they remained a menace and made many
more sinkings.

At the end of October the escorts withdrawn from the Home Fleet
started to return to Scapa Flow, and in particular the 17th Flotilla of
'O' class destroyers, prepared for the restarting of the next series of
winter convoys to Russia, the first two due to sail in November.

Obdurate of the 17th Flotilla remained for a while in the Atlantic
with a support group and so would not be available for the
November or December convoys to Murmansk. So far the captain of
Obdurate had not achieved his ambition to sink his own U-boat
although he had with great skill and determination contributed,
while commanding the *Wild Swan* and now with *Obdurate*, to the
demise of several enemy submarines. His telegraphist, D.S. Goodbrand, in 1943, wrote a pen picture of his commanding officer:

> 'Most of you have never been to sea before, therefore you are a liability,

not an asset, to this ship. Eighty percent of you are green as grass. It is my intention to whip you into such shape that in three months' time you will be one of the smartest destroyer crews afloat. . . ' These were the first things the Skipper said to us on reaching my last ship, haggard from the long sleepless train journey starting at Plymouth, weary with carrying our kit-bags and hammocks through the mud of a Glasgow dockyard.

In no time at all it was made clear to us who was to be the new master of our souls and arbiter of our destinies.

The Skipper was a strange mixture of fiery temper and cynical aloofness. The story of him and his ship is the story of a combination dedicated without rest to engaging the enemy on every possible occasion.

My memories of him are many and varied. Out of a mass of unformed details, trivial in their incompleteness, a few concrete images appear merging gradually into a definite mental picture of the man himself. It was this way, once you had made contact with him you never forgot him. You meet some people, are momentarily engrossed with them, their dress, features, manners of speaking, etc., then forget them as a matter of course. They simply don't stick in your mind.

Not so the Skipper. . . .

The way I remember him best, it would be action stations on a freezing rough day in the North Atlantic or somewhere between Iceland and Archangel. An asdic contact has been obtained and along with another destroyer we are detached from the main convoy escort to hunt for possible U-boats.

The Skipper crouches over the binnacle, bulbous and duffel-coated, an alert ear cocked for the informative echoes that 'ping' from the asdic apparatus in a corner of the bridge. A sub-lieutenant stands by translating them into ranges and bearings. The two ships exchange signals, manoeuvre, converge on a bearing. Depth-charges! Boom – boom! The deadly articulation of sound underwater, debris of spray flung skywards, descending whitely, the air throbbing. The Skipper looks hopefully astern, beyond the creamy frothing triangle where the screws thresh, seeking the black surfacing hull that he has waited for for so long. But there is nothing. The ship lurches crazily in a beam sea. More depth-charges.

'Port twenty', says the Skipper down one of the many voice-pipes that writhe round the compass-platform.

'Twenty of port wheel on, sir!' sings back the coxswain from the wheelhouse.

The Skipper murmurs something inaudible, stamps his heavy seaboots and puts his gloved hands in the pockets of his duffel-coat. . . . Stooping over his compass he is like a rock against the reeling background of storm, welded there, shrewd in the ways of his ship. The wind is icy wild, lashing into the sombre cloud-stippled Arctic sky. . . He is intent on the business of killing Germans. His purpose is fixed and unalterable. This is his job and nothing will stop him doing it. His eyes are close with grimness and the look on his face akin to the lunatic rage of the sea.

'Steer two – two – oh!' The U-boat hunt goes on.

And that is the way I like to remember him best.

This is also the reason I came to admire the Skipper. He was a disciplinarian of the old school, an unsmiling strategist with his roots deep in the naval tradition: he stopped our grog and our shore-leave; he sent many of us to 'chokey' for periods ranging from ten to ninety days; he emphasised on every occasion the unbridgeable gulf that existed between our respective worlds . . . Yet I came to respect him because in pursuit of his ambition and because he hated Germans, he brought his destroyer safely through every imaginable danger, hardship and vile condition of service afloat, for which, incidentally, we paid amply in overdoses of seasickness, strain and fatigue. I admire him because he is the type of man who is responsible, to use that well-worn phrase, for winning the war at sea. And looking back to the loneliness in which he commanded, I think he was greater than we knew.

Albert (Bill) Bishop joined up, as a new entry in November and was sent to Shotley, HMS *Ganges*. The boys' training establishment seemed to be little changed after four years of war:

I joined HMS *Ganges* November 1943 and the first thing they did was to give us a hair-cut, I came out looking like a convict, then we had our photos taken holding a number, mine C/JX 657706 for our pay books. . . . Next day Saturday, we then had medical and dentist and lost two teeth. . . . We had our first TAB injection then told that the rest of the day was ours but not to take our jumpers off before turning in. . . . Next morning we had to turn out in trousers and gym shoes and after breakfast up over the mast with stiff sore arms. A very tall mast and we were scared, but it went off OK and being Sunday the rest of the day was ours. . . .

If our instruction in seamanship and parade drill did not go well, we had to double round the parade ground with a Long Lee-Enfield; the double march was called the Shotley Shuffle. For gunnery we drilled on an old 6″ mounting with 100-lb shells. For punishment it was called 'holding the baby', standing for five minutes with a shell held in your arms in the loading position or if it was for the whole crew, we had to run up 100 steps carrying the shell. . . .

After divisions my class was marched to the swimming baths, we had to lie on benches face down and were shown how to do the breast stroke, then ordered to undress we were marched to one end of the pool and told, 'This is the shallow end, 3ft', then marched to the other end and told, 'This is the deep end, 15ft'. The instructor pointed to me and ordered, 'Right, Lofty (I was 5′ 11″)'. I said, 'I can't swim'; then I was in with the help of a Royal Marine Instructor. The test for those who could swim and the standard for us who still had to learn later was to swim two lengths in a duck suit and then float for three minutes'. . .

Training complete; we did the exams and then the passing our parade; all those who had passed the swimming test went on leave. I hadn't, so with a dozen left behind I went to the pool. The officer in charge said, Ordinary Seaman Bishop, put on a duck suit and get in there and if you pass the test you will catch the London train. I passed and they took me by truck to Ipswich station; the lads all gave a cheer and called out, 'Good Old Bish always last but gets there in the end.'

Eric Harlow had long completed his (ex-*Ibis*) survivors' leave and his courses after return to barracks. He was now serving in the destroyer *Obedient* and was a watchkeeping coxswain of the ship's motor cutter. One day in December 1943 he was duty coxswain in the destroyer anchorage, Gutter Sound, Scapa Flow; spending the whole forenoon on routine trips to the base and to other destroyers in the anchorage. It was a typical very cold winter's day with the sound full of white horses whipped up by a stiff northerly breeze. There were many other boats going about their ships' business and like the other coxswains, Eric, muffled up to his eyes against the cold, stood up in the stern sheets of the cutter as he guided it back and forth between his ship and shore. Quite suddenly he thought that he recognised the cox'n of a passing destroyer's cutter;

I hadn't seen him for a couple of years, but the cox'n in the passing boat could only be Harold, to the surprise of 'Postie' sheltering under the canopy with 'Stokes', I brought the cutter round and chased the other boat blowing my whistle. The stoker in the other boat looking aft saw me and tugged at his cox'n's duffel coat to draw his attention and he slowed down. When I got alongside it was Harold; he was a watchkeeper in the *Obdurate*; we were both in the same flotilla. Later on the way back to *Obedient*, I stopped at Harold's ship and with the permission of the OOD went forward where I shared Harold's tot and we arranged to meet ashore at the canteen that evening on Flotta Island. This we did, enjoyed a few jars together and caught up with our news.

In the Mediterranean, *Mauritius* was having a break from her bombarding task and had in fact spent the major portion of the month of December in Taranto harbour before sailing for Malta on the 23rd. From Malta on Christmas Eve the cruiser sailed for Gibraltar and arrived on the afternoon of Christmas Day. There she stayed for three days, before sailing into the Atlantic to join a squadron of cruisers forming a patrol line north of the Azores to intercept German blockade runners, which were known to be trying to reach the Bay of Biscay enemy-held ports.

Mauritius arrived too late to intercept the blockade-runner *Alsterufer* which was sunk by rockets of a Czech Liberator aircraft on the 27th. She was also unable to assist the cruisers *Glasgow* and *Enterprise* when they fell upon eleven enemy destroyers and torpedo boats which had set out to escort the *Alsterufer* into the Gironde. One German destroyer and two torpedo boats were sunk by the gunfire of the British cruisers.

The year ended with the Allies in the Pacific making landings at Bougainville, in the Gilbert Islands and New Britain. On the Eastern Front the Germans had been driven back across the Dneiper River and the city of Kiev had been recaptured. On the Russian convoy route to Murmansk two more convoys had been successfully passed through without loss. The German operation to intercept Convoy JW55B with a strong surface force, consisting of the battle-cruiser *Scharnhorst* and six destroyers, failed with the sinking of the battle-cruiser.

The Germans in the Mediterranean remained in isolated control of the Dodecanese and Aegean islands and had stopped the Allied advance north in Italy at the Garigliano river.

CHAPTER SIX

1944

On 1st January 1944, *Mauritius* was ordered to remain at sea for a further 24 hours and search for survivors from the sunken German ships. The search proved to be unsuccessful and the cruiser called into Plymouth to refuel. Captain W.W. Davis obtained permission to send his men on 48 hours' leave; starboard watch left for their two days' leave at 0630 on the morning of the 3rd, every man expecting to return to de-ammunition ship in preparation for a refit, and then long leave. What they did not know was that their captain had not been able to dissuade Their Lordships from returning the cruiser to the Central Mediterranean war theatre, and that it had been an accident that brought the ship to Plymouth to refuel; she had been destined to refuel in Gibraltar and it was the extra 24 hours of search in the Bay of Biscay that had prevented this happening.

Lower-deck was cleared at 1000 hrs on the 3rd and Captain Davis tried to explain to the port watch why his ship had to return to Mediterranean: *Mauritius* had been away from the United Kingdom for seventeen months and although she had seen action almost continuously since July 1943, she was one of a few ships that had not suffered casualties or damage; her fire power was badly needed, and so on.

Starboard watch returned from leave at 2400 hrs on the 6th with no leave breakers and the port watch left at 0630 next morning, leaving behind them a disappointed starboard watch. Discontent began to mount, stores and mail for passage to the Mediterranean started to arrive in large quantities clearly confirming that the ship was under orders to return to the battle zone. It seemed that many men were frustrated in their hopes of getting leave after six months of continuous action, in which the discipline code had still been strictly applied. Warrant No 131 had been read before the ship departed from Malta.

Discontent started to be expressed by physical manifestations; late on Friday evening, after pipe down, a fire was discovered in the stokers' bathroom; it took half an hour to extinguish and its cause could not be explained by accidental causes.

Port watch returned to leave at 2400/8th and the next day, Sunday, *Mauritius* proceeded down the Hamooze in a stifled atmosphere of tension, her ship's company in a sombre and uneasy mood of semi-fear for the consequences of an action of protest to which they were committed. The cruiser anchored at 1232 in Plymouth Sound, 004 degrees Breakwater Fort 5 cables. Hands went to dinner and steam remained on main engines with engine and boiler room watches closed up.

One of the early indicators of trouble came to John Edward (Nobby) Clark, a watchkeeping crew member of the cruiser's cutter; his 24 hour duty finished at noon after a 24 hours that had allowed no rest:

> I was in the 1st motor cutter's crew, having had the first leave of 48 hours, I finished my duty at Sunday dinner time with everyone knowing we were going back to the Mediterranean; my last boat trip was with the last bags of mail for ships in the Med Fleet . . . the unrest started when someone told me not to turn in after my all night duty but to lash up and stow.
>
> The hands were piped to tea at 1530 and to clean into the dress of the day. At 1600 the pipe was evening quarters, no one turned to, only the petty officers; it could have been the captain's first clue of trouble.

Down in the engineroom Chief ERA William Lewis was to have a catalystic shock:

> We were on the control platform when my right-hand man, a quiet sober responsible leading stoker suddenly moved across the engine-room and they all sat down. I went over to him and asked what was going on? His astonishing reply was that they were on strike and so was the whole lower-deck of the ship. He said that all the boiler-room stokers were also 'on strike', I checked and this was so. I told the leading stoker that this was impossible; you cannot have a strike, it is only mutiny. I could do nothing to shift them. We cut off telephone communications to Seaman and Stoker messdecks but found that they had organised a system through the fire-main connections which passed through the water-tight bulkheads. . . We senior rates sailed the ship but after 36 hours we were all totally exhausted after the bad storm in the Bay of Biscay.

On the cruiser's forecastle Lieutenant Patrick U. Bayly DSC, whose appointment to the cruiser brought him to join *Mauritius* on 3rd January, found himself faced with the task to weigh and secure the starboard anchor and forecastle with only the assistance of the chief stoker on the capstan, the petty officer captain of the forecastle and a few petty officer volunteers. Patrick Bayly, who remembers the incident with great clarity, retired from the Royal Navy as Vice Admiral Sir Patrick Bayly, KBE, CB, DSC.

The fair log for *Mauritius* has an entry for calling the ship's company to evening quarters at 1630 hrs; at 1705 hrs the clearing of the lower-deck to be addressed by the captain, then at 1730 hrs securing for sea. Despite these entries in the cruiser's fair log it appears the ship's company obeyed none of them and remained in their messes. 'Nobby' Clark continued his recollection of the messdeck resistance;

First the padre came down to the mess-decks to talk to us, he was not liked and soon left without getting any replies. Then the commander, who selected the CW candidates sitting worried at their mess table. They had been told to turn to if ordered to, and they did but no one else. After the commander, came Commissioned Gunner Mr Mole who was very popular, but he could not shift anybody. Then there were four people guarding the closed messdeck bulkhead doors. The telephones were cut off, but we were able to contact the whole ship by using the fire-main connections through the water-tight bulkheads. Came a huge banging on the doors; when challenged it was the Royal Marines coming to join us.

ERA 3rd Class A.R. Russell;

When the time came for us to depart the sailors, stokers and some of the Royal Marines refused to go to stations and battened themselves into the seamen's messes. Communication with them was via the firemain fixtures through bulkheads beside the doors which were knocked up.

The chief and petty officers prepared the ship for sea and we left to anchor in the Sound. *Glasgow* was in the Sound and, I was told, had trained her guns on us, a very tense and dramatic moment. I remember that the WRNS brought one of our boats back to the ship which was hoisted inboard by our aircraft crane.

Bandsman Ian Connel remembers the incident;

When side and cable parties were piped to their stations, no member of either party took any notice. We were then ordered to clear lower-deck, but the seamen and Royal Marines stayed below and closed their hatches. I as a member of the band actually went onto the quarter-deck. Eventually the ship put out to sea. Captain Davis cleared lower deck on arrival at Gibraltar and said no action would be taken against any of the ringleaders, whom he said he knew, provided we would all agree to follow him through thick and thin and that we would be returning home in three months. There was a show of hands and everyone on the quarter-deck agreed.

The cruiser's log records that at 1900 hrs the ship went to dusk action stations and the ship's company closed up. At 0405/10th the port anchor was found 'to have been carried away' (no doubt because of the failure of the fo'c'sle party, to turn to, in Plymouth Sound). It took an hour and 25 minutes in a violent Bay of Biscay gale to secure the anchor. On arrival at Gibraltar Captain Davis cleared lower-deck and informed his men that he would have to inform the Commander-in-Chief Gibraltar of the events that had occurred in Plymouth Sound; he said he would state what he believed were special circumstances and that he hoped that the ship's company would support him in the future.

Three hours later Captain Davis cleared lower-deck again and informed the ship's company that the cruiser was to return to the Italian war zone, have very little leave but nobody would be victimised.

Able Seaman/LTO(W) David M. Skin; 'A few ringleaders were sorted out and dropped off at Malta and we were sent as a punishment without shore leave back for a prolonged period in the battle zone.'

Able Seaman Skin is correct; the ship's log records that *Mauritius* was, after 24 hour call in Malta, back in the Bay of Naples bombarding the coast road near Terracina. She remained in the area for the remainder of the month engaging shore batteries and mobile artillery units deployed by the Germans to slow the Allied advance in Italy. Yet in Malta on 22nd January Warrant 135 was read and a seaman was discharged into detention quarters.

A destroyer in the Mediterranean battle area was also being teased into a near mutinous situation. *Laforey* had survived a multiplicity of air, sea and off-shore actions with many casualties and damage to the ship. Her men were being subjected to the trauma of senior officer changes, Captain R.M.J. Hutton DSO, DSC had departed and was succeeded by a man of special distinction, Captain H.T. Armstrong DSC, a younger man who had created a formidable destroyer flotilla, the 17th DF, which his successor a few weeks after transferring command was to elevate into naval history in the Battle of the Barents Sea. He was much younger than Captain Hutton, consumed with ambition and considered by his contemporaries to be destined for an eventual First Sea Lord, so perhaps it was predictable that he would not endear himself to his new flotilla or to his flotilla

Battleship *Ramillies*.

Bob Burns DSM with his family, on survivors' leave from *Laforey*. March 1944.

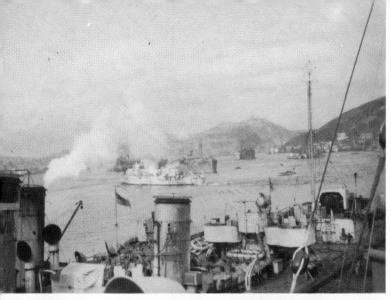

Oribi. A scene of St John harbour, Newfoundland

Oribi. A mess-deck bridge school.

Oribi. Polyarnoe, Russia

leader, *Laforey*. His effect on the experienced and battle-hardened chief and petty officers in *Laforey* was unfortunate.

> His first address to the ship's company was to say that the Mediterranean war was a two-penny half penny affair and wished to take the ship into the far east where the real war was going on. This did not go down well with those who had not seen their loved ones for years and we knew he had been home on leave after his time in *Wren*, *Maori* and then *Onslow*.

So wrote the GI, Bob Burns.

Captain Armstrong did nevertheless save his ship from a complete collapse of morale. Before he had joined, the ship, in Captain Hutton's command period, had acquired an appalling moronic character, a Dominion officer who, in Petty Officer Bob Burns' words:

> . . . in a few short weeks had demoralised a happy ship's company with a succession of cock ups, his crowning disaster was to inform the Red Watch that the pre-war British navy consisted of 'the scum of the back streets of the industrial cities, glad only to be in the service for a feed and good clothing'. When Captain Armstrong joined he found the lower-deck on the very verge of mutiny. . . There were all the real threats of a wash-deck locker burial.

Buck Taylor, the coxswain, and two other senior petty officers with the Buffer, saw the captain, and to his credit this officer who had destroyed a happy ship was given a pier-head jump at Syracuse into the base HMS *Elissa*.

The destroyer *Obdurate* formed part of the escort to Convoy JW56A whch sailed from Loch Ewe on 12th January. The convoy of 20 ships had a bad start when in the teeth of a hurricane five ships had to turn back, and then on the afternoon and evening of the 26/27th three ships were torpedoed. The *Obdurate* was herself damaged by a new German torpedo, a homing device called the T5 by the enemy and the Gnat by the Allies. Telegraphist D.S. Goodbrand writes of the convoy:

> 1700 hours, leaving harbour Seydisfiord we are fifth in a file of destroyers steaming in line ahead down the fiord, on either side of which snow-covered crags rise steeply.
> Once outside the boom we assume an arrow formation. Land recedes; a grey chasing mist has rolled down from the ice-locked hills and hidden the entrance to the fiord. Sea and sky have become a vast, uniform grey-

ness. No sunset ushers the Arctic night. A final signal flickers redly from the bridge of the flotilla leader, then it is dark. The trip has begun. Our speed it seems is sixteen knots; our first job is to pick up the convoy.

On the messdecks loudspeakers blare forth BBC short-wave programmes. Men off watch spend their time in a variety of ways. Some play cards, a few write letters, others read – thrillers, Lin Yutang, the Hornblower tales of C.S. Forester – prepare meals or try to snatch the odd hour of sleep before going on watch.

Seamen coming down from the upper deck, bloated with winter-clothing, bring a damp Arctic smell with them into the stuffy messdecks. The ship rolls a little, caught in a moderate swell and instinctively we adjust ourselves to the new movement. The talk, mainly about the present trip, is realistic, unsentimental. Several men are sceptical about our chances in the event of contact with Norwegian-based enemy capital ships. The general attitude seems to be one of hoping for the best plus commonsense recognition of the routine dangers to be encountered.

There is a 'buzz' that we shall pick up the merchant ships at noon tomorrow, Sunday. Meanwhile we are advised to sleep fully-clothed and to wear our lifebelts constantly.

1100 hrs, Sunday. Bad weather. Grey, roaring seas cascade along the upper deck, wash over the bows as the ship butts her way through. Numbers of men are seasick. The stench in the heads is nauseating. Later on the weather grows calmer. At 1300 hrs the merchant-men are sighted breasting the horizon, a mirage of scattered hulls and smoke littered sky. We overtake them swiftly. They are mostly American, a few British. Liberty ships, tankers, ammunition ships. One or two have locomotives lashed to their decks. Disposed in five columns they move comfortably within the protective ring of screening destroyers. The next two days pass peaceably enough.

Midway between Spitzbergen and the German U-boat base at the North Cape, is Bear Island. The threat of ice-pack moving south at this time of year forces the convoy to steam well below Bear Island to within twenty-minutes flying time of the Norwegian coast. This area, ideal for enemy air and under-sea attacks on our shipping, is the chief danger-spot of the whole Arctic supply route. Noon on the fifth day finds us due south of Bear Island, ready for any emergency.

Trouble is not long coming. At 1400 hrs our listening devices detect the presence of U-boats in the vicinity. The weather is extremely cold. Ships loom weirdly out of a shifting sea-mist. During the next three hours the attack develops in earnest. There has been some strain and excitement. Thankfully we hear the alarm bells ring for action stations, then rush to our posts.

Destroyers race to investigate submarine contacts, plough through the lanes between columns of merchant vessels, frenziedly dropping depth-charges.

'Buzzes' fly round the ship. 'Tin-fish just missed us!' 'Sub got a merchant packet, went down in seconds!' The W/T office is constantly receiving signals. Latest reports indicate possibly fifteen subs operating against the convoy.

1800 hrs. A bridge starboard lookout sights a U-boat on the surface. We chase it at twenty-five knots, alter course to attack from a favourable angle. The U-boat submerges at 1,000 yards. Seconds later there is a terrific explosion on our starboard quarter. We have been torpedoed!

The ship rocks, vibrates, steadies herself. A report is radioed immediately to the senior officer. The shock has brought men racing up from below decks with inflated lifebelts ready, if necessary, to abandon ship. The Engineer Officer goes aft to inspect the damage, then reports to the bridge. Five flattened torpedomen are helped shakily to the sick bay. The starboard engine is out of action, screw gone, propeller-shaft twisted, maximum speed reduced to ten knots. We rejoin the convoy.

Supper. The messdecks are loud with chatting and argument, the reaction from the past moments of nervous strain. In vivid, intensely personal accounts we relive the incident of torpedoing. Most of us feel shaken, some exhilarated at our providential escape, others depressed.

About midnight I am awakened by sounds of ammunition being taken from a forward magazine. 'B' gun is firing star-shell. Latest news circulates quietly in the messdeck. It seems that three merchantmen are sunk and escorts are busy picking up survivors. All night the rumble of depth-charges alternates with the steady double-crump of star-shells. . . .

A North Russian port. We arrived safely after a three day running fight with U-boats.

The snow-covered landscape, hemmed in by glittering white tundra, is busy with trudging uniformed Russians. The people are friendly. Soviet soldiers and marines like our cigarettes. We exchange them for curious glass-handled knives and red-star badges bearing the hammer and sickle. Temporary repairs are effected by the ship's crew, helped by a few Russians, over two or three weeks, adequate dockyard facilities being non-existent.

Civilians are not much in evidence. What few children there are seem to be evacuees from the Ukraine. They are tough, boisterous, like to laugh. Equipped with horrific photographs of German atrocities to wave in front of our noses and voracious appetites they invade our messdecks at meal times, swinging on the hammock rails and tumbling over each other like young bears in their bulky parkas in their haste to squat at table or on the seat-lockers, 'filling their boots' with grub laughingly shared by the hands then foraging even for scraps in the 'gash' buckets, each grinning mouth a bottomless pit – orphans of the Hitlerian storm.

Outside the cold almost stops you breathing. A vivid brown moon burns over the tundra. Youngsters sleigh down the primitive streets. A guard, watching us pass, jabs his bayonneted rifle into the air shouting the equivalent of 'Up Hitler'. A column of Red Army men and girls in uniform holding hands file out of the theatre and through the snow towards their respective barracks, regimented even in leisure. . . . These are my last impressions.

Then our thoughts turn towards the voyage home.

The destroyer *Petard*, after many months of almost constant action in the East and Central Mediterranean and more recently in the Dodecanese, had been transferred with her sister ship *Paladin* to the East Indies Fleet. On 12th February the two ships, with the cruiser *Hawkins*, were escorting a trooping convoy of four ships from Kilindini to Colombo. At noon the Commodore's ship, the 7,300 ton *Khedive Ismail*, was torpedoed by the Japanese submarine *I27*; the ship sank in three minutes, leaving very many of her crew and passengers numbering more than 1,000 struggling in a glassy smooth sea. The submarine placed itself beneath the survivors where she was driven to the surface by the destroyer's depth charges.

Captain Sam Lombard-Hobson writes of the action in his book *A Sailor's War*:

> *Petard* was transferred to the Far East fleet where she soon found herself in a frightful situation, so vividly described in Nicholas Monsarrat's *Cruel Sea*, of being over a submarine which had just torpedoed and sunk a passenger ship. To destroy the Japanese U-boat, Egan had to cut through the swimmers, and drop a pattern of depth charges in their midst. The anguished cries of men and women in the water haunted him for long afterwards; and, sadly, my old school mate was driven to take his own life. . .

One survivor, Petty Officer P. Crabb was asleep in the petty officer's mess in the *Khedive Ismail* when the torpedoes struck:

> As soon as the torpedoes struck, immediately she listed over and everyone made a dash for the companionway, except for yours truly and Petty Officer Harper. We both made for two ports which were open. I remember scrambling through and hobbling down the ship's side, I was recovering from a broken leg, stepping over the rolling chock and diving into the sea. By the time I surfaced the ship had gone.
> I swam to a green smoke canister some 30 yards away. Hanging on to this I looked about me; there were several other survivors either swimming or hanging onto whatever floated.
> The convoy had disappeared by this time and it seemed that we were left to our own devices. 200 yards away there were two lifeboats from the ship, one was upside down. Survivors were all making for them so I decided to do the same. I am almost certain that the submarine passed under us as there was quite a turbulence of water and a wake left behind.

* Reproduced by kind permission of Laurence Pollinger Ltd.

This was the scene when *Petard* and *Paladin* arrived at high speed. The sub must have been picked up on their asdics because they started to depth charge some 300 yards away. I distinctly remember one charge from a thrower exploding just above the surface of the sea. It's a very strange experience to feel shock waves coming through the water and the almighty thump in the stomach.

Before the convoy had departed from Kilindini the cruiser *Hawkins* had sent over to the *Khedive Ismail* a party of signalmen and telegraphists to supplement the commodore's communications staff. Only one of the *Hawkins* men, Leading Signalman W.R. Harwood, survived the sinking and later the destroyer's depth charge attack:

> Of the two WRNS survivors, one was rescued from below decks of the *Khedive Ismail* by me personally and we were picked up from an upturned lifeboat by the *Paladin*. The WRNS refused to leave me until we boarded the *Hawkins* at Addu Atoll.
>
> A sad end to the story was that WRNS Nora Munro died about four years later; her death was connected with the incident.

Her temporary repairs completed in Murmansk, *Obdurate* had limped home on one screw and now waited at Hebburn-on-Tyne for orders to proceed for her major refit:

> 8 Mess, 0100 hours. Snores emanate from slung hammocks that touch ever so slightly, such is the lack of space. The solitary light-bulb glows feebly behind its mask of blue paint, solicitous of the blackout. Portholes are closed; all is at rest. Then I wake to a noise. Peeping over the side of my hammock I discern two shadowy figures descending the ladder from the seamen's messdeck, pussyfooting, trying not to disturb their messmates sleeping below. Jack the Tel. and Charlie the Chef are returning after a night on the booze. I watch them unseen. They put their heads together in maudlin conclave. Mischief is afoot, I can smell it – hear it in their stifled chuckles and frantic whispers. What are they up to? Suddenly all their consideration for others had vanished. They stumble over a bucket, point through the darkness. 'Let's do it,' says one. 'Go on then,' says the other. They utter a cracked and crooked laugh, cut short as each in turn makes admonitory shushing noises. Silence. In the dim light it is hard to tell which is which. Then as my eyes grow more accustomed to the gloom, I notice the taller Jack stooping under the oblivious hammocks as he shuffles towards tableware reposing in racks screwed to the bulkhead. The chef lurks behind him, urging him on, sotto voce. Jack noiselessly opens a drawer and extracts a large breadknife. Then he turns and creeps towards the hammock in which he knows sleeps the leading writer, a fellow of aloof and sickly outlook with many enemies

and the flames of his ardour fanned by Charlie the Chef in the role of Avenging Angel, brings down the breadknife's blade like a guillotine and begins sawing energetically at the clews of the offender's hammock.

The wail of the leading writer as he hits the deck might have warped a plank. The indignation of the roused sleepers knows no bounds for a space, then subsides into low mutterings under a barrage of expostulation from the petty officer of the watch who, attracted by the din, peers down into 8 Mess from the upper hatch-opening. 'What's going on down there?' he hisses. No ripostes. The two inebriates have disposed themselves flat on the locker-tops behind the mess-tables and feign sleep. Despite their addled heads, fumed by the brown ale of Geordieland, they know which side their bread is buttered.

Eventual silence; not even the ticking of a clock. The target for tonight lies where he is fallen in the ruins of his hammock, not daring to move. The petty officer departs, grumbling. The blue light on the deckhead burns on, signalling a victory for the oppressed.

Who would be a leading writer?

Later in Plymouth *Obdurate* prepared to pay off and her ship's company packed to move into the barracks at Devonport, HMS *Drake*: Signalman Colin Watson recorded:

The Yeoman of Signals, who was the finest I ever knew, sent a message to our messdeck, to my oppo and me, both signalmen who had served the full first commission in *Obdurate*, requesting the pleasure of our company and ending with, 'Bring bottle'.

We arrived with our bottled 'Neaters' and found the Yeoman and Navigating Officer there, already with a few tots inside them, sitting on the deck. We joined them shared our rum, talked of the good and bad times and toasted *Obdurate*. . . The crew paid off and returned to Devonport Barracks. I never sailed again in Arctic waters, but of the ships I served in, the *Obdurate* remains a special memory.

Able Seaman William E. Hope recalls:

Giving a wrong age by some three months, I volunteered for the RN mainly, because I wanted to go to sea, the other reason was that I had no wish to be called up for the Army. I enjoyed my ten weeks of seamanship training at HMS *Collingwood* in Fareham, Hants. On completion, I was drafted to a dispersal camp, in the Portsmouth area, I think the name was Stockheath. From there I was drafted to HMS *Oribi*. To join *Oribi* I had to travel to that Naval paradise Scapa Flow, accompanied by some fifty other ratings, all very eager to go to sea. On arrival, I found that *Oribi* was still out on sea-duty; consequently I was billeted on board the *Greenwich*, a depot ship for the sea-going ships.

Eventually, *Oribi* came steaming in and I was, along with two other HO ODs, transferred to this beautiful sleek-looking destroyer. A short induction by the chief coxswain, and I was guided to Mess One, just one bulkhead door away from the forward paint shop. I was a little apprehensive, being the greenest of green, I weighed up the crowded mess-deck, tried to answer the many questions flung at me from all sides. They all looked like seasoned sailors, and some of their comments were enough to make me wonder whether I was doing the right thing. In a rather squeaky voice I asked where do I sling my hammock? A voice with a broad Geordie accent replied, 'Sling the f. . . thing over the side, you won't need it on this bastard.'

There was nowhere to run, so I started to learn all about life on the lower-deck of a wartime destroyer. I did learn, sometimes the hard way, but I was taken in hand by a three badge seaman, who quickly taught me the ropes and life became that much happier. The three-badger looked after my welfare like a father. He held the position of the ship's 'Tanky', a man that could always produce a bottle of ship's rum for any occasion.

My first taste of sea-time was on a convoy to Russia, I had already been warned of what to expect, I listened to every word, after all these men knew about it, stormy seas, U-boats, dive-bombers, sinking ships and the ice-cold temperatures. Well, maybe it was the rough weather, or maybe all the U-boats had been sunk but apart from the cold weather I was more fortunate than my predecessors, I only suffered wet clothes lack of sleep and a bad dose of chilblains. The experience did me a power of good. I had found my way around the ship, I learned how to do dhoby-ing in a galvanised bucket, I was shown how to make a Manchester Tart when it was my turn to be 'Cook of the Mess.'

My action station was the pom-pom as a loading number, I became adept at keeping the ammunition belts going in a continuous flow, in spite of gashing my fingers on numerous occasions. My cruising station was on B Gun, again as a loading number; the monotony of this was broken by one hour spells as look-out on the bridge wings; on one occasion I was so tired, that my head fell forward, and I bashed the bridge of my nose on the binocular stand; apparently, I had nodded off. Fortunately the officer of the watch had not spotted my offence and I was greatly relieved to scurry back to B Gun-deck, when my relief arrived.

I can't really remember our guns being fired in anger during that trip but I do remember the rough sea: life-lines were rigged, and venturing along the upper-deck was quite frightening, the bows of the ship seemed to disappear into deep waves, and I often thought that we were taking on the role of a submarine; however, the ship came through it all with hardly a scratch. It was a different story down on the mess-decks, the deck was almost as wet as the upper-deck, mess-tins, crockery, articles of clothing, paper-back books, cigarette-ends were all swilling around the deck, it would appear that the porthole and deadlights were not too secure, consequently water had seeped in and flowed down the ship's side, flooded the seat lockers spilling over on to the deck, and as the ship rolled on her beams, little rivers of sea-water rushed from side to side. Before anyone could sit down to a meal, the mess had to be cleaned up – not that we sat down to food very often. In rough weather, the main meal consisted of a concoction called 'Pot Mess' which could be prepared by the greenest 'Cook of the Mess' just a matter of emptying cans of Irish stew, peas, tomatoes, potatoes, carrots, packets of dried soup into the largest mess-fanny, with a suitable quantity of water, add seasoning and whip it down to the galley for boiling. When the hands came down to dinner, the fanny was to be found swinging from a hook in the deck-head. Each man would grab a mug, dip into the fanny and your meal was taken standing up, whilst clinging to a stanchion for safety. This was a favourite meal when the weather was rough.

If meals were a bit haphazard, finding a place to sleep was a lottery. Most of the good places were reserved by the senior hands, God help the man who pinched their billet. I was rather fortunate to find a vacant space on the deck just outside the bulkhead door leading to the paint-shop, at least there was no danger of anyone putting their big feet on my head whilst I was sleeping. It seemed that no one slung their hammock whilst we were at sea, however, after many sleepless nights I did start to get used to the idea, but I never got used to the idea of sleeping on a wet deck; my mattress consisted of an oil-skin coat, which gave some protection against the little rivulets of sea-water which flowed with the movement of the ship. If you got four hours' sleep you were doing well, you could always catch a few winks whilst on watch, according to your watch-station, but I found it very difficult, being on B Gun which was directly under the watchful eye of the Bridge Officers. Like most men, I dreaded the sound of the 'action bell'; there was no problem of getting dressed, because we slept in our clothes, with our life-belts close at hand, usually being used as a pillow, grabbing this most precious item we would run like hell to our action station, (mine was the pom-pom). The gun was already loaded; it was matter of making sure the ready-use locker was open and then waiting for instructions; more often than not it was a false alarm and a quick return to your cruising station or back to the mess for a quick cup of 'kye' and get your head down again.

There was a number of great characters onboard *Oribi*; names escape me now, but I do remember the coxswain, a very efficient man, hard but always fair, he didn't always follow the strict lines of discipline, but would readily sort out anyone who stepped out of line. On one occasion there was a fight on the mess-deck between a three-badged Killick and the GI. Strangely, the two contestants appeared to be the best of friends. However they came to blows; when the fight came to the notice of the coxswain, he came to the mess-deck, took in the situation, then casually turned and secured the bulk-head door and let the fight take its course. The GI and the Killick eventually retired, bloody and bruised, to the PO's mess, no doubt to share a glass of ship's rum.

'Wings and Bash', these were nicknames given to mess-mates. I recall in *Oribi* the first time I heard the expression 'Bash'. I was very young and very green compared with my mess-mates. I found the going a bit tough at first, then the 'Tanky', a three-badge seaman, took me in hand to show me the ropes, and everyone started to refer to me as 'Tanky's Bash', but then there were remarks passed that, that I did not care for very much. For instance 'Has Tanky shown you the golden rivet yet?' I was green but I had been in the Navy long enough to understand the meaning of their remarks, so one day I had to prove to my mess-mates that I could look after myself, and just to prove that I was no hammock-warmer for 'Tanky'. At that time I suppose I was a little too sensitive but I overcame that but not before a fellow mess-mate and I came to blows; yes, I got the worst of it, but I did earn some respect. Strangely enough, shortly after the scrap, I was called 'Wings' which was later changed to 'boat-hook', following an incident in the ship's motor cutter when I accidentally broke a Boat-hook and almost injured the captain.

In South Africa at the radar school in the base HMS *Assegai*, Tom Guard had passed out as petty officer (Radar),

My pal and I passed out top of the PO course and as a reward we were lent to the Royal Indian Navy – a reward we could have done without but on the other hand I had seen enough action at sea. . . . We came from Durban to the Indian sub-continent by an ex-merchant navy ship and a few days after landing we took the train to Bombay. Four days very comfortable because we had a very large compartment with padded sleeping benches. We could claim four annas a day for soda water to clean our teeth! . . . It was while we were in Bombay one afternoon having a cup of tea that we heard the loudest explosion ever and saw a huge mushroom of fire – an ammunition ship had gone up in the harbour. We went back to *Braganza* where everyone was falling in – I had been in the AFS and NFS before the war and in the early days of the war too, during the blitz on Manchester and Liverpool, and so I was put in charge of a pump and off we went. I have never seen such carnage – I don't know how many lives were lost – I know some WRNS working on the dockside were all killed and pieces of the ship were blown miles away and I saw molten metal running down the side of a building. I believe that Bombay lost most of its fire-fighting appliances which were being used on a cotton fire in another ship at the time. Also on acetelene welder was actually burning a hole in the cotton ship when the ammo ship blew up. He was thrown into the water but saved! This was in March 1944. We were moved up to the new school on Manora island and we were the only two Royal Navy ratings in the place. We were housed in the Gunnery School and got ourselves a 'Nice Number' in the officers' cabins. The desert was on one side and the sea on the other and gradually we 'acquired' such things as a punkalouver, carpets, bookcases, radio etc, and it was home from home. After a few weeks theory we took the ratings to sea for practical training. They had the *Madras* and another corvette, we would be out for a week and call in at Bombay. We had a mess made especially for us in these ships and a special place where we eat our food – apart from the other Indian sailors. Just think of it! You know in these boats and all the Royal Indian Navy ships there were all kinds of religions – living happily together inboard in their own separate messes.

Mauritius since her rather ignoble departure from Plymouth in early January had been in action very many times commencing with a day long bombardment of Formica in Pozzuoli Bay on 5th February; this task, with German aircraft making frequent attacks on the cruiser, continued until her last action in the Italian campaign which lasted six hours on 3rd March north of Naples against German artillery and infantry positions.

The cruiser returned to Malta for a stay of twelve days prior to sailing to the United Kingdom on 24th March. While she remained in Malta the toll of punishment warrants continued; eight were read bringing the total to 144 since the ship was commissioned in 1941.

Mauritius returned to the UK via a call at Algiers and Gibraltar, then north to Cape Wrath via the Pentland Firth to Chatham where the ship's company were sent on long leave and the dockyard prepared the ship for her role in Operation *Neptune*, the maritime section of the invasion of Europe, *Overlord*.

The destroyer *Laforey* was sunk on 30th March by three torpedoes fired by *U-223* (Lieutenant Gerlach) at the end of a long hunt by *Laforey, Tumult, Hambledon* and *Blencathera*. The destroyers had driven the U-boat to the surface in a position south of the island of Stromboli and it was trapped in the light of star shells fired by the hunters. For some inexplicable reason Captain Armstrong ordered his searchlight to be exposed and allowed the doomed U-boat to find its last target. *Laforey* sank in seconds, and with her eight officers and one hundred and seventy nine ratings were killed or drowned. Her ship's company totalled 224. Robert Burns was one of the few survivors:

Captain Armstrong hastened the demise of our ship by the injudicious use of the searchlight even though the target was clearly illuminated by star shells. He was not popular with the crew because he played down the long war in the Med as a twopenny half penny skirmish. . . Lieutenant Stocker RN, [who had only recently joined the ship], swam towards and joined a small group round my red lifebelt light and one young ordinary seaman, not long in the ship himself, asked him, 'Won't you get into trouble, sir, losing the ship so soon after joining?'

The highly political and volatile atmosphere in the Greek forces exploded into open mutiny in the old cruiser *Georgios Averoff* and four escort ships in Alexandria and Port Said on 8th April. The revolt was put down by loyal elements of the Greek navy on the night of 22nd/23rd April, but outbreaks of trouble continued over the next few months. HHMS *Apostolis* was one of the four mutinous escort vessels, Leading Signalman Lerigo was still part of the British liaison team,

1944 saw us continuing on our Port Said to Gib routine, but unknown to us, trouble was brewing. The ship remained as filthy as ever, but now we were used to all this.

On our way back from Gib we were asked quietly by the liaison officer to avoid any arguments or political discussions with the Greeks, (not many of those anyway) he would explain later. All seemed normal as we made our way to Port Said.

We duly arrived and to our complete astonishment, the Greek ensign was hauled down and the red flag replaced it. *Saktouris* followed suit and other ships of the Greek fleet already in harbour were flying the red flag. None of the liaison staff were treated other than normal. We were in the middle of a mutiny. I don't think it did much for us RN ratings, but this time nothing surprised us, after all 'Fred Karno's' navy had nothing on this lot. . . Nothing could surprise us and when we sailed from Port Said in company with *Saktouris*, again flying the Greek ensign and escorting a tanker to Alexandria; this was a strange mutiny. We arrived in Alex: the mutiny was resumed and *Apostolis* secured with a British frigate, *Nadder*, alongside.

We RN ratings transferred to the *Nadder* and the Greek officers put ashore. The Greek ships were in complete revolt. Many people tried persuading the crews to give up, including the Greek archbishop of Alexandria, who ended up excommunicating the lot of them. Finally some weeks later loyal Greek forces stormed the ships and re-occupied them.

Eventually after being screened, the crew, minus several ringleaders, returned to the ship. The same officers and senior rates returned. This would never had happened in a disciplined service, one supposes.

Apostolis returned to the fleet, but the authorities it appeared, decided *Apostolis* and *Saktouris* were in need of a sharp lesson. Instead of a cushy run we were despatched to Italy and the Adriatic. It brought them down to earth with a bump.

Leslie Stevenson did not leave with the main party of liaison ratings and when he did it was not to return:

Mutiny, we were not the cause, gunfire – the RN arrived. I left at the dead of night with bag and hammock and crept onboard the *Delphinium* which had touched alongside. . . . I was put into Sidi Bishr transit camp for a month, from where patrols were sent into Alexandria to deal with Greek outbursts.

May 1944 saw the North Atlantic almost clear of U-boats after the heavy losses they had experienced since their return to the Western Approaches in January 1943 had been sunk in the months of February, March and early April.

In the Arctic only two more convoys had been passed through to Russia, one each in February and March and without merchant ship losses. The destroyer *Mahratta* had been sunk with heavy losses while escorting the February convoy.

The German counter-attacks in Italy at the Anzio salient had been repulsed, the long struggle to capture Mount Cassino had ended and the Allied army was advancing north.

Shipping losses in the Indian Ocean which commenced to increase in the months of February and March had ceased and the Eastern Fleet had attacked Sabang and Soerabaya. Allied island landings continued in the Pacific and two landings had been made in New Guinea. The Russian armies in April re-entered the Crimea and Sebastopol had been recaptured in May. Within the United Kingdom the huge build-up of land, sea and air forces was nearing completion for the invasion of Europe.

On the morning of 6th June the Allied landing and invasion of Normandy commenced and hundreds of thousands of seamen, soldiers and airmen were involved in a titanic struggle against a highly skilled and determined enemy. Not every serving member of the Royal Navy was committed to the ships of the invasion fleet in Operation *Neptune*; numbers of men were still in training establishments or barracks waiting for their next draft chit. Telegraphist D.S. Goodbrand was one of these and wrote a light-hearted account of his activities on that fateful 'D' day when the Allied world held its breath:

Cap-flat-a-Back
6 June 1944: The Second Front . . . the greatest fleet ever assembled. . . Allied military might poised to breach Hitler's Atlantic Wall. . . The invasion awaited by a breathless world. What wartime serviceman has not at one time or another been asked by the curious young: 'Where were you? What did you do on D-Day, the glorious Sixth of June?'

SUPREME HEADQUARTERS
ALLIED EXPEDITIONARY FORCE

Soldiers, Sailors and Airmen of the Allied Expeditionary Force!

You are about to embark upon the Great Crusade, toward which we have striven these many months. The eyes of the world are upon you. The hopes and prayers of liberty-loving people everywhere march with you. In company with our brave Allies and brothers-in-arms on other Fronts, you will bring about the destruction of Nazi tyranny over the oppressed peoples of Europe, and security for ourselves in a free world.

Your task will not be an easy one. Your enemy is well trained, well equipped and battle-hardened. He will fight savagely.

But this is the year 1944! Much has happened since the Nazi triumphs of 1940-41. The United Nations have inflicted upon the German great defeats, in open battle, man-to-man. Our air offensive has seriously reduced their strength in the air and their capacity to wage war on the ground. Our Home Fronts have given us an overwhelming superiority in weapons and the munitions of war, and placed at our disposal great reserves of trained fighting men. The tide has turned! The free men of the world are marching together to Victory!

I have full confidence in your courage, devotion to duty and skill in battle. We will accept nothing less than full Victory!

Good Luck! And let us all beseech the blessing of Almighty God upon this great and noble undertaking.

DWIGHT D. EISENHOWER

Eisenhower's D-Day Message

The heroes – those who came back – had a tale to tell. Those who remained at home, the sport of a different Fate, such as myself, were less forthcoming, having much in common with Shakespeare's lay-a-beds on another occasion.

The Sixth of June? I remember it well, but hardly with pardonable pride. There were whispers, of course, vague generalizations, rumours of impending Armageddon, but it was a well-kept secret, perhaps one of the best-kept secrets of the war. So when I went 'ashore' on liberty from the stone frigate near Plymouth where, with other communication ratings ex-*Obdurate* (after she had paid off in April) I was awaiting draft, I had no inkling of the imminent clash of destinies a few miles across the channel. Nor, it seemed, had somnolent Plymouth at ten o'clock in the morning, about which time I leapt from the jeep whose driver, bound for Devonport's naval barracks on business of his own, had cheerfully offered me a lift outside the camp gates, and found myself in Drake Circus at the eastern end of Union Street, that thoroughfare remembered with affection by matelots of many Allied nations.

The sun shone mildly as I walked between two rows of rubble and ruined buildings created earlier by the Luftwaffe, my only thought being to enjoy the relaxed congenial atmosphere of the local YMCA canteen with its tea and sticky buns. But this was not to be my day.

Keeping one's nose clean was well-known to be the first dynamic principle of life in the armed forces, and doubtless always will be. Forget it, and you were in trouble. Irresponsibly, lulled by the peaceful scene – people and traffic were scarce; I might have been strolling through a country village – I thoughtlessly moved my newly-bought cap to the back of my head (a position beloved of Jolly Jack on the spree) to prevent the rim chafing my forehead and thus, while heroes fell and guns roared on the other side of the channel, entered blissfully into the minefield which besets all those who transgress the KRs and AIs, consciously or otherwise.

Arriving at the YMCA canteen I was only slightly discomposed (my thoughts being elsewhere) to be greeted by the sight of a Naval Patrol consisting of a PO, a Leading Hand and two ABs, immaculate in white blancoed caps, belts and leggings, issuing from the entrance. They regarded me with interest, rather like a crowd of anglers assessing a prize trout. Warily I made to enter the canteen, observing through the half open door the tea and buns-dispensing staff busy at their allotted tasks. It was impossible, without summoning the aid of a magic I did not possess, to escape the notice of this grim-faced quartet who stood four-square, barring my way.

'Your cap,' said the PO casually. I fumbled self-consciously with the offending headgear.

'It's flat-a-back,' added the killick, his jaw tightening.

'Sorry,' I mumbled nervously. The two ABs looked deliberately over my left shoulder. A milk-car trundled by. Three American sailors pushed past us on the pavement with modest apologies.

The PO gazed after them disdainfully. He sniffed. 'Naval regulations,' he began, 'do not permit. . . ' The rest of the Patrol looked speculatively in the direction of a naval truck parked nearby, satisfaction vying with hostility on their well-scrubbed faces. My heart sank. I was their first catch of the day.

'Name?' asked the PO. I told him. 'Pay-book, pass?' I produced them. 'Camp or ship?' I co-operated with eagerness, hoping for at least a morsel of human kindness to soften the iron of Naval tradition, a hope that plainly receded as, my documents passing from hand to hand, the look in the eyes of my captors grew progressively colder and icier.

With the knowledge that I was not only an HO, which was bad enough, but also a Wireless Telegraphist, which was infinitely worse to men happy to have press-gangs and who were apt to regard any naval personnel of even my own slender technical accomplishments much as, I suppose, an 18th century Westphalian peasant might regard a modern day oil rig or space module – the disposition of my naval patrol took on a new dimension of rigour, and I knew my doom was sealed. 'Gentlemen of the Service' we might be, we communication ratings, to those who worked manually in the bowels of a ship afloat, but to a Naval Patrol ashore, rooted as they were in decades of dealing with the descendants of *Bounty* mutineers, such attitudes of lower-deck indulgence bordered on heresy. To the PO this was quite evident.

'Apprehended in Union Street, Plymouth wearing cap flat-a-back contrary to naval regulations,' he intoned. 'You'll be taken back to yur camp and charged. . . '

They escorted me to the truck with the gravity of undertakers. Nelson had won again. Which was as it should be.

Farewell, Liberty and sticky buns. With nonchalant expertise the killick spun his wheel as we screamed through Drake Circus and out into the countryside, now redolent with menace and seeming hidden dangers. I affected a distant coolness as if it was all happening to someone else that belied my true feelings as events blurred sequentially into arrival at the camp with its wire fence, flag-poles and scattering of Nissen huts. The main gate opened and closed. The truck stopped. In a body we entered the guard-house where everyone seemed to be drinking mugs of tea in a guarded and reserved manner. Their eyes lit up with anticipation on our appearance. My patrol seemed quite at home and the PO made his report.

I remember the Officer of the Watch. 'Off-cap!' The charge read out with becoming if chilling solemnity. 'Cap flat-a-back. . . ' (Eyes widening with shocked disbelief.) Sentenced to one day's chores in the guard-house. 'On-cap! About turn! Quick march!' Polish the brass – mop the floor – polish the brass – clean cells – polish the brass. The longest day darkened into night as the quarterdeck brass gleamed like Solomon's temple and fair stood the wind for France.

A year later, on a few hours' liberty from another ship, over a Tom Collins in the bar of the Elphinstone Hotel, Madras, I recounted this episode to one Signalman Evans, a harum-scarum lad from Lydney, Glos. who had spent D-Day on board a frigate loaded with troops who splashed from landing craft onto mined beach-heads as a first blood-soaked step towards unseating a tyrant. Grinning appreciatively, Signalman Evans finished his drink.

'Your round,' was all he said.

Eric Smith with his friend and shipmate Nobby, from *Ganges* and *Ajax*, had gone to the Gunnery School at Chatham and qualified;

The gunnery course lasted until May, when both 'Nobby' and I passed out with good marks, were now ready and looking forward to going to sea again. Meanwhile Nobby had married his childhood sweetheart. Before 1939 no one under the age of 25 could draw marriage allowance for a wife. It therefore followed that hardly any young sailor could afford to get married, or if they did and the union produced children, then the family would have to exist solely on the sailor's pay, which in the case of an AB for instance, was only 21/- (old shillings) per week, plus the extra 3d per day for the likes of a GC badge or non-substantive rate. In mid-1939 when the Government decided to start calling up young men for the forces, it was found that many of these young men, then between 19 to 20 years were in fact married, and so many of them complained about their straitened circumstances to MP's and the Press. It was obvious that something had to be done. Their Lordships obviously could not give to a conscript without giving the same treatment to a regular rating. I remember Cassandra, columnist with the *Daily Mirror*, was most vociferous in getting this particular part of KR & AI's and the Naval Discipline Act altered. We had a few married men under 25 years on board and I remember that few of them ever went ashore and if they did it was usually just to a sports fixture or a cinema. . . .

In actual fact when the revised King's Regulations and Admiralty Instructions – November 1943, BR 32/1943 was issued in 1944 there were no changes to the rules governing payment of marriage allowance to men under 25 years of age, the rule, article 1767, continued to be only suspended for the period of hostilities. There were no changes whatsoever to the schedules of summary punishments. Corporal punishment of up to 25 lashes continued, only suspended indefinitely, as No 2 in the order of summary punishments.

More important, the re-issued KR & AI, gave no changes in the pay rates which had been in force since 1919, later amended so that men joining the service after 5th October 1925 received a 25% cut, an action that was the prime cause for the Invergordon mutiny in 1931, when the Government of the day decided to impose a 25%

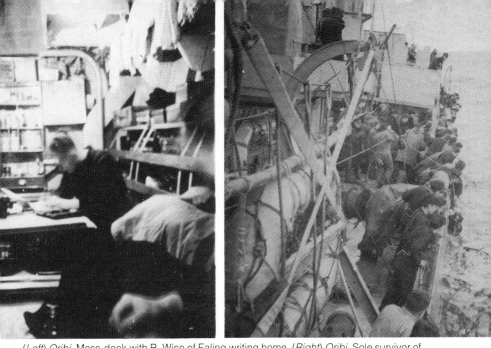

(*Left*) *Oribi*. Mess-deck with R. Wise of Ealing writing home. (*Right*) *Oribi*. Sole survivor of U365, the commanding officer being rescued, December 13th, 1944.

Oribi, 1944.

(*Above*) *Oribi.* After VE
relaxing in the Tivoli Ga
Copenhagen.

Magpie. Christmas 19

Magpie. An intercepte
blockade runner crowe
refugees trying to reac
Palestine.

reduction in pay rates on men who had signed engagements prior to 5th October 1925.

Pay rates had not changed therefore while civilians on war work received inflated pay rates which had in fact created a greater disparity between servicemen and civilians than existed in the 1914-1918 war which was the cause of great discontent in the WW1 fleet.

There was also another dimension; pay received by American servicemen bore no relation with the British rates of pay which remained unchanged for 25 years; this was a special cause of friction and discontent. The British servicemen, at this stage of the war, had a poor regard for the fighting ability of their powerful, dollar rich, ally whose fighting prowess did not match up to their numbers and massive support of modern equipment. Reports of the American achievements against the Japanese fleet and land forces in the Pacific were still hardly known by the men of the British fleet in the Mediterranean and Home Fleet.

In an attempt to prevent the mistakes of the past being again repeated, Captain Russell Grenville RN wrote and published a book in 1944, *Service Pay*. In this book he traced the history of pay to the men serving in the fleet and emphasised the fact that over the last 150 years Government had only increased naval pay rates after a mutiny or the threat of one.

Captain Grenville considered that unless immediate radical changes were made to current conditions of service and pay that serious trouble could again occur in the Fleet. He made detailed and strong recommendations for change, for example to increase the pay for an able seaman at the age of twenty from 4/- per day to 14/6 per day with similar increases for all other ranks and to commence from April 1944.

In the preface of this book Captain Grenville wrote;

> The fighting services are the nation's defenders, to whom it is under a very special obligation, its own civilian liability to air-bombing notwithstanding. The national honour is therefore involved in whether the nation adequately acknowledges that obligation in ways other than inexpensive flattery.
>
> There are those who think that it does not; who suspect that the fact that the men of the services are under military discipline improperly utilised by the Treasury to their financial disadvantage.

Ordinary Seaman A. Bishop had arrived in Alexandria in a troopship RMS *Duchess of Bedford* and had been transferred ashore to the base HMS *Sphinx* to commence training for an operation and to become involved unknowingly in the continuing obsession of some politicians and military commanders to retake the Aegean islands. They could not wait for the Russian advance, the invasion of Normandy and the Allied advance north in Italy to commence syphoning away the German island garrisons to defend the homeland. They seemed intent on squandering lives.

Then 200 of us were drafted to special commando style training; we were fitted out with battle-dress, rifle, mess-tins, water bottle etc., and were called the 'Jaunt Party'. After 10 days of this hard training we were taken to Alexandria dockyard and boarded the cruiser *Aurora* and taken to the Greek island of Melos. My pal 'Aussie' was not with us. Off Melos we joined the cruiser *Black Prince* and escort *Emperor* and a couple of Hunt class destroyers. The island was bombarded by the warships and Hell Cats from the carrier, we were loaded into landing craft and taken ashore.

I was in the first boat and one of the first two to step ashore and almost stepped onto a dead German. I didn't like this and wondered what was in store for us. We soon found out; we were shot at by a sniper. Nobody was hurt except the Jerry who was soon disposed of. We had a snoop around and found a safe spot and settled in and made our first meal, we made tea in biscuit tins, we boiled the water, put in two tablets that made the water taste like chloride of lime, then emptied a packet which contained tea, milk and sugar. It didn't taste very good at first but we soon began to like it. We carried small tents big enough for two.

We had a week there and several times came under heavy fire, at one time I heard bullets passing me and we had to call in Hell Cats to help us, at one time the B17's had a go. Jerry got the better of us and Commander Denis decided that we got off. We withdrew to the beach under fire and made our way out to the destroyer *Easton*. We lost one landing craft. We were transferred to the *Aurora*, given a tot of rum and the chaplain gave a service for those of us who got back safely. Then it was a shower, a good meal and crashed our swedes. On the whole it was a rough time and some of us thought that the raid was a mistake.

Back at *Sphinx* they laid on a party for us, plenty of grub and free beer, the camp dog did OK; he got drunk as usual and his legs went in all directions. I was sorry to find that my pal 'Aussie' had got a draft to another submarine. I had a week in the camp guard then was drafted to the 'M' class fleet destroyer *Marne*. At last I am going to be a sailor. She is a lovely-looking ship with closed in gun turrets, one funnel and a lattice mast and she is a unit of the 3rd Destroyer Flotilla.

I was put in 1 mess, 1st part of port watch, my action station is loader on the left gun, 'A' turret and my part of ship is fo'c'sle. My job is shell room and Ready Use locker sweeper also 'A' turret. There were two of us joined the ship, both from the 'Jaunt Party'; his name was Peter Edward Pearson, PEP I called him and we became oppo's. . . . We sailed that same evening for the Greek islands and on the second day we had a force 10 gale and found that these ships did not behave too well but I was lucky. I found that I was a good sailor. I didn't get to know many chaps for a while except the gun crew as we spent a lot of time at 2nd degree of readiness and watch keeping was four on and four off.

We carried the flotilla padre and one quiet morning on patrol we had just done cook of the mess and were saying prayers on the upper-deck by the torpedo tubes, fairly close inshore to the island Cos when a shell burst besides us, someone shouted 'Bloody Hell' and we were at action stations in 30 seconds flat and fired a few rounds back. It was quite hostile round these islands and we would spend a lot of time closed up and sing songs like:

We had to join, we had to join old Churchill's navy
Ten bob a week, nothing to eat
Long baggy trousers and blisters on your feet etc, etc.,

When in the turrets cookie would come round with sausages in sandwiches so thick that you need an opening of 4" to take a bit and kye so thick that you could stand a spoon in it. If Lofty Miles was off watch he would make flap jacks.

We kept patrolling you would sometimes make a bombardment and then we went into the island of Symi for fuel and water. Bartered with the natives for hen fruit, fruit and veg. When we went to move a chain had fouled our prop shaft and that gave us a chance to get a couple of hours' sleep. When we left it was blowing a gale and some of the chaps who had been drinking the local brew went rather funny colours and those who were very bad were put in the captain's report.

During the patrol one evening our radar picked up two small ships at about 2300 hrs; we chased in and put the 20" lamp on them and Jerry tried to shoot it out. Our pom-pom fired and one boat seemed to explode and caught fire, the second surrendered. It was full of Christmas supplies and a 88mm gun. We took some cigars and put on a prize crew after taking off the Germans, then escorted it to just off Symi and recovered our chaps next morning.

Having no cells the prisoners had to stay on the mess-decks with us. This was the first time I and several others had met the enemy and found them to be like us, just a bit older. They would not let us work; they did everything for us and we got to know each other by name. One said to Pep and me that only the British could treat an enemy so well and it was a long time that he had been so happy. After a few days they were transferred to a cruiser returning to base. They shook hands with everybody and the CO thanked us all for our kindness and told us that we had kept up the tradition of the Royal Navy.

We bombarded Pescopi on Xmas eve and the Captain, Lieutenant-

Commander P.A.R. Withers said we would go into Symi next day. It got up a full gale during the night and we arrived at about 1400. The smell of the tinned turkeys cooking in the galley and the fuel oil did not mix well but we all had a bottle and I realised that this is a happy ship. We worked and played hard, we had a skipper who kept a tight clean ship but at the same time looked after his men. He was proud of us and would chat to us. Talked to me about my Dad often. He was a Yeoman of Signals who had lost his ship, the *Sikh*, and had been taken prisoner of war at Tobruk. He was repatriated after 7 months and stayed on as an instructor at Gibraltar.

On Boxing Day an Army captain and five soldiers boarded us, he was Captain Harding (of the SBS). For several weeks we would land this party at night and then pick them up in the morning, they were destroying installations which we were also shelling ready for troops to land to take the islands. We were all sad later that Captain Harding had been killed in the Far East.

William Hope was concluding his first year in the Navy;

Christmas 1944, *Oribi* was operating from Greenock; the great liners were still engaged transporting troops and equipment across the Atlantic and our job was to give escort support to the liners for about 24 hours then return to Greenock. I was the youngest member of the crew, so on New Year's Eve I was given the honour of ringing out the old year and ringing in the new. By this time I had been given a job as bowman in the ship's motor boat, it was something I really enjoyed, but on my first trip I earned a rollicking from the skipper. We had been called away to take the skipper to the *Queen Mary* for a conference. The coxswain was steering the boat alongside the ship's gangway. Captain Ingram was descending the gangway; to hold the boat, I tried with my boat-hook to hook on to a guard rail. I missed, my boat-hook somehow got tangled in the gangway, it snapped the wood shaft, the hook part dangled from the gangway guard rail, the other piece flew from my grasp giving the skipper a nasty smack on his leg causing him to slip down the remaining steps. The air was blue and I felt like jumping over the side to escape his wrath.

As an able seaman, I became more useful in the ship and I was really enjoying life, then I blotted my copy-book.

CHAPTER SEVEN

1945/1946

The New Year commenced with the Germans fighting rearguard actions on all fronts. Paris had been recaptured in August 1944 by the Allies who were driving towards the Rhine. In September the enemy commenced using rocket missiles against Britain. The British had landed in Greece and the Germans had withdrawn from the Balkans. Now in January 1945 the Russians were advancing through East Prussia and Czechoslovakia. In the Far East British land forces had recaptured most of Burma from the Japanese and the Americans in mighty sea, air and land battles continued to expel the Japanese from widely scattered Pacific islands as they closed in towards Japan.

In European waters the cruiser *Mauritius*, under the command of Captain W.W. Davis, had achieved a unique record. She was the only British major warship to have taken part in the four invasions of Sicily, Salerno, Anzio and Normandy. The ship had bombarded the enemy on over 250 occasions. After D-day, *Mauritius* continued as part of the bombarding squadron of major ships until the end of July 1944. She was then deployed to operate off the French Bay of Biscay coastline and badly mauled an enemy convoy of four store ships and a tanker escorted by a destroyer and two 'M' class minesweepers. A week later she sank a convoy and its escorts, two 'M' class minesweepers, three flak ships and three merchantships. The cruiser finished the year on offensive sweeps off the Norwegian coast.

December also saw the reading of warrants continuing, numbers 231 and 232 were read during the month, making it an extraordinary average of 58 warrants per year since commissioning. In spite of this feature of the ship's life style and the break-down in discipline in Plymouth Sound, in January 1944, the cruiser had since July 1943 established a formidable reputation as a fighting machine and had fought many actions with no casualties to her ship's company.

Mauritius fought her last action in company with the cruiser *Diadem* on 27th January. The cruisers engaged three Narvik class destroyers 50 miles NW of Bergen; in an inconclusive action at high speed the destroyers escaped behind their smoke screen. *Mauritius* had one man wounded, her first casualty, from one shell hit by a destroyer.

The war was not quite over in Italy. The destroyer *Marne* after a spell in the Adriatic supporting Yugoslavian partisans was now in the Ligurian sea in the extreme north of Italy bombarding Spezia and Genoa. Able Seaman A. Bishop was still a member of A turret's crew:

> The skipper cleared lower-deck to tell us that we were going to bombard La Spezia and Genoa, we would join up with a Hunt class *Tetcott* and a tug to get us clear if we got damaged. On the way we found a spent German torpedo, stopped and away duty sea boat. I was stroke oar. We put a strop round it and towed it to the ship, it was a bit tricky because run out Jerry torpedoes act as mines. But all was well we hoisted it inboard. . . . We met the other ships and did a 'dummy run' before going in for the night. The Americans lent us some films including a 'Donald Duck' and gave us some fags, some of them liked our 'ticklers' so we made up a couple of tins.
>
> The tug left at midnight and we went four hours later and met up in the target area. *Tetcott* took up her covering station and we ran in. We came under heavy gunfire but we were still out of range. When we did open up there was a hell of an exchange of shells and *Tetcott* was damaged, we kept on firing while she withdrew signalling 'Good Luck'. There was a big explosion ashore and things went quiet. We withdrew then and stood down, cleaned guns and returned to normal watch-keeping setting course for Leghorn. We were all moaning about being the only bloody ship left in the navy, but what we didn't know was how close the end of the war was. In harbour it was the same routine, off loading empty cordite cases and taking in fresh ammo'. One advantage of working from a front line base was that there was plenty of fresh water. We had tea, and I emptied the dishing up water when a spoon rattled down the gash shute and all the lads together sang,
>
> 'Tinkle tinkle little spoon, knife and fork will follow soon.' It's fatal to make a mistake.
>
> We had next day in and those without special jobs rubbed down the rust patches and treated them with boiled oil and red lead. The salt on the funnel was cleaned off by defaulters during the first dog watch, the ones with one day number 16 punishment.
>
> On our next bombardment we went too close and ran aground and had to clear lower-deck to jump up and down on the fxle until the ship began to bounce and she came off under full power. On another occasion we broke down, there was water in the fuel, all we could do was to wallow off Portofino with black smoke belching out of the funnel. There was hell

to pay over this because the fuel had come from an Italian tanker, but it did give us a run back to Malta and into dry-dock to repair the damage from running ashore and leave to both watches. . .

It was a nice trip back to Leghorn; we joined up with *Meteor*; she was the canteen boat (being the junior commanding officer) but was our chummy ship. Everything seemed to have changed; we had very little opposition from Jerry; in fact we would take turns with *Meteor* to have a shoot and when Jerry fired back they fell short or passed over the top. When *Meteor* was shooting we would sit outside the turrets in the sunshine and watch her or we would watch the RAF Typhoons making rocket attacks. Then on 5th May, my birthday, we were shelling and got a check fire order. We waited for quite a while and the skipper said that something was going on and we could stand down and have a smoke. Cookie brought along the tea. We were lying stopped off the Italian coast and about an hour later the captain said over the loud hailer and intercom, 'Lads, the war is over'. We hugged each other, shouted, laughed and cried, the whole ship went mad. Then came the order, unload and clean guns, then ship the gun tampions! The ship headed for Leghorn, we dressed ship as we entered, sirens going and an American band played us in with other Yanks waiting with cases of beer.

What a welcome – I'll never forget it. A strange feeling, a destroyer with blistered paint on guns lying quiet, but *we* weren't. I was duty watch and had to do shore patrol with Petty Officer Gus. We met the *Meteor*'s patrol and then joined up with the American patrol. Beer was free everywhere and we all got drunk, when we returned to the ship everyone was plastered, even my oppo Pep, and he never drank much. Several of the chaps had black eyes but had no idea where they got them. A statue with a soldier on a horse, in town, had been painted red; the Wops said it was British sailors did it. The biggest trouble inboard was getting each other's tight jumpers off.

Next day the Captain cleared lower deck and thanked everyone for working so hard and told us that the rest of the 'M's would be joining us next week and finished up by saying, 'You buggers had a good time ashore last night, reports are still coming in, but never mind this time.' We gave three cheers for a good captain.

My promotion to AB had come through and was back dated 12 months so I picked up £25. I was rich so I had some good runs ashore and not being much of a drinker was able to do a bit of shopping. We now had all the fighting 'M's' together and took part in a VE service and a march past in the Yankie stadium in Leghorn. We then sailed for different ports to take part in VE parades, we went to Cannes in the south of France and had two super days. The ship was for the first time open to visitors and the GB News got us to pose with the 'bints'. This was shown in cinemas all over the UK and several chaps got 'Dear John' letters.

Leslie Stevenson had returned from the East Mediterranean in the troopship *Reina del Pacifico* and from July to December 1944 had been on the staff of Commander in Chief Plymouth in Mount Wise Head-quarters. In January he had been drafted to his second corvette, the *Stonecrop*, whose commanding officer was nick-named 'Trunky' by his ship's company.

Stonecrop was one of the many ships at sea on VE Day in the English Channel,

> VE Day we were in the English Channel collecting U-boats, eerie, foggy, thought the odd one might torpedo us. . . . Trunky gave us all a free tot. 'Have what you like', he says. Drunken ship steered by someone I guess. . . Then Sunday in harbour at Divisions, Rig of the day or any gear, took mugs of tea to the service. He gets into, 'Oh Lord have mercy on us, miserable offenders' gazing at us all sipping tea!. . . .

In the Skagerrak, a black night full of menace, patrolling an ill defined enemy swept channel through a dense minefield two destroyers *Opportune* and *Obedient* waited for incoming U-boats arriving to surrender. Able Seaman S. Birtley was in the *Obedient*:

> probing into the Skagerrak the straits between Norway and Denmark, pitch dark night unidentified ships show up on Radar, we carefully approach, closed up at action stations, fire star shells over them to light up the area. Two fishing boats out from Denmark come alongside, information from them is that a German cruiser is shelling Copenhagen. We pass down cigarettes and a bottle. Probably medicine! We proceed further along the Skagerrak. Before morning we hear that the German war is over.

Not everyone was at sea when VE day arrived, W.E. Hope was blotting his copy-book:

> In May, *Oribi*, was having a refit in Immingham docks and this meant my first long leave, only, I took longer than I was entitled.
> I got myself involved with a girl-friend and stayed at home. VE day came and went, then having seen the folly of my ways, I gave myself up to the local police. I had no money and my travel-warrant had expired. I served 21 days at the Royal Naval Detention Quarters, Preston. The strict discipline and exercise did me no harm at all and I went back to *Oribi* a wiser person.

The *Marne* spent many weeks visiting Greek ports where the ship had problems with the civil war factions, then showing the flag at Istanbul, Italian ports, Algiers and Tangiers after a refit at Malta. Bill Bishop continues his narrative:

We left next day with *Musketeer* for Gibraltar in a force 8 gale and passed the *Scout* getting washed down. As we entered Gib with porpoises leading us in the destroyer *Kimberley* was coming out. My Dad was in her going home for demob after 28 years in the Royal Navy. My Winger Pep and I had a run ashore and were lucky to see some rock apes but were disappointed because they were so small. We both bought some silk stockings and underwear and had big eats, a couple of drinks then back onboard. *Sheffield* had come in and next day we shoved off to Casablanca. When we arrived *Sheffield* had her Royal Marine band playing Rule Britannia. *Musketeer* and us picked up a pilot, then passed one each side of the cruiser to take the lead and we hit a tug rolling it almost over, three of her crew going over the side. As it bounced down our side, Jimmy the One Lieutenant Prescat Deci known as the 'Screaming Skull' were shouting out, 'Watch the bloody paintwork!' We went into the inner harbour, turned to starboard then went astern dropping the hook and secured stern to the wall. '*Muskie*' started her run in and was close enough to put a gang-plank over; she almost clouted us then stopped. Her Captain shouted across, 'I've bloody well gone aground'. So she tried to pull herself off with her hook only to find that it was foul of a wreck. It took divers the rest of the day to get it free, then half the night to get her back. Our skipper said, 'French pilots, I've shit 'em'.' We found Casablanca not the place we hoped for. We left *Sheffield* and *Musketeer* there and returned to Gib. . . .

We then went to Cannes again and went ashore to do some shopping as the buzz was that we were going home to the UK. The following day Pep and I returned ashore and little Ron came; we had a couple of drinks but found the grub a bit dear so decided to return to the ship. We were passing the centre one of three very big hotels when an American officer standing in the doorway said, 'Would you lads like to come and join us for a drink?' Inside it was a big dance, drink, grub, the lot Yankee style, all high ranking officers and we three AB's were made to feel like the rest. One USAAF officer said, 'We are taking a B17 to Manston Kent for the weekend, and you can come. We'll arrange transport to and from home for you'. They got in touch with the ship but were told that we were leaving for Nice tomorrow.

We had a wonderful night, they had laid on a room for us and next morning we were called with a cup of tea and on the bedside tables we each had a box with our name containing 200 fags and about a 4 months ration of chocolate and sweets. Outside a Jeep waited and took us back to *Marne* in time for breakfast.

Lofty Miles said, 'Billy, if you fell into a sewer you'd come out smelling of roses'. That day we left for Nice with a short stop at St Raphael.

Marne returned to Malta for a boiler clean and to change from wartime matt grey to a peace-time high gloss pale blue-grey overall colour. The ship's company numbers were reduced and men sent home to be demobbed.

> We were now down to 197 crew. Christmas Day, the junior rating did the rounds in the captain's uniform and the captain dressed as an ordinary seaman. There were sippers for all the officers and they in turn gave the messes a bottle. They were well slashed as they went back along the portside; in the afternoon some WRNs came inboard and somehow one lost her black French knickers; they were flying from the masthead. Buffer Nash got drunk, walked along the upper-deck, passed wind and had an accident so some of the lads put a fire hose on him. It was the first peace-time Christmas and everyone went wild.
>
> After the dicky refit we went to Palestine in a hurry to intercept ships carrying immigrants. This was a hell of a job stopping ships loaded with Jews from all over Europe; most were small, very old overloaded craft. Some had dead inboard; we had to take some off, transfer others to merchant ships and send them to Greece and Italy. We also gave them food and water. We went into Haifa and half the ship's company went to Jerusalam; when they were away someone blew up one of the large petrol tanks. We had to make a quick exit; there were four destroyers in. *Musketeer* collided with us in the scramble; she broke her 'A' bracket and returned to Alex. The rest of us split up to patrol for 48 hours doing double watches. We went back to Haifa and the remainder of the crew was brought out to us. Trouble on land was getting bad and the Pongos were having it rough. You would think that after the bloody war we had all been through, people would want to settle for peace.

After leaving the *Oribi*, William Edward Hope was again in serious trouble:

> You would think that having spent one period in Detention Quarters at Preston, I would have learned my lesson, but, no I went and made the same mistake again. I went AWOL.
>
> I had been drafted to HMS *Suffolk* for passage to the Far East. *Suffolk* was in Liverpool, I joined her and was set to the ship's working party, loading stores etc, and taking advantage of evening shore leave, I got a lift to Manchester, my home-town, saw my girl-friend and didn't return to Liverpool for a couple of days, unfortunately *Suffolk* had sailed. I was adrift for a few more days then gave myself up to the Military Police at Ardwick Barracks, Manchester. Eventually an escort arrived from Portsmouth and I was taken to RNB *Victory*. I was given some stick by the Regulating staff there; the war was still being fought by the Japanese, and the RPO suggested that I was too scared to go out East. It took about

two weeks for me to be 'weighed off'; my warrant was read and I was given 72 days at Kingston, Royal Naval Detention Quarters.

The reception at Kingston was something to remember. In the receiving room in front of a couple of POs and a Marine Colour Sergeant I was ordered to lay out my kit for inspection, I did not respond quick enough, so one of the POs grabbed my kit-bag and spewed out my kit over the floor, leaving me to collect it and lay it out as for muster. My hammock mattress was then cut open at the seams, the filling pulled out presumably searching for razor-blades. I then had to strip off my uniform and was taken to the showers and a hair-cut; on completion I was allowed to dress in my white duck-suit and was issued with a new pair of boots. A visit to the sick-bay for a short-arm inspection and carrying what was left of my hammock, toilet gear (minus a razor) and a house-wife I was escorted to a cell, my first task being to repair my hammock mattress.

The furniture in my cell consisted of a bed-board, (scrubbed white by previous inmates) a small table and stool, a galvanised bucket (burnished) and a toilet metal-pot complete with lid (also burnished) a bible, and a copy of the prison standing orders. There was a bell-push on the white walls, with the instruction 'To be used only in extreme emergencies'.

The daily routine never varied, I woke up each morning to the ear-shattering noise of the 'Centre Dust-bin' being hammered by the duty PO at 0530 doors were unlocked and the order rang out 'Stand by your doors' at the sound of the first whistle, you would spring out of your cell clutching your potty, at the next whistle turn right march to the ablutions and swill out then return to your cell, to stand behind your door. At the next whistle out you would spring to march to the centre to collect a razor blade and return to your cell. Having completed your ablutions, you would proceed to scrub your cell furniture and floor with the water used for ablutions. You had something like thirty minutes to complete this task.

Fully dressed, you would once again stand behind your door, waiting for the order to 'slop out'. Eventually you would go through the same routine for the purpose of returning razor-blades and collect your breakfast. Breakfast consisted of porridge (no milk or sugar) two thick slices of white bread with a small pat of butter and a mug of tea.

Following morning prayers, we were detailed off for cleaning duties, the corridors had to be scrubbed, all metal-work had to be burnished. The rest of the day was spent on the parade ground, where we would double around and around with a rifle, the exercises were designed to bring you up to a high standard of physical fitness. In wet weather the drills were carried out in the corridors. Obviously the prison officers were bored to tears and it was very often that the inmates were blamed for the officers having to be there, so, it followed that we were there to be punished and punished we were. There were some prisoners who were very fit, and the PO would select the fittest to lead the running, the pace would be stepped up and heaven help you if you failed to keep up, should you allow your rifle to droop from the required position, a quick rap from the PO's stick would soon bring it up on your shoulder.

Your first break came with lunch, collected and taken back to your cell. Two potatoes baked in their jackets and a stew. This seemed to be the standard diet followed by semolina and a mug of tea. You were aching to lie down but the use of bed-boards was forbidden till 2000 hours.

1300 hours and it was back to the dreaded parade ground, and if you were really unlucky you would find that your regular PO was off-duty and he was replaced by one of the Marine prison officers, consequently you would find that he had no love for matelots in DQs. By the end of the session the Lee-enfield rifles felt as heavy as a 4″ gun.

1600hrs and we were back in our cells, completely exhausted. The last meal of the day was collected at 1630 hrs, usually two slices of bread, butter and jam with tea (I'm a little bit vague about the actual time of this meal). However, on certain days you were allowed to select two books from the Prison library, which could be exchanged once a week. On occasions you were given tasks to do in your cell, sewing, or rope picking. (oakum). Sunday was a rest day, normal routine till 0930 hrs then we had a cell inspection by the Commander of the Prison, any faults found could result in loss of remission. A church service followed the inspection. Meals did show some improvement on Sunday. For the rest of the day you were confined to your cell, with nothing to do but read.

The main difficulty was not being able to talk to anyone, the only chance you got to chat was in the library or in the ablutions, but the PO was always ready to pounce on any offenders.

2000 hours cell doors were opened for 'Slopping out' and collect a bucket of water ready for the morning ablutions, boots complete with laces were put outside your cell door for the night and lights out took place at about 2030 hours.

It took time, he recalls, to adjust to this sort of life, and some people found it too difficult. He heard of attempted suicides having taken place in Kingston maybe but he says he had no facts to substantiate this. There were some hard-cases there, people who were intent on getting out of the Navy at any cost, and during his time there were incidents of two men who went beserk in their cells. Smoking was prohibited in there but cigarettes were smuggled from cell to cell. One of the cushy duties was to be detailed off for work in the kitchen, when they could supplement their diet with anything that was going spare. Very often the prison officers would turn a blind eye to their pilfering of food.

I suppose conditions at Kingston were similar to all other establishments of this nature, but having spoken to ex-army men I am led to believe that

Military Detention Quarters were not as disciplined as the Naval quarters, be that as it may, they were not designed as recuperation centres.

I guess any normal person could get through the rigorous exercises and rifle drill and even put up with the meagre diet, but the treatment by some of the officers was often mean and petty. For example:- Mail, once you had served 14 days of your sentence you were allowed to write a letter home, by making a request, you would be issued with one sheet of paper and a pencil, on completion the letter would be censored and despatched to the appropriate address in an envelope bearing the stamp of RNDQs. Fourteen days later you would be advised that mail was available for you and you would be told who the letters had come from, mother, uncle, or girl-friend and you would be allowed to receive the one you had requested, after it had been censored by the duty officer; having received a letter, fourteen days later you would have the choice to write or receive.

Should you make any mistakes on the parade ground, the unfortunate offender would be made to stand at attention with arms outstretched holding a rifle. Talking was strictly forbidden, scrubbing corridors on your hands and knees, a quick word with another in-mate and an officer's boot would find your bucket and a duck-suit would be soaked with the contents of the bucket; it was just too bad if you were not due for a clothes change (allowed once a week). Cells were often subject to a spot check, anyone found to be hoarding food from a previous meal would be subject to a lock-in at the next meal-time. Other minor offences could result in a loss of remission, (one third of your sentence).

There was a hard core of men who were the real 'hard cases' determined to get their 'Services no longer required ticket' they were serving much longer sentences, the bread and water diet in solitary confinement seemed to have no effect on them, because they were rarely seen outside their cells. Another class of inmate was the homosexual; for reasons best known to the officers, these prisoners were rarely seen doing punishment drills but they did come in for some rough treatment from the other inmates, especially at 'slopping out' times. Whilst in there I met the former coxswain of the *Oribi* and though he did me no favours he did try to make me see the error of my ways.

However I got on with serving my sentence, with no complaints, until, I reported sick with a septic foot. Unfortunately they refused to treat my foot and classed me fit for punishment, doubling around the prison yard was agony, so in an effort to obtain treatment, I slung down my rifle and refused to obey orders. The Marine Instructor took me inside; I was given three days solitary on bread and water, but I did not get the treatment I needed.

Within two weeks I had done nine days on bread and water in solitary confinement and then fortunately for me I received a visit from the Medical Officer from the Royal Naval Barracks, Portsmouth; he gave instructions for my foot to be treated, which by this time required lancing. I did not complain of my treatment. . .

Looking back, my actions may seem foolish, but at the time I felt they were justified. More so when some ten days later, I was taken out of my cell at five-o'clock in the morning down to the central office, I was ordered to dress in my blue uniform, my kit-bag and hammock were brought to me, and I was informed by the duty officer that I was being drafted to Australia (later I learned that I was undergoing a Shanghai draft).

Handcuffed to a sentry escort, I was then transported to Southampton and taken on board the *Aquitania*, locked in a cell and when the ship had been at sea for twenty-four hours I was released and advised that the remainder of my sentence would be remitted when I reached HMS *Golden Hind* in Australia.

For my part I have no complaints about my treatment; I got what I deserved and was prepared to accept the consequences of my actions. I felt at the time that I didn't deserve solitary and the bread and water diet, but being a prisoner there was very little I could do about it, maybe the 'Shanghai draft' and remission of sentence was some sort of redress.

The voyage to Australia, he recalls, was for the most part uneventful; on board there were sailors and soldiers going out to relieve men from various Far East stations and a large contingent of wounded Australian airmen. When the ship arrived at Capetown, the quarantine flag was flying from the mast, and no one was allowed ashore. But the Australians had other ideas – they went ashore by any means available; not to be outdone some of the British troops followed them, and it took some twenty-four hours to get everyone back on board.

The *Golden Hind* Naval camp, just outside Sydney, he remembers as a sailors' paradise, a dispersal camp for men arriving to join the pacific fleet and men who were waiting for passage home to the UK. Whilst waiting for a draft, he became part of a dockyard working-party. Every day they were taken down to the dockyard to work on various ships, and Hope worked for some time in the *Implacable*, which was involved in returning troops to Australia from the Pacific Islands, many of whom had been wounded or prisoners of the Japanese.

Eventually I was drafted to the *Belfast*; to join her I had to take passage in *Chaser*, a banana-boat aircraft carrier to Hong-Kong, but *Belfast* had sailed to Shanghai, so I was transferred to HMS *Argonaut*. But navy communications were up the creek because *Belfast* had sailed again; however a month of travel and passage in the *Manxman* I caught up with *Belfast* in Hong-Kong where she was taking on stores for a 'Show The Flag' exercise starting with a first call to Sydney.

Life on board a cruiser, especially one bearing the flag of Admiral Sir Denis Boyd, was a bit more pusser than life on a destroyer; it was more like living in RN Barracks; however, I soon got used to the routine and having proved to the Master at Arms that I was no 'Skate' I settled down to enjoy life and the experience of visiting such places as New Zealand, Fiji, Japan, Manus, Singapore and many other places that I had only read about. Everywhere the ship called, was a new experience, dances were laid on for the crew, week-end leave with families in Australia and New Zealand were arranged. The crew of *Belfast* were not always the best ambassadors. On occasions we met up with ships of the American Fleet, and somehow there was always confrontation, I had heard many stories from my shipmates about the 'Battle of Shanghai', when, it was alleged that American sailors searched the streets of Shanghai for British troops with the intention of beating-up the Limeys. It was a well known fact that the British forces resented the Americans, pay and conditions, and didn't take kindly to their arrogant boasting. It was only natural then, that some 'Jack-a-shore' was always ready to shove his fist into any American sailor's face, especially after a few pints of the local brew. I was on shore patrol duty in Hong-Kong, and we always worked in conjunction with the American Military Police as it was easier to get around in their Jeeps. This particular evening we were called out to quell a riot in one of the well-known drinking houses, as usual the trouble involved American and British sailors; aided by troops from the local barracks. The MPs steamed in wielding their batons and when it was soon evident that the batons were aimed at the British sailors, this only inflamed the situation, so just to even matters we got stuck in with sticks (we carried helving tool handles, bound at one end with a metal band); needless to say the metal ends only found American bodies. Order was eventually restored, with quite a few arrests and a few cases for the hospital truck.

I don't think anyone volunteered for shore patrol duty, but I found my name on the duty list far too often; maybe it was because I was 6' 2" in height, unfortunately I was only about 10 stone 6lbs, wet through. Sometimes shore patrol had its humorous moments. Bag-shanty Patrol provided most of these, Wanchai was the out-of-bounds brothel district. Twice each evening we would raid one of these establishments, kicking down doors and charging in we opened every cubicle; the unfortunate men would be lined up, in all states of undress, mostly naked but still wearing shoes or boots, collect all their pay-books and of course report them. However, any American found in this situation were often cruelly ridiculed by their MPs; quite often they were beaten-up and arrested.

On the other hand the 'Yank' could be quite generous; on one occasion the *Belfast* put into Otaru, a northern port in Japan. The currency on board ship could not be spent ashore, so a nearby American Military base sent a fleet of Army trucks to collect our liberty-men, and take them to their base where everything was laid on for our benefit, drinks, food, cigarettes and entertainment; in return the officers of *Belfast* gave a quarter-deck cocktail party for our hosts.

Since his last ship had paid off, Telegraphist Goodbrand had tried without success to get a draft back to the 17th Flotilla:

Saga of an LST.
I never heard another shot fired in anger after April 1944.

In November, after two abortive drafts to destroyer *Onslow* and converted merchant ship/aircraft carrier *Slinger* each cancelled within three weeks on over-complement grounds, I became part of a C & M party which left Devonport to take over a US Navy LST at Belfast.

The boat had been used in the invasion of Normany and there was a party of Yanks on board. They proved to be a fine bunch and did all they could to make the transfer as painless as possible. We fed at the same trough and their rations were superb. The rest of our complement were due to arrive in two weeks' time.

In the ship's hold, designed to carry tanks, trucks and other vehicles, departed Yanks had left huge jumbled mounds of discarded uniform clothing, a sort of Government Surplus dealer's delight, the choicest items of which were quickly snapped up by the C & M party, attracted by their flamboyant novelty. . . .

Two weeks later we recommissioned the ship, the White Ensign supplanting the Stars and Stripes. Our skipper, a middle-aged RNR veteran with beard to match and a chronic thirst, came up trumps. The mainbrace was spliced, the Yanks left for pastures new and we awaited the rest of our crew.

They arrived next day, about ninety of them, mostly pontoon ratings with talk of 'combined ops' in the offing. They stowed their gear, heard the buzz and with glistening eyes, their ancient piratical instincts on fire, descended like locusts into the hold. Within fifteen minutes not a shred of old Yankee cast-offs remained; the plate was licked clean. Needless to say, we were soon back on pusser's fare, a traumatic change for the C & M party.

Thus for a few hectic weeks we flaunted odds and ends of leftover USN uniforms. To no avail. The wardroom grew affronted by this intemperate display and ordered the crew to surrender all items of apparel foreign to the Royal Navy. It was done and we thought of other things, chiefly the rain and when we would be ready for sea and what new horizons awaited us beyond the dingy, mud-spattered confines of the dockyard. . . .

We tied up at a dilapidated wharf. It was VE-Day and everyone got 24 hours leave. Apart from little volunteer groups of 'caretakers' the crews of all ships in company descended avidly on Liverpool. Mid-morning we watched Labour's elder statesman Stafford Cripps, lean, tall and ascetic-looking, mount the steps of the grimy Town Hall to address the citizenry. Up we marched from the bowels of the earth like troglodytes blinking in the sun, winding in procession through streets and alleys converging on the huge square, proudly wearing their auras of six years, grim endurance under the bombs and vicissitudes of Hitler's War like badges of trade, and flaunting their banners of guild and union with all the beribboned pride of the professional working-classes, determined that the era of air-raid shelters was over for ever and the march to the promised sunny uplands of peace and prosperity had begun. Flags and bunting misted the grey roofs and flapped in anarchic breezes against the pedantic oratory from the Town Hall steps. It was a tableau lifted straight from the 19th century and impressive as a millennium. The propaganda swelled like a hot-air balloon, the doyen of British socialists toyed with his beaming cohorts and the cheering was loud and predictable. We left this mutual admiration society at the height of its tidal euphoria and sought the relaxation of pubs. In the evening we found ourselves in a vast ballroom, lit up like neon signs, clasping unknown hands and waists as we danced the night away and singing 'Auld Lang Syne' in a frenzy of victorious sentiment. Europe's war was done. The Japanese sideshow seemed worlds away. No more would nation strive against nation: sense and equity would see to that. How young we were, like innocents wandering in the grief of time. But how good it was to be alive and young then, witness to the 'brightness dropping from the air', appropriate to our generation, like our fathers before us. . . Back on board we got out our tropical kit while the atom bomb slept undreamed of in the near-future.

Next day three LSTs left the Mersey and in line abreast sailed south down the Irish sea towards Gibraltar and the Med. It was a dream of a cruise. Crossing the Bay of Biscay at a peaceful 12 knots, we went ashore at Gib in whites; gaped at the honey-coloured battlements and 16th century palaces of Malta; rode camels at Port Said where astute boot-blacks of tender age crawled unseen under our pavement café tables to cover our shoes with white chalk, thus blackmailing us into business using, astonishingly, the braw accents of Glasgow and Aberdeen; sweated down to Suez and called at Aden.

I went ashore in white ducks scrubbed stiff as boards, dreaming through a tangle of bazaars and relishing the pungent, atavistic smells of Araby. . . .

At Trincomalee we swam and fished and made limited forays into the hinterland. In mid-June we arrived at Madras, our base for the remainder of the war. If the wardroom knew the reasons for our presence there, these were never disclosed to the lower deck. For the next six months the three LSTs pottered about the Bay of Bengal like absent-minded beachcombers paddling in a lagoon. Vizagapatam, Rangoon, Singapore and even Bangkok presented themselves to our curious eyes but our innate Britishness offset the allure of Oriental wonders. The Skipper contracted a disease in Singers and we left him there in hospital. . . . In his absence [we] went into a large rock which could literally be seen for miles near the entrance to Vizag harbour, thus dislodging the starboard door which occasioned great hilarity among the sailors. Retreating to

Madras after loading up with RAF personnel bound for Blighty, makeshift repairs were attempted, but for the rest of the commission we dithered about the Bay like a fretful seagoing dinosaur with one eye open and one closed.

In between trips we spent long weeks at Madras, and shore-leave being frequent learned to explore and enjoy this vivid outpost of declining Empire at will, revelling in new sights, sounds and experiences. The days slipped by; even Hiroshima made little impact on us as we got on with our personal lives in the web of naval routine and thought only vaguely, if at all, of the future.

There were incidents. . .

Adab the laundryman who performed marvels of industry and was well thought of on all sides was found using the crew's shower facilities by Signalman E. who abused him roundly and chased him viciously all round the ship to everyone's amazement.

One of the tels, a married Yorkshireman, popular and fond of his rum, had a birthday, drank 'sippers' at a variety of indulgent mess-tables and vanished for two days, finally being found snoring lustily under a pile of discarded hammocks outside the POs' mess.

The senior signalman, aged 25 from Ormskirk, and I were made up to leading rates and collected an increase of pay. He would have made an ideal shop-steward in industry. On unassailable principle he defended his two juniors like a fierce elder brother (though one was older and married) and inevitably got his way, right or wrong, when POs steered clear of his acid wit; and I never knew him to lose an argument with an officer. A remarkable chap.

One afternoon after dinner a fight, laced by fumes of 'Nelson's blood', broke out in the seamen's mess-deck. Two pontoon ratings went at it hammer and tongs for almost thirty minutes, exercising an old grudge. Uproar and mayhem garnished with colourful oaths. Much crockery broken.

Returning to the ship late after a night out in Madras I once walked into a bizarre theatrical performance. A few yards inside the dock gates two giant Indian policemen armed with truncheons were belabouring a groaning figure writhing on the ground. They rained blows and kicks on their victim with evident satisfaction watched by a half-moon of up to 300 Indians impassive as the stones they sat on. It was an eerie sight: only the thud of blows and the moans they elicited disturbed the silence of the night. I walked slowly towards this grim tableau and seeing my approach the policemen delivered parting kicks to the man's ribs then melted into the darkness. The onlookers gave no sign. I raised the man up from the ground and shakily supported him towards the ship-lined wharves. His head was a mass of blood which soon covered my shirt front. When he stopped moaning I discovered he was an Irish marine: it was the usual story of drink and disorderliness with authority taking needlessly vicious advantage of his helplessly arrogant condition. I looked round but the turbanned audience had drifted away; the show was over. My lost sheep pointed to his ship and I left him at the foot of the gangway, he insisting on this, and watched him making laborious shift to climb aboard keening wild tribal airs after the manner of Mayo men. Back on my LST curious eyebrows were raised at my crimson shirt but nothing was said.

Our first sight of Singapore. The harbour was a forest of sunken ships of every description from sampans to battle-wagons: hulls, masts and smoke-stacks splaying upwards at all kinds of crazy angles as we snaked cautiously through this nautical graveyard to an anchorage surrounded by the grim detritus of war, the paraphernalia of old battles. Ashore there were good canteens and cinemas. The place was slowly coming alive after the Occupation, and we were strangers to the misery that had gone before. Several good runs ashore.

Rangoon. We visited the famed Shwe Dagon pagoda with its golden spire and marvelled at the tumult of squadrons of crows rendering the streets hideous with their cawing din.

Once at Singapore an AB and myself after a night out returned late to the jetty to be informed that we had delayed the ship's sailing by one hour. The liberty boat awaited us manned by a disgruntled crew. We piled aboard scenting trouble and headed for LST 5 at anchor in mid-harbour. Climbing the rope ladder thrown over the ship's side, the first face we saw belonged to the coxs'n; he was boiling with rage, spluttering incoherently in his Westcountry idiom. In double-quick time we were weighed-off, passing swiftly through the hands of the officer of the watch, first lieutenant and skipper whose face darkened with anger as we whipped off our caps. Considering the enormity of our crime we got off lightly with only ten days' stoppage of pay and leave. We were bound for Bangkok but neither of us saw it. Confined to the ship we hung wistfully over the deck-rail watching liberty boats depart for the fleshpots full of expectant shipmates who had kept their noses clean. All we two saw of Bangkok, jewel of the East, was a party of Jap pow's labouring stoically on a wharf; stocky, brawny men they appeared, their role of conqueror reversed for once as history rolled over them, as it had rolled over so many others.

A Blighty election was looming and we all received voting cards which were religiously completed. The first time most of us had ever voted, I believe, giving rise to mild repartee between slung hammocks before 'lights-out'.

It was VJ night and the ship's company had been invited to a dance and festivities at the Governor's palace in Madras. Predictably, Sig. E. and I got drunk at the Elphinstone bar and had to be escorted by our mates to the palatial venue where a hundred daunting steps confronted us. Dragged up to the ballroom entrance to the Coxs'n cast one viperous look in our direction and rapped out an order. Two brawny ABs threw us over their shoulders and deposited the outcasts urgently on a nearby lawn where we slept the night away, oblivious to the celebrations. About 2 am we were collected, slung into a launch and hoisted aboard ship where we slept profoundly under mess-tables till dinner-time. So much for VJ night.

Later in the year we loaded up with troops (including Gurkhas), tanks and trucks and joined a mini-fleet reputedly under Mountbatten's direction which concentrated on a stretch of palm-fringed beach somewhere between Malacca and Penang. Rounding up stray pockets of Japanese soldiery, said the buzz. It was a peaceful afternoon, the text-book operation drawing no hostilities. Tanks were manned, vehicles filled with infantry and the line of LSTs leisurely approached shore to disgorge men and material onto the sand. The last thing I saw was a lorry-load of pongos crashing through the undergrowth with one of them swigging beer from a bottle, his right leg dangling carelessly over the rear-board of the truck. 'And the best of British!' we called after them. Then we returned to base. This operation was the nearest thing to a war situation we had encountered since arriving in the Far East. . . .

Early in December replacements arrived for 15 or 20 of us, including the two married members of our mess and myself, who were due for demob. Before leaving the signals officer invited the three of us to his cabin, gave us whisky and wished us well. Then we lucky ones shook hands with our shipmates and No 1, left the ship at Madras with our hammocks and baggage and caught the train for Bombay. An uncomfortable journey lasting two days. Flies, heat, railway stations full of unfortunates, begging and parading their sores. We stayed a week in a Bombay barracks then boarded the trooper *Ile de France* bound for Southampton, breaking the voyage only to spend a few hours ashore at Durban where we were greeted by the legendary Perle Mesta, singer of songs dear to the hearts of Allied servicemen.

A leisurely sun-soaked cruise was overtaken by sterner weather as we approached the Channel and the English winter. Southampton docks. We disembarked in January snow to catch the Plymouth train for Devonport Barracks where I met a submariner with whom I had enlisted on the same day back in '41, also a signalman from the old Arctic days on destroyer *Obdurate*. However, my large suitcase full of 'rabbits' which I had guarded with religious zeal ever since leaving Madras was stolen from the storage depot in Jago's in which I had placed it for safe-keeping. Sad. But the demob process was painless enough, my demob suit adequate and soon I was on my way north to Manchester, home and the uninspiring job I had been glad to escape from four years, nine months and five days previously when the world was young and my head as parochial as the proverbial parish pump. . .

The adventure was over.

The cruiser *Belfast* had remained with the Pacific Fleet and W.E.

Hope recalls the Hong-Kong Sew-Sew Women and Christmas Day rum in the *Belfast*:

One of the customs in Hong-Kong was to allow Chinese women on board while the ship was at anchor. Their purpose was to repair sailors, uniforms, sew on badges etc,. But once inboard the 'Ladies' had other ideas on how to earn the Hong-Kong dollar. Following an incident in one of the seamen's messes, later known as 'Rose Cottage', the Master-at-Arms made absolutely sure that the Mesdames Sew-sews were all old enough to deter any sailor's amorous thoughts. . .

Rum was the cause of many strange incidents in the ship, Christmas Day in Hong-Kong 1946, the day that the youngest rating changed rig with his captain. The officer-of-the-day was carrying out the duties of the quarter-master, he piped the call, 'All hands who haven't done so and wish to do so, may do so now'. Minutes later a very drunken rating staggered onto the quarter-deck and proceeded to urinate over the side. Needless to say he found himself quickly on Jimmy's defaulters list.

William Hope's time in the *Belfast* was coming to an end;

In 1946 a new Admiralty Fleet Order meant that the Royal Navy was slowly getting her ships and crews back on a peace-time routine. The Royal Marines had a base at Stonecutter's island near Hong-Kong, and it was to this base that the crews of *Belfast* were sent for some physical fitness training. Living under canvas for two weeks did not go down very well with men whose only exercise had been confined to a dance-hall on a shore run. However, we survived and the Royal Marines had a field day giving 'Jack-me-hearty' the run-around.

December 1946, I, like all other men in the ships at Hong-Kong at the time were sent to the Naval Hospital for chest X-rays, Tuberculosis seemed to be rife amongst the Chinese, so as a precaution, mass radiology was ordered.

Unfortunately I was the only one from *Belfast* confirmed with T.B. in both lungs. I couldn't believe my luck, everything looked black, here I was, not yet twenty-one and firmly believing that I was going to die of this terrible disease. My mess-mates tried to make sure that I went out happy, my wake turned into a celebration, out came the treasured stores of ship's rum, the next day I was despatched to hospital still in an alcoholic daze. Two months later I arrived at Southampton in the hospital ship *Oxfordshire*. Twelve months later, after nine months in a civilian sanatorium, I was discharged from the navy.

The next eight years I spent in and out of various sanatoriums; in 1956, I had major chest surgery but T.B. spread and I had to undergo abdominal surgery. It was 1960 before I could really start my working life again. Occasionally I need further treatment, but I have learned to live with this and although I am now once again unemployed, I enjoy life.

I often look back on the few short years I spent in the Royal Navy and count them the happiest days of my life. I do regret the period of indifference when I went AWOL but I put it down to the inexperience of youth. I am one of the lucky ones: my eldest brother was a Royal Marine regular; he went down with his ship, the aircraft carrier *Glorious*.

*

A long and terrible war had come to an end; worldwide, millions of men women and children had perished, victims of the brutalities of a total and global war.

In the British and Commonwealth fleets 74,000 officers and men had been killed and a further 30,300 seamen had died serving in ships of the merchant fleet. 2,972 warships, large and small, had been sunk by enemy action or natural hazards: major ships (431), auxiliary and minor vessels (1115) and landing ships and landing craft (1326). The Merchant fleet had lost 5,150 ships of which 2,820 had been sunk by submarine attacks.

Now forty years on, a great many survivors of the crews who manned the ships of the Royal Navy, including many whose health was permanently broken by wounds, injury or disease, tend to look back to their service and experiences in the war at sea with nostalgia and pride. The appalling physical discomforts which were the lot of the majority who served in the older and smaller ships, stern and strict administration of an outdated code of discipline and the wholly inadequate, anomaly-ridden pay scales, unchanged since the 1919 rates were reduced in the 1920's by 25%, play only a minor and supporting background to Jack's recollections when he gathers at reunions with elderly shipmates.

The fears of many wartime observers, including Captain Richard Grenville, never matured, which centred on the possibility that unrest over pay could spill over into a repeat of naval history, mutiny as a necessary precursor to achieving pay justice. In fact the radical proposals made by Captain Grenville in his 1944 book were ignored and it seems probable that the Government, the General Staff and the Admiralty in particular, traded or gambled on the fact that this war was on the whole popularly accepted as inevitable and as a clear cut fight for survival. The 1939/45 war did not require the vast weight of State-created propaganda of the 1914-18 years, to popularise and justify the war.

The naval casualties of the Second World War were greater than the numbers who died at sea during the 1914-18 war but it seemed that the men of the World War Two British navy accepted with greater tolerance the hardships, the injustices in pay and the many mistakes and excesses of the 'Establishment' which conducted the course of the war.

The same kind of indefinable support for the Second World War surfaced briefly during the 1982 Falklands conflict and was recognised by many of the veteran Jacks.

GLOSSARY
Lower-deck expressions and phrases

Ackers	Any foreign currency.
Air ships in a fog	Sausages and mash.
An awning	Pie crust.
Andrew	The Navy.
Baron	A rating flush with money, a lavish spender, rich.
Babys heads	Dumplings.
Blackcoated workers	Stewed prunes.
Bootneck	A Royal Marine.
Bunts or Bunting Tosser.	A Signalman.
Burgoo	Porridge. A foreign language.
Cackle Berries	Eggs.
Chinese wedding cake.	Rice pudding.
Clacker	Pastry or a pie crust.
Crab fat	Paint, a compound or any sort of paste/mixture.
Crusher	A Regulating Petty Officer (R.P.O)
Dabtoe	An important rating.
Dear John letter	A letter from a girl friend or the wife to say that she has found someone else.
Dustmen	Stokers.
Gophers	Soft drinks.
Gulpers	A large draft from a proffered rum tot.
Hookey	A Leading Seaman or rate.
Jack Dusty	A Stores rating.
Jankers	Summary punishment carried out in a ship.
Jaunty	The Master at Arms.
Jimmy or Jimmy the One.	The First Lieutenant.
Kye	Ship's cocoa.
Links of Love	A string of sausages.
5/8th Nuts and Bolts merchants	Engine-room Artificers.
OOD	Officer of the Day.
OOW	Officer of the Watch.
Oppo	Friend or shipmate.
Pass the slide	Pass the butter.
Poultice Wallopers	Sick bay attendants.
Pusser(s)	Anything official and all naval store items and issues.

Rubber baron/shark	A mess-deck money lender.
Sail hatch	Backside.
SBA	Sick Birth Attendant.
Scribes	Writer ratings.
Sea Buffaloes	Royal Marines.
Sin Bosun	The Chaplain.
Sippers	A small sip from a shipmate's proffered tot.
Skate	Backslider, a useless individual.
Snoring horn	The nose.
Sods opera	A ship's concert party.
Sparker	A Telegraphist.
Sprog	Inexperienced, young or a new recruit.
Straight rush	Roast meat on potatoes with Bisto gravy.
Tanky	An able seaman or Royal Marine assistant to Jack Dusty.
Ticklers	A hand rolled cigarette made from Pussers issue tobacco.
Tiffey	An Artificer.
Train smash	Herrings in tomato sauce.
Rose Cottage	A mess set aside to isolate men who have caught a sexual disease or infection ashore.
Ukkers	Ludo.
Winger or Wings.	A young or junior rating befriended and taken under the wing of an older man.

Sources

Contributors of written material
S. Birtley, A. Bishop, R. Burns, T. Bywater, J.E. Clark, I. Connel, P. Crabb, S. France, S. Francis, J. French, D.S. Goodbrand, J. Harlow, E. Harlow, S. Lombard-Hobson, W.E. Hope, W.R. Howard, W.F. Larham, R. Lerigo, W. Lewis, G. Male, A.H. Ridout, W. Sands, G. Sims, C. Smith, E. Smith, L. Stevenson, F. Risdon, A.R. Russell, P. Vine, C. Watson.

Contributors who gave interviews or exchanged correspondence
F. Barber, S. Bark, R. Bone, W. Buckley, C. Buist, N. Bussi, E. Chantry, S. Connor, J.W. Crossley, J. Crowther, H. Davey, G. Elson, W. Evans, G. Haddon, H. Harlow, L. Howes, E. King, J. Lakie, J. Lancaster, R. McGarel-Groves, C. Money, J. Rycroft, J. Saunders, D. Skin, E.L. Smith, S. Webb, J. Williams, A. Willis, L. Worrall, A. Wood.

Bibliography

The War at Sea, Vols I, II & III (Parts I & II)	SW Roskill, HMSO.
Naval Life and Customs.	J. Irving, Sherratt and Hughes.
Chronology of the War at Sea, Vols I & II.	Rohwer and Hummelchen.
A Sailor's Odyessy.	Viscount Cunningham of Hyndhope, Hutchinson & Co.
Kings Regulations and Admiralty Instructions, BR 31/1939 & BR 31/1943.	HMSO.
Service Pay.	Captain Russell Grenville, Eyre & Spottiswoode.
London's Navy.	Gordon Taylor, Quiller Press.
HMS COVENTRY. A narrative.	George Sims, HMS *Coventry* Old Hands.
The Royal Naval Medical Service, Vol II.	JLS Coulter, HMSO.
History of the Second World War, The Mediterranean and Middle East, Vol III	ISO Playfair, HMSO.
Dabtoes.	Eric Smith, unpublished.
A Sailor's War.	S. Lombard-Hobson, Orbis.

Public Records Office. Ship Log Books.

Ajax	ADM 53	107360	December 1939.
Cairo	"	115471	June 1942.
Coventry	"	115674/5	July and August 1942.
Frobisher	"	115952/3/4/5/6/7	July to December 1942.
Mauritius	"	114640/1/2/3/4/5/6	June to December 1941.
		116235/6	January and February 1942.
		116237/8/9	April, May and June 1942.
		116240/1/2/3/4/5	July to December 1942.
		117894/5/6/7/8/9	January to June 1943.
		117900/1/2/3/4/5	July to December 1943.
		119857/8/9/60	January to April 1944.
		119861/2/3	May to July 1944.
York	"	113511	December 1940.

Appendix

THE KINGS REGULATIONS AND ADMIRALTY INSTRUC-
TIONS. BR 31/1939 and BR 31/1943.
Article 538 paragraph 2 – Approval and Formal Reading . . . The Warrant
should be forthwith dated and formally read by the Commanding Officer to
the accused. As a general rule the formal reading is to be carried out on the
quarter-deck and should be preceeded by the Article of War under which
the offence falls.

Punishment number.	Warrant Punishments.	Appropriate Offence. Article 540. Table I.	Other punishments that can be added to the warrant. Table II.
2	Corporal Punishment. Max; 25 lashes.	Suspended indefinitely,	Article 543 to 549
3	Imprisonment. (Civilian prison) Max: 3 calendar months	Violent assault. Fraud or cheating.	5,6,7,8,12,13, 14 & 21.
4	Detention. (Max: 3 calendar months)	Absence, breaking out of ship. Desertion. Making false charges. Giving false evidence. Drunkenness at sea or on duty. Neglect of duty, skulking. Smuggling liquor on board. Selling or making away with medals or clasps. Selling clothes or bedding. Wilful disobedience. Riotous behaviour. Using provoking language tending to create bad feeling or disturbance. Wilfully breaking, wasting or injurying public stores.	ditto.

		Wilfully destroying or injuring the clothes or effects of persons in the RN or others. Maliciously throwing anything from aloft, down hatchways into engine-room etc. Striking or interrupting a sentry. Negligently using fires or lights.	
5	Dismissal from HM service	As part of any or separate from the above offences.	5,6,7,8,12,13, 14 & 21.
6	Dis-rating or reduction in rank.	Drunkenness. Trafficking in wine, beer, spirits. Gambling. Lending money at interest. Cursing, swearing, obscene language. Disrespect towards superiors. Injury to or wasting stores.	6,7,8,10 only.
7	Deprivation of Good Conduct Badges & Good Conduct medal.	Intent to deceive. Leave under false pretences. Committing a nuisance. Skulking, neglect of duty.	8,10,11,12,13.
8	Reduction to 2nd class for conduct. (Max: 6 months)	Examining another man's locker or bag. Sleeping in another man's hammock or bedding. Fighting, quarrelling or assaulting. Culminating offences or a series of small offences. Not obeying the lawful orders of a sentry.	8,10,11,12,13, 14,15 & 16.
9	spare	*******	******
10*	Solitary confinement in a cell or under a canvas screen. (Max: 14 days)	For any of the offences listed under punishment numbers 6,7 & 8.	12,13,14,15, 16 & 21.
11	Extra work or drill. (Max: 14 days)		14,15,17.

12	Stoppage of leave. (Max: 3 months)		ditto.
13	Reduction to 2nd class for leave. (Max: 3 months)		ditto.
14	Deductions from pay for improper absence or unfitness for duty through drink.		15,17.
15	Stoppage of grog. (Max: 30 days)	For habitual drunkenness longer stoppage, payment for non-issue.	17.
16	Extra work not exceeding 2 hrs per day.	*****	*****
17	Reprimand by Captain.	*****	*****
18	For Marines, extra guard.	*****	*****
19**	For boys only. Birching on the bare breech.	Max: 24 cuts.	12,14.
20**	For all boys. (including band boys RM under 18 years) Caning.	Caning on the breech. Max: 12 cuts.	ditto.

Note. Punishments 11,12,13,14,15,16,17 & 18 are summary punishments that do not require warrants.

* No 10. Cells or under canvas punishment afloat. Low diet (bread and water) for the first three days. No bedding for the first four days, thence only on alternative days. (Without bedding the offender sleeps on a board shelf with a wood block pillow and dressed in a canvas suit). Exercise after the first three days, one hour per day. Reading, the bible or instructional material.

** Article 585, BIRCHING and CANING OF BOYS.
BIRCHING. The punishment of birching is to be confined to boys rated as such, and to boy buglers and band boys when embarked, and is to be inflicted with the birch as issued by the dockyard, and is never to exceed 24 cuts or blows; it is to be inflicted by the ship's police in the presence of the executive officer, a medical officer, two or more petty officers, and all the boys.

The punishment is to be awarded by warrant, and in ships not carrying the flag or broad pendant, the approval of the Flag Officer or Commodore is necessary.
CANING. Caning on the breech, duck trousers and pants being worn, is limited to boys rated as such and boy buglers and band boys when embarked and is to be inflicted with a light and ordinary cane. The number

of cuts or blows is not to exceed 12, and the punishment is not to be carried out in public. Unless he attempts to break away, the boy to be caned should not be secured but should stand and bend down to grasp a chair or other firm object. Caning is intended for the serious offences of theft, immorality, drunkenness, desertion (in special cases as an act of leniency) insubordination, or gross and continued disobedience of orders. In the absence of the Captain, the Commanding Officer is not to order caning to be inflicted, unless the Captain shall be absent from duty by permission or superior authority for more than 48 hours.

INDEX

Index